Pandemics, Pills, and Politics

Pandemics, Pills, and Politics

Governing Global Health Security

Stefan Elbe

JOHNS HOPKINS UNIVERSITY PRESS   BALTIMORE

This book was brought to publication with the generous assistance of the European Research Council.

Johns Hopkins University Press
2715 North Charles Street
Baltimore, Maryland 21218-4363
www.press.jhu.edu

Library of Congress Cataloging-in-Publication Data

Names: Elbe, Stefan, 1975– author.
Title: Pandemics, pills, and politics : governing global health security / Stefan Elbe.
Description: Baltimore, Maryland : Johns Hopkins University Press, [2018] |
    Includes bibliographical references and index.
Identifiers: LCCN 2017043199 | ISBN 9781421425580 (pbk. : alk. paper) |
    ISBN 9781421425597 (electronic) | ISBN 1421425580 (pbk. : alk. paper) |
    ISBN 1421425599 (electronic)
Subjects: | MESH: Global Health | Health Policy | Security Measures—trends |
    Influenza, Human—drug therapy | Pharmaceutical Research
Classification: LCC RA418 | NLM WA 530.1 | DDC 362.1—dc23
LC record available at https://lccn.loc.gov/2017043199

A catalog record for this book is available from the British Library.

Special discounts are available for bulk purchases of this book. For more information, please contact Special Sales at 410-516-6936 or specialsales@press.jhu.edu.

To Alexander

And we must come together to prevent, and detect, and fight every kind of biological danger—whether it's a pandemic like H1N1, or a terrorist threat, or a treatable disease.

—President Barack Obama

We will seek to advance access to and effective use of technologies to mitigate the impact from outbreaks of infectious disease, regardless of their cause.

—US National Security Council

Our nation must have a system that is nimble and flexible enough to produce medical countermeasures quickly in the face of an attack or threat, whether it's one we know about today or a new one.

—US Secretary of Health and Human Services

Contents

Preface

Can a pill strengthen national security? The suggestion may seem odd, but many governments around the world have come to believe precisely that. Several states now consider the ability to rapidly develop new medicines and vaccines critical to their national security. In an interconnected world, security is no longer about armed force alone; it also entails protecting populations against a broad spectrum of biological dangers. The spread of a new pandemic, a bioterrorist attack, or even an accidental laboratory release could all cause mass deaths, crippling economic shocks, and widespread societal disruption. Governments are therefore working more closely with companies to develop a new range of pharmaceutical defenses, or "medical countermeasures," to better protect their populations against such threats.

Yet the quest to secure populations *pharmaceutically* is proving fiendishly difficult to implement in practice. It is also generating a maelstrom of policy dilemmas and controversies along the way:

- What are the major challenges in developing new medical countermeasures against deadly—but also highly unpredictable—diseases?
- How do the power dynamics between pharmaceutical companies, governments, and other actors play out in this quest to develop new pharmaceutical defenses?
- Will authorities ever get to a point where they can rapidly make lifesaving new medicines available to their populations in response to future outbreaks?

In this volume, I explore the growing entanglement of pharmaceuticals and security through an in-depth study of the world's most prominent medical countermeasure: Tamiflu.

Billions of Tamiflu capsules were stockpiled by governments around the world in the fight against pandemic flu. Tens of millions of people have taken the antiviral drug. Yet Tamiflu also attracted scientific controversy about its effectiveness for pandemic preparedness. It provoked suspicions about undue commercial influence in government decision making about stockpiles. It even found itself at the center of a prolonged political battle over who should have access to the data about the safety and effectiveness of medicines. Through the prism of Tamiflu's previously untold story, this volume reveals the major challenges involved in securing populations pharmaceutically and explores how governments are designing extensive new medical countermeasure regimes to overcome those challenges. At the heart of this pharmaceutical turn in security policy, I argue, lies something deeper: the rise of a new molecular vision of life that is reshaping the world we live in—including the way we now imagine and practice security.

Acknowledgments

This book would never have come to fruition without the support of my family, for which I am deeply grateful. Louiza Odysseos has been a loving, constant, and inspiring intellectual companion to this project over many years. Our three children too showed great patience in the finishing stages of the book, while I inevitably juggled (and often fumbled) the competing demands of authorship and fatherhood. Both my mother and my mother-in-law eased the journey immensely by frequently volunteering to help with childcare so that I could undertake the travel required for carrying out the research project on which the book is based.

The book has also benefited greatly from extensive discussions and exchanges with Anne Roemer-Mahler and Christopher Long, as we worked together on a larger research project exploring the role of pharmaceuticals in security policy over the past couple of years. Along the way, many other friends and colleagues similarly provided intellectual inspiration and helpful feedback, in particular the members of the Global Health Section at the International Studies Association, the Global Health Working Group of the British International Studies Association, and the European International Studies Association. Here at the University of Sussex, the work has also benefited from generous feedback and engagement by members of the Department of International Relations, the Centre for Global Health Policy, and the university's wider Global Health Group. The book is much richer for all of their helpful engagement. Any errors of fact or interpretation remain, of course, entirely my own.

I would also like to thank, in particular, the many people who agreed to participate in the research process. A number of leading practitioners in international organizations, industry, governments, and nongovernmental organizations provided valuable insights into many of the key themes that form the focus of this book. Some did so through their participation in a stakeholder workshop held at the Royal Institution in February 2014. Many others did so by agreeing to be interviewed for this project. They are too numerous to be listed here (and several wished to remain anonymous), but they have my gratitude for being so generous in time and spirit, often agreeing to quite long and detailed interviews about their involvement with Tamiflu, and sharing their fascinating stories about their encounters with the medicine. Finally, I would also like to thank Karis Petty of the Centre for Global Health Policy, who provided valuable help in the final stages of compiling the manuscript.

The analysis presented in this book is shaped extensively by my disciplinary background in international relations. Themes like security, power, political economy, globalization, governance, and biopolitics thus reverberate throughout the pages to follow. Yet the material also touches upon other debates in the social sciences around global health, the politics of knowledge, the study of businesses and management, the wider role of pharmaceuticals in society, and so forth. Several of these themes have been explored separately in other articles that may also be of interest to readers:

- Stefan Elbe, Anne Roemer-Mahler, and Christopher Long (2014), Securing Circulation Pharmaceutically: Antiviral Stockpiling and Pandemic Preparedness in the European Union," *Security Dialogue* 45(5): 440–457;
- Stefan Elbe (2014), The Pharmaceuticalisation of Security: Molecular Biomedicine, Antiviral Stockpiles, and Global Health Security, *Review of International Studies* 40(5): 919–938;
- Stefan Elbe, Anne Roemer-Mahler, and Christopher Long (2015), Medical Countermeasures for National Security: A New Government Role in the Pharmaceuticalization of Society, *Social Science and Medicine* 131: 263–271;
- Anne Roemer-Mahler and Stefan Elbe (2016), The Race for Ebola Drugs: Pharmaceuticals, Security and Global Health Governance, *Third World Quarterly* 37(3): 487–506.

The research leading to these results has received funding from the European Union's Seventh Framework Program (FP/2007–2013) ERC Grant Agreement n. 312567: "Pharmaceuticals and Security: The Role of Public-Private Collaborations in Strengthening Global Health Security."

Abbreviations

BARDA	US Biomedical Advanced Research and Development Authority
CDC	Centers for Disease Control and Prevention
CPMP	Committee for Proprietary Medicinal Products
EMA	European Medicines Agency
EUA	emergency use authorization
FDA	Food and Drug Administration
HHS	Department of Health and Human Services
MERS	Middle East respiratory syndrome
MUGAS	Multiparty Group for Advice on Science
NAO	National Audit Office
NICE	National Institute for Clinical Excellence
NPAE	neuropsychiatric adverse event
PREP Act	Public Readiness and Emergency Preparedness Act
PRIDE	Post-Pandemic Review of Anti-Influenza Drug Effectiveness
SARS	severe acute respiratory syndrome
SNS	Strategic National Stockpile
TRIPS	Trade-Related Aspects of Intellectual Property Rights
WHO	World Health Organization
WTO	World Trade Organization

Pandemics, Pills, and Politics

1

Encapsulating Security

Pharmaceutical Defenses against Biological Danger

An epidemic of epidemics—that would certainly be one way to describe our experience of the twenty-first century so far. Hardly a year has gone by of late in which the alarming discovery of a new outbreak has not dominated media news cycles at some point. The epidemics have exotic names and enigmatic acronyms, and they are fast becoming too numerous to list—like HIV/AIDS, SARS, H5N1, H1N1, Middle East respiratory syndrome (MERS), Ebola, and Zika. Together they have made the question of how to better protect populations against lethal infectious disease outbreaks politically much more urgent. Governments now take such outbreaks so seriously, in fact, that they even consider them as threats to national and international security. In an increasingly interconnected world, they fear, lethal infectious diseases could rapidly spread around the world—and potentially cause devastating shocks to populations, economies, and societies. National security strategies are evolving in response to such shifting threat perceptions. Once considered the preserve of issues like war, terrorism, and weapons of mass destruction, security agendas today also explicitly warn of biological threats and dangers.

How can governments better protect their populations against such deadly outbreaks? Clearly their traditional state arsenals of military force, nuclear deterrents, or clandestine intelligence capabilities will offer little protection against an "invasion" of lethal microbes. Governments will also have to acquire some very different capabilities to better manage such health-based threats. That is why they have already begun to work much more closely with private companies to develop a new range of *pharmaceutical* defenses, such as antivirals, antibiotics, next-generation vaccines, antitoxins, antibodies, and antidotes. Their political aspiration is to have an array of such "medical countermeasures" readily available for distribution to the population in advance of the next outbreak. If the outbreak is caused by a new disease, then governments also want to have the capability to rapidly develop *new* medical countermeasures in response. In either case, the proactive development, stockpiling, and distribution of new medical countermeasures for the purposes of civilian biodefense has become a political objective for many governments in the twenty-first century.

Yet governments also encounter serious and protracted obstacles when trying to procure such new pharmaceutical defenses. The development of new medicines is largely the preserve of the pharmaceutical industry, and the companies that make up that industry are mostly driven by commercial logics and market forces—*not* by security concerns. To most of those companies it is unclear why they should prioritize the costly development of new medical countermeasures against highly unpredictable security threats when they could make much more money focusing on products with larger, already existing, and more defined commercial markets. From the outset, the quest to develop new medical countermeasures thus pits two very different logics against one another: a political logic whereby governments wish to secure their populations against emerging biological dangers and a commercial market logic that does not naturally prioritize the development of such products. Whose interests will ultimately prevail in this standoff between governments and pharmaceutical companies? Is it actually possible in practice to align the competing logics of pharmaceutical development and security policy? Will governments ever be able to persuade the pharmaceutical industry to develop new medical countermeasures so that lives could be saved during future outbreaks?

This book explores the growing interplay of pharmaceuticals and security that is unfolding today in the quest to develop new medical countermeasures. In opening up this world to more sustained study, the book shows that the quest to secure populations pharmaceutically generates a unique set of challenges that differs in crucial respects from those usually encountered in more routine pharmaceutical development. How, for example, will the development of such medical countermeasures be financed without a regular commercial market to sell them into? How can such products against highly lethal diseases obtain regulatory approval—especially if they cannot be properly tested in human clinical trials because the pathogens are so rare or dangerous? Who will be liable in the event that harmful side effects later surface during the widespread use of a new medical countermeasure during an emergency? Developing new medicines is complicated and risky at the best of times; it is even more so when it comes to creating new medical countermeasures where processes of pharmaceutical production have to be aligned more closely with security logics.

The policy challenges surrounding medical countermeasures are so numerous, complex, and intertwined that governments can procure them only by extensively adapting their pharmaceutical policies and practices. There is no single "magic bullet" policy option available to them. Instead governments are having to design whole new pharmaceutical regimes dedicated specifically to this purpose—like the new emergency medical countermeasure enterprise taking shape in the United States. This book therefore also maps the extensive, multistakeholder, and rapidly evolving medical countermeasure enterprise being built in response to those challenges today in the United States—with its bespoke funding streams, legal frameworks, regulatory procedures, partnerships, and even whole new institutions emerging at the intersection of pharmaceuticals and security. The book analyzes, in short, both the nature of the policy challenges involved and the new institutional formations already taking shape for their future governance.

At the heart of this pharmaceutical turn in security, the book concludes, ultimately lies something much deeper. More than just a growing preoccupation with an array of biological dangers, this "pharmaceuticalization" of security policy also signals a much more fundamental epistemic shift in our understanding of life. Recent advances in the life sciences are promulgating a new "molecular" vision of life, in which biological existence is seen to be governed by the complex interplay of molecular processes that can be increasingly well understood and intervened upon. This significant shift in our underlying understanding of life is already producing powerful fears about a number of new biological threats that lurk at the molecular scale, against which governments wish to better protect their populations in the twenty-first century. At the same time, this molecular vision of life is also opening up the possibility for industry to develop new pharmaceutical defenses mitigating those biological threats through the careful design of a range of new molecular interventions. The rise of this molecular vision of life thus forms the deeper epistemic backdrop against which the pharmaceutical turn in security policy is unfolding today. Put differently, security is changing in the twenty-first century because the way we are imagining life is also changing.

Biological Danger: The Political Rise of Global Health Security

Diseases now feature prominently on the security agendas of many countries. That is not to say that all health issues are also seen as security threats. Far from it, though there is certainly a pivotal subset of diseases attracting more extensive and sustained security concern. That is because these diseases could rapidly cause significant levels of death and morbidity, could inflict severe economic shocks, and could provoke widespread fear and societal disruption in the population. There is no exhaustive, definitive, or even agreed-upon list of exactly which diseases make up that subset. Yet they tend to be diseases that are both potentially lethal and highly infectious. Many governments perceive such diseases no longer as merely conventional issues for clinical medicine or public health but also as more pervasive threats to national and even international security.

That governments should become more concerned about such biological dangers is understandable when viewed against the backdrop of some of the most seminal international political events unfolding in the twenty-first century so far (Hester forthcoming). Upon closer inspection, it turns out that many of these events were caused by (or linked to) new infectious disease outbreaks. The global spread of HIV/AIDS, for instance, was significant enough politically to prompt the United Nations Security Council to officially designate a disease as a threat to international peace and security for the first time in its history. Not long thereafter governments had to hold their breath and scramble once more—this time in response to the spread of a potentially lethal new coronavirus causing severe acute respiratory syndrome (SARS). The virus—for which there was no cure—had emerged unexpectedly out of southern China. From there it rapidly fanned out across Southeast Asia and many other parts of the world on the back of an increasingly globalized aviation network—generating widespread fear and economic losses along its path.

No sooner had the SARS threat dissipated than governments were put on outbreak alert once again. This time the alarm was triggered by the re-emergence of deadly human infections with a highly lethal strain of "bird flu" (H5N1) in Hong Kong, which then also began to spread across Asia. A flurry of high-level pandemic preparedness activity soon ensued. Yet few experts at the time guessed that the next pandemic flu virus would not, in fact, emanate from birds in Southeast Asia. Instead it came from a novel H1N1 "swine flu" virus spreading in the Western hemisphere. On 11 June 2009, the director general of the World Health Organization thus grimly proclaimed in a live international broadcast anxiously watched by people around the world that the first influenza pandemic of the twenty-first century had arrived. Fortunately, most countries weathered this 2009–2010 H1N1 pandemic much better than initially feared.

Even after the milder-than-expected experience of H1N1, however, the frequency of new international outbreak alerts has not let up. Concern continues about a new coronavirus spreading in the Middle East and beyond (MERS). Lethal human infections with a novel influenza virus (H7N9) have been repeatedly reported in China, raising the specter of pandemic flu once more. The world recently also had to watch in dismay as the largest and deadliest outbreak of Ebola in history grimly unfolded across a region of Africa where it had not traditionally spread. At the time of this writing, international health organizations are also raising further concerns about the spread of the Zika virus in South and Central America, which only months before virtually no infectious disease experts would have flagged as a major concern. As globalization incessantly increases the speed, frequency, and density of connections between formerly distant places, the fear of new infectious disease outbreaks rapidly spreading around the world has risen to the forefront of many governments' security agendas. In epidemiological terms, governments now have to expect the unexpected. Such unpredictable and naturally occurring outbreaks thus form one pivotal axis of biological danger confronting the world today.

The closely related specter of bioterrorism only serves to further compound this political sense of deep microbial unease. What if a hostile group were to target a population by intentionally releasing a lethal infectious disease agent so as to cause widespread suffering, death, and disruption? In the West, political concerns about the threat of terrorism were already escalating in the run-up to 11 September 2001. Amid the seismic international political repercussions of those day's events, it is all too easy to forget that only a week later several letters laced with lethal anthrax spores were mailed to prominent political and media leaders via the US postal system. The letters had been made to appear innocent—as though they were written by school children. The precise origins of the deadly anthrax contained in those letters remains subject to contrasting accounts. Yet there can be no doubt that the letters had transformational political consequences for security policy. Especially in the United States, the letters rapidly moved political calculations on bioterrorism to a new register of "not if, but when and how extensive" (Franz and Zajtchuk 2002: 493). Since that time, Western intelligence agencies have also repeatedly warned about the stated intention of groups like Al-Qaeda and ISIS to launch a bioterrorist attack on Western targets. Moving forward, governments would therefore have to consider a second axis of biological danger as well—the simmering threat of bioterrorism (Enemark 2017).

These twin biothreats of natural and intentional disease outbreaks are increasingly accompanied by a third vector of microbial concern. That is because the number of government, scientific, and private laboratories around the world carrying out scientific research on such dangerous pathogens is continuing to grow. With such a proliferation of geographical sites, groups, knowledge, and technologies, concerns about an accidental release or a laboratory safety lapse are rapidly gaining in political salience. There are certainly historical precedents for accidents occurring in laboratories. In China, two researchers were exposed to SARS coronavirus samples that were incompletely inactivated. The researchers subsequently transmitted the virus to others, leading to several infections and one death in 2004 (GAO 2016: 1). Accidents have also occurred at highly respected laboratories, such as the US Centers for Disease Control and Prevention (CDC), where accidents with anthrax and flu viruses occurred as recently as 2014. In 2015, it was further revealed that a Department of Defense laboratory had inadvertently sent out live *Baccillus anthrax*—which causes anthrax—to nearly 200 labs around the world over the past 12 years (GAO 2016: 1). Such incidents mean that the sources of microbial unease are today at once natural, intentional, and accidental. Taken collectively, these three axes of danger convey the impression that the world confronts an unsettling and complex terrain of potentially unbounded biological threats at the outset of the twenty-first century.

In some respects, it probably does not really matter much if a future outbreak were to be caused naturally, deliberately, or accidentally. If people wake up to either eventuality one morning, governments would certainly need to act swiftly and decisively in order to protect their populations and to stem the debilitating spread of fear. That also explains why several governments have already become much more focused on how they would actually protect their populations in such an eventuality. The new term they have coined for this political endeavor is "health security" (Elbe 2010; Davies, Kamradt-Scott, and Rushton 2015). Following the 2001 anthrax letters, for example, ministers from Canada, France, Germany, Italy, Japan, the United Kingdom, the United States, and Mexico—along with representatives of the European Commission and the World Health Organization—convened in Ottawa for their first meeting of the newly formed Global Health Security Initiative (GHSI). The new political initiative was set up to counter the threat of bioterrorism but quickly evolved and expanded to encompass pandemic threats within its domain. The GHSI may have consisted of only a small number of countries, but it sent a powerful political signal that the professional worlds of health and security were beginning to converge much more closely in order to better confront such biological dangers in the future.

Nor would it take long for the notion of health security to gain much wider traction in the international political system. That same year, the European Union similarly created a new high-level (albeit initially informal) Health Security Committee to strengthen health security across the territories of the European Union. The new committee, consisting of representatives from EU countries, was later formalized and given proper legal underpinning (Kittelsen 2013). In 2007 the World Health Organization (WHO) too helped to drive the international political process forward by developing a working definition of global health security—understood as "the activities required, both proactive and reactive, to minimize vulnerability to acute public health events that endanger the collective health of populations living across geographical regions and international boundaries" (WHO 2007: ix). Politically, WHO's involvement in global health security was significant because it signaled a further geographic expansion of such health security concerns—especially beyond the confines of high-income countries. This would enable the international community to eventually move to a position in which, by 2016, 55 countries from around the world had signed up to a geographically much wider and more diverse Global Health Security Agenda (White House 2016). Beyond Europe and North America, the international list of countries joining the broader initiative now also included ones from Central and South America, Asia, Africa, and the Middle East (McCarthy 2014).

The rapid international political rise of this notion of global health security should not be read to imply that all countries around the world embrace this fusion between health and security concerns and accept it uncritically. On the contrary, there has been—at times even vehement—political resistance to the notion of health security in some diplomatic quarters (Aldis 2008; Kamradt-Scott 2015). Nevertheless, the proverbial genie is out of the bottle, and the notion of "health security" today widely permeates official policy and international political discourse. Indeed, many governments around the world now routinely acknowledge the significance of health security threats (Elbe 2009, 2010), include them in their intelligence community threat assessments, and are also integrating them into their security strategies (Cabinet Office 2008, 2010; Kittelsen 2013: 7; Livre Blanc 2013; National Academies of Sciences, Engineering, and Medicine 2017; White House 2002, 2006; Wizemann et al. 2016: 17). The protection of civilian populations and economies against an array of biological dangers has become a key political objective for several governments in the twenty-first century (Hester forthcoming).

Pharmaceutical Defenses: The Quest for New "Medical Countermeasures"

Yet what can governments actually do to strengthen health security? New outbreaks are notoriously difficult to predict and could emerge from almost anywhere around the world. What is worse, such outbreaks nowadays have the potential to spread very rapidly across the globe, via planes, ships, trains, and all the other international networks of circulation that characterize our age. The magnitude of the international political challenge of strengthening global health security cannot be underestimated. Several governments are therefore already routinely undertaking a wide range of preparedness activities to mitigate such biological threats.

Governments work, for instance, with epidemiologists and mathematicians to better model the risks involved. They frequently stage elaborate high-level simulation exercises to test cross-government response capabilities. They develop advance protocols for the risk communication, messaging, social media, and public outreach strategies they would likely utilize during an outbreak. They have also agreed to comprehensive and legally binding international norms governing the international reporting of new infectious disease outbreaks. They have even developed new surveillance systems drawing upon complex automated algorithms—such as searches performed on the widely used commercial Internet search engine Google— to scan an array of data sources for early warning signs of a new outbreak occurring anywhere in the world (Roberts and Elbe 2017). Governments, in short, are simultaneously deploying a plethora of strategies in their efforts to strengthen health security.

Yet for those countries with the requisite resources and technical ability to do so, there is also one further—and particularly pivotal—area of health security that has attracted protracted political attention: the development of new *pharmaceutical* defenses. Access to a new array of medicines and vaccines would be highly desirable for governments during such a crisis. After all, there can be no certainty that all—or even any—of the aforementioned preparedness activities would successfully contain a future outbreak. In the event that these strategies fail, or are simply activated too late, it would still be extremely desirable for authorities to have some medicines and vaccines readily at hand that they could fall back upon to protect their populations. Indeed, recent experiences with outbreaks like SARS, pandemic flu, and Ebola will have left government officials under no illusion: in the immediate aftermath of an outbreak there will be overwhelming popular demand for—and political pressure to supply—medical interventions to protect people against the threat. What is more, widespread access to such pharmaceutical defenses could also help minimize the immense socioeconomic disruption associated with infectious disease outbreaks, as governments might not even have to impose the much more restrictive and unpopular public health policies of the past, such as quarantines, travel bans, school closures, and so forth. The ready availability of a safe and effective pharmaceutical intervention would mean that the various flows of people, goods, and services necessary for sustaining social and economic activity could largely proceed during such an emergency (Elbe et al. 2014b).

All of this means that several governments are now trying to proactively acquire a new range of such pharmaceutical defenses to protect their populations. The central idea here is for governments to stockpile a number of relevant medicines and vaccines for known diseases in advance of a new outbreak so that they can readily and rapidly be made available to the population during a crisis. In addition, governments also want to build a more flexible infrastructure so that they can quickly develop new pharmaceutical defenses once a new biological threat materializes. "Our nation," extols the US government in this vein, "must have the nimble, flexible capability to produce medical countermeasures rapidly in the face of any attack or threat, whether known or unknown, novel or reemerging, natural or intentional" (PHEMCE 2013). As the quotation reveals, "medical countermeasures" is the name that governments have given to this very specific political endeavor to develop, acquire, stockpile, and rapidly distribute such pharmaceutical defenses against an array of health security threats.

The precise definition of the term "medical countermeasures" is still far from settled. The influential Institute of Medicine (IOM) in the United States, for instance, defines such a measure as "a drug, biological product, or device that treats, identifies, or prevents harm from a biological, chemical, radiological, or nuclear agent that may cause a public health emergency" (IOM 2010: 5). The European Union considers them "any medicines, medical devices, or other goods or services that are aimed at combatting serious cross-border threats to health" (Mielczarek 2015). Others still have defined them as "vaccines, antimicrobials, therapeutics, and diagnostic that address the public health and medical consequences of chemical, biological, radiological, and nuclear events; pandemic influenza; and emerging infectious diseases" (Marinissen et al. 2014: 284). Technically, the term "medical countermeasures" thus encompasses quite a broad range of different medical products. In its most common usage, however, the term tends to refer mostly to pharmaceutical interventions—such as antibiotics, antivirals, antitoxins, antidotes, and next-generation vaccines—that could rapidly be administered to populations in response to a biological threat or widespread health emergency.

This concept of "medical countermeasures" is certainly not one that ordinary people are likely to encounter while going about their daily lives. Yet it is actually an intriguing concept that is worth pondering a little longer—not least because it manages to capture at least three significant political developments at once. First, the rise of this notion is, in and of itself, a revealing sign that the societal role of pharmaceuticals is broadening in the twenty-first century. Pharmaceuticals are becoming significant well beyond the realm of routine medical care where the majority of people are most likely encounter them and are also attaining a greater political relevance for the purposes of defense and security policy. Here the concept of "medical countermeasures" effectively begins to constitute—and also analytically separate out—a new category of pharmaceutical products that possess a special, elevated, and even exceptional political significance because they are potentially relevant to ensuring a country's national security during a crisis or emergency. In the first instance, the rise of the term "medical countermeasures" is thus a potent political signal that pharmaceuticals are becoming much more central to security policy at the outset of the twenty-first century.

The idea of "medical countermeasures" is also fascinating, secondly, because of the terminology it musters. The concept textually embodies the progressive epistemic fusion of the two professional fields of medicine ("medical") and security ("countermeasures"), attempting to seamlessly blend key vocabularies from both communities into a single notion. Here the term begins to form a fascinating intersection, or bridge, between these two different social fields, giving rise in the process to a fascinating new and interdisciplinary policy space where the respective concerns of pharmaceuticals and security begin to interpenetrate each other, and can also come into direct tension with one another. If we wish to explore the messy entanglements that can arise from the closer interplay of the pharmaceutical and security logics, we need to look no further than the world of "medical countermeasures." That policy space, we will see, is proving to be anything but neat, smooth, and seamless; it is full of knots generated by these entanglements.

Finally, the term also signifies a considerable expansion in governments' political ambition when it comes to the scope of such pharmaceutical defenses. There are, of course, much longer-standing government and military efforts to develop pharmaceutical defenses to protect members of the armed forces—especially those about to be sent into battle—stretching back well into the twentieth century. Today, however, the political referent for these investments in medical countermeasures is moving well beyond the military. It is now considerably broader and also entails the civilian population (F. Smith 2014). Consider the Public Health Emergency Medical Countermeasures Enterprise (PHEMCE) established in the United States in 2006. PHEMCE is an interagency initiative for coordinating federal agency activities specifically on medical countermeasures. Explicitly citing the need to defend American citizens against health security threats, PHEMCE takes the government lead in "protecting the civilian population from potential adverse health impacts through the use of medical countermeasures, which are medicines, devices, or other medical interventions that can lessen the harmful effects of these threats" (HHS 2012).

That explicit focus on *citizens* marks a significant historical shift from the earlier—and predominantly military—focus of medical countermeasure development in the United States. After the Second World War, medical countermeasure development was driven mostly by the Department of Defense (DOD) with a clear focus on the military (Wizemann et al. 2010: 101; Wizemann et al. 2016: 21). In 1998, however, President Clinton changed this designating the Department of Health and Human Services (HHS) as the lead agency for responding to medical emergencies related to weapons of mass destruction. Whereas DOD had largely focused on pre-exposure prophylaxis (before sending soldiers into theater), the government now wished to see greater focus on the area of postexposure prophylaxis and treatment. The government also wanted the programs to be available to a much broader range of potential recipients than just the military—including populations with special medical needs like children, the elderly, immune-compromised persons, and so forth (Wizemann et al. 2010: 101). Although DOD continues to work on protecting its forces against exposures to threats like brucellosis, plague, botulism, tularemia, etc., the notion of "medical countermeasures" today points toward a much broader political aspiration of governments to better protect their entire populations against emergent biological danger. It signals, in short, nothing less than a deliberate and decisive move toward more widespread *civilian* biodefense. That at least is the overarching political vision being articulated now in relation to medical countermeasures and health security.

Implementing the Vision: The US Medical Countermeasures Enterprise

What happens when governments actually try to implement this political vision and set about the more practical task of procuring such new pharmaceutical defenses? Things tend to get very tricky, very quickly. From the outset, governments trying to develop new medical countermeasures encounter a hornet's nest of new policy tensions and dilemmas. One fundamental challenge that governments have to confront, for example, is how to persuade commercially operating pharmaceutical companies to even contemplate taking on the development of such new medical countermeasures.

The task of pharmaceutical development is complex, costly, and risky. It is also work largely carried out today by the private sector operating according to market logics. How can governments incentivize these essentially commercial entities to develop new medical countermeasures, especially when the companies could make much more money pursuing other medicines with larger commercial markets? Exactly how much would it cost to develop such new medical countermeasures? Who would carry those costs? How will newly developed medical countermeasures be paid for, acquired, stored, and maintained? And how would they be administered to the population during a crisis? These are just some of the many practical and sensitive questions that arise for governments in the quest to acquire new pharmaceutical defenses.

From the perspective of the pharmaceutical companies, there are many additional—and equally thorny—questions that immediately arise. Why should they prioritize medical countermeasures when they can make a much greater financial return by focusing on other products? It usually takes many years, even a decade or more, to develop new pharmaceutical products. What assurances will pharmaceutical companies have that future governments will still be interested in buying these products once they are finally developed years down the line? By that point in time, new governments will probably have been elected, and their political priorities may well have changed, yet companies will already have sunk significant financial sums into their development. Given the scientific and technical complexity of new drug development, who will end up carrying the inevitable costs of failure—especially when initially promising new drug candidates fail at a later stage of the development process? Even if a product is successfully developed, how can a company then secure a good price when the government is the only likely customer for the product? And what would happen to companies if the future use of the medicine suddenly generates harmful side effects? Who will then have to deal with the potentially enormous financial risks and in some cases even legal liabilities? From the commercial side, too, there is thus no shortage of complicated questions that rapidly arise in the quest to develop new pharmaceutical defenses. These industry concerns, moreover, cannot be easily ignored, irrespective of one's personal view of the industry. That is because of the central, nearly monopolistic role that private companies enjoy in developing new pharmaceutical products. As two observers put it, when it comes to developing new pharmaceuticals, private-sector companies practically "own the ball. If you want to play, you must play with them" (Buse and Walt 2000: 552).

More questions still arise from the perspective of citizens, as the potential future users of such medical countermeasures, and in whose name they are to be developed. Can citizens trust that their government will carry out its duty to properly evaluate the safety and efficacy of new medical countermeasures, especially when the government may have partnered extensively with industry, and perhaps even invested financially, in order to get them developed in the first place? During a crisis, will enough medical countermeasures be available for all of those who need them? If not, who will get access to the scarce supplies first, who will make those decisions, and how will they be made? In more practical terms, how will people actually be able to obtain such medical countermeasures in a crisis, and how quickly will they be able to get them? Might the government even force people to take such medicines against their will in order to protect public health? More broadly, does the channeling of extensive public funds toward the development of new medical countermeasures mark a reasonable and cost-effective use of public treasure, given the considerable uncertainty underlying the prospects of such an event occurring and the many other areas where there is pressing demand for scarce resources? From the perspective of the public, too, there is no shortage of difficult questions that quickly arise.

On the one hand, then, it is certainly easy enough to understand the wider political vision animating the growing political interest in medical countermeasures. After all, when faced with exposure to a potentially lethal infectious disease outbreak, who would not want to have access to a lifesaving medical intervention that has been proved to be safe and effective? On the other hand, putting that vision into practice is extremely challenging and quickly gives rise to a number of formidable policy tensions. Can any government or multinational company successfully navigate all of these complicated issues and actually get new medical countermeasures developed in the twenty-first century? Whose interests will ultimately prevail in this endeavor—those of governments, those of pharmaceutical companies, or those of the public? What powers do these different actors and stakeholders have at their disposal in terms of shaping the overall outcomes? Or, to put it more succinctly, is it actually possible to implement the medical countermeasure vision in practice?

Some governments have certainly been very determined to do so, and none has tried harder than that of the United States. Through a lengthy and iterative process of trial and error, the US government has gradually tried to work its way through many of these complicated issues over the course of the past decade. In the end, the government found that the only way it could persuade at least some commercially operating companies to develop new medical countermeasures is by introducing an extensive array of new programs, measures, and laws addressing their many different concerns. It was not likely to happen if pharmaceutical markets were simply left to their own devices. Over time, and in a piecemeal fashion, the US government has thus gradually built what is now effectively a whole new government-backed pharmaceutical regime geared specifically to the commercial development of new medical countermeasures. For short, it is called simply the medical countermeasures enterprise.

That specialized pharmaceutical regime for medical countermeasures today consists of a number of interrelated elements. The first step in building this new enterprise entailed setting up new government-funded pharmaceutical stockpiles. In 1999, the US Congress thus tasked the federal government with creating a new National Pharmaceutical Stockpile. In the event of an emergency, the new pharmaceutical stockpile would supply states and communities with large quantities of essential medical material within 12 hours of a government decision (Prior 2004). It was initially supported with a comparatively modest allocation of $51 million. The first deployment of these 12-hour push packages occurred during the events of 11 September 2001 and the subsequent anthrax incident (Nicholson et al. 2016: 7). The program was later codified in the Public Health Service Act of 2002, which also increased funding for the stockpile (Nicholson et al. 2016: 7).

In 2003, the new stockpile was then renamed the Strategic National Stockpile (SNS) as it evolved into a much wider "national repository of antibiotics, chemical antidotes, antitoxins, life-support medications, IV administration and airway maintenance supplies, and medical/surgical items" (IOM 2010: 6). Thus, by 2006, the push packages contained in the SNS reportedly occupied 124 cargo containers, weighed 94,424 pounds, and required 5,000 square feet of floor space (Prior 2004: 7). The year 2009 then witnessed the greatest ever deployment of the stockpile to date, with more than 12 million antiviral regiments distributed during the H1N1 influenza pandemic (Nicholson et al. 2016: 8). Since that time, the stockpile has continued to grow significantly, and by 2016 the total SNS inventory was valued at approximately $7 billion—with more than 900 separate line items, spread across six large facilities in different locations (which remain classified) (Nicholson et al. 2016: 2). Dedicated pharmaceutical stockpiles operating outside of the normal pharmaceutical supply chain thus form the first element of the new US medical countermeasures enterprise.

New government funding streams form a second such element. Congress has been funding the SNS to the tune of $500–625 million per year (Nicholson et al. 2016: 11). Yet in 2004 the US government also allocated earmarked public funds explicitly for the purposes of purchasing new medical countermeasures through the BioShield program. The program established a secure source of public funding worth $5.6 billion so that the US government could bulk purchase newly developed medical countermeasures. The federal government essentially leveraged public funds in order to constitute a new government-backed pharmaceutical market for medical countermeasures. That, it hoped, would further accelerate the research, development, purchase, and availability of effective medical countermeasures (IOM 2010: 6). The BioShield program also showed that the US government did not merely wish to stockpile existing pharmaceutical products; it wanted to encourage and invest in the commercial development of a number of *new* pharmaceutical defenses as well.

As a next step, the US government then adapted some of the legal frameworks governing the development and deployment of medical countermeasures. For example, it introduced comprehensive new liability protections against injury compensation claims for manufacturers of such medical countermeasures. These legal safeguards are against compensation claims that could be reasonably anticipated to surface during the mass administration of a new medical countermeasure—especially if unexpected but harmful side effects suddenly surface from the product. In the United States, earlier legal protections had already been introduced through the National Childhood Vaccine Injury Act of 1986, which focused on financial liabilities of vaccine manufacturers from injury claims. In the name of strengthening health security, such protections were now extended to medical countermeasures more generally through the Public Readiness and Emergency Preparedness Act in 2005. These legal changes were intended to mitigate industry concerns about lawsuits that could conceivably arise if a newly developed medical countermeasure ended up generating harmful side effects following its mass deployment.

Finally, the US government also made adjustments to some of the regulatory approval processes governing the development of new medical countermeasures. In recognition of some of the unique challenges that can arise when seeking regulatory approval for new medical countermeasures, the government decided to introduce a new pathway for granting regulatory approval for such products. Called the "animal rule," this novel procedure was developed by the US Food and Drug Administration (FDA) in May 2002. The rule would essentially allow sponsors to gain regulatory approval for their new medical countermeasures on the basis of animal studies that model the disease in human beings, rather than directly through extensive human clinical trials. Separately, the government also introduced a new emergency use authorization procedure, allowing the government to deploy an unapproved medical countermeasure during an emergency or to use an approved medical countermeasure for purposes other than those for which it was initially approved. The extensive adaptation of these legal frameworks thus formed another pivotal element in the new medical countermeasure enterprise built by the US government.

It soon became clear, however, that all of these policy changes still remained insufficient to lure many pharmaceutical companies into the area of medical countermeasures. So the government decided to make one last roll of the dice. It went a big step further and created a whole new organization dedicated specifically to the development of new medical countermeasures, the Biomedical Advanced Research and Development Authority (BARDA). Established in 2006, BARDA's explicit mission is to develop and procure needed medical countermeasures against a broad array of public health threats, whether natural or intentional in origin. The new organization's primary strategic goal was to create an "advanced development pipeline replete with medical countermeasures and platforms to address unmet public health needs, emphasizing innovation, flexibility, multi-purpose and broad spectrum application, and long-term sustainability" (BARDA 2011).

BARDA's role would also go considerably beyond helping companies to develop new medical countermeasures, however. The manufacturing and distribution of medical countermeasures would be additional—but equally significant—goals of BARDA. Today the organization is further tasked with maintaining an "agile, robust and sustainable U.S. manufacturing infra-structure" and "a ready capability to develop, manufacture and facilitate distribution of medical countermeasures during public health emergencies" (BARDA 2011). In many ways, the creation of BARDA thus marked an im-plicit admission by the US government that the successful development of new medical countermeasure capabilities would not be possible by relying on commercial market logics alone. It would also require new forms of state-backed institutionalization and intervention.

Since its inception, BARDA has emerged as one of the world's most so-phisticated enterprises dedicated specifically to the development of new medical countermeasures. It can now provide pharmaceutical companies working on such medical countermeasures with a wide range of advanced development assistance—such as designing late-stage clinical trials for safety and efficacy, advising on manufacturing processes, optimizing prod-ucts for storage and longevity, and so forth. Overall, its efforts have al-ready contributed to the federal acquisition of tens of millions of doses of medical countermeasures. Under Project BioShield alone, the US govern-ment has been able to add 12 new products to the nation's emergency stockpile (HHS 2014: 3). BARDA claims that since its inception it has also been involved in 24 products that have been cleared, approved, or licensed (Hatchett 2016b: 5) and that it has also supported more broadly the re-search and development of more than 180 medical countermeasures (Fass-bender 2016). All of these developments indicate that it is possible to work through some of the challenges that arise in the quest to secure popula-tions pharmaceutically, even if doing so has taken a lot of time and effort, as well as a considerable amount of trial and error.

Thanks to these extensive efforts and investments, the US government today finds itself at the international forefront of the quest to develop new medical countermeasures. Yet this does not mean that the United States is the only government with such a heightened interest in acquiring new phar-maceutical defenses for its population. It is more difficult to obtain an accurate international picture about related medical countermeasure devel-opments unfolding in other countries because much of this information remains classified. However, it is clear that many other governments have become much more interested in acquiring pharmaceutical defenses for their populations—albeit usually on a smaller scale. For example, in the United States' immediate neighbor to the north, the Canadian government now similarly maintains a National Emergency Stockpile System (PHAC 2012). In the Southern Hemisphere, the Australian government too created a new National Medical Stockpile as early as 2002. It reportedly contains a strategic reserve of essential vaccines, antibiotics, and antiviral drugs, as well as chemical and radiological antidotes (Australia DOH 2014). The items are kept in various strategic locations across Australia, which are not publicly released for security reasons (PHAC 2012).

Similar developments have also been unfolding in Europe. The government of the United Kingdom created a UK Strategic Stockpile in 2001, again containing a range of antibiotics, vaccines for anthrax and smallpox, botulinum antitoxin, and so forth—placed around the UK for delivery within two hours (Lightfoot 2009). The UK stockpile now contains more than 20 products (not including items that are already used by the National Health Service for routine applications) with a replacement value of around £147 million (Cole 2013: 11). In 2013, moreover, the European Union as a whole also established a new legal basis for member states jointly procuring medical countermeasures—showing a move toward greater coordinated action on meeting cross-border health threats in the European Union (EU 2013).

The precise international picture may remain somewhat murkier then. Yet all of these parallel stockpiling activities can leave no doubt that the United States is not the only country investing in new medical countermeasure capabilities today. While it certainly appears to be well ahead of the game internationally, there are also many other countries around the world (mostly high-income ones with the requisite resources) that similarly believe that a government's highest political priority—ensuring national security—today demands the capability to proactively develop, acquire, stockpile, and mass-distribute a range of pharmaceutical defenses. Like the United States, moreover, these countries also continue to grapple with the many complex challenges involved in actually developing such new medical countermeasures.

Tamiflu: A Medical Countermeasure under the Magnifying Glass

All of these issues and tensions around medical countermeasures will likely be of great international political significance in the event of a future outbreak. In fact, the question of how many people around the world would survive such an outbreak could well depend upon how thoroughly governments, companies, and citizens understand (and indeed tackle) these issues in the years ahead. And yet we know surprisingly little about the detailed processes surrounding the development, acquisition, and use of medical countermeasures today. The complicated policy challenges engulfing them are not widely understood, especially outside the specialist community directly involved in their development. Nor are there many scholarly analyses of the processes through which some governments are already beginning to respond to these challenges. Generally speaking, these issues have not been the subject of sustained attention by researchers so far.

There is certainly a growing body of scholarly work focusing on health security more broadly, especially coming from the field of international relations and security studies (for an excellent overview see Rushton and Youde 2015). That literature has greatly refined our understanding of health security and the political processes unfolding around it (Davies 2008; McInnes and Rushton 2013; Nunes 2014); but it has not to date focused very much on the prominent role of medical countermeasures—with the notable exception of one insightful study on the history of vaccines in biodefense (Hoyt 2012). That is a fairly a significant gap in the scholarly literature, given just how central pharmaceutical interventions have recently become to debates on global health security.

Conversely, there is also a much wider social science literature examining the role of pharmaceuticals in society more broadly today, especially emanating from the disciplines of sociology and anthropology (Abraham 2010; Clarke et al. 2010; Lakoff 2005; Petryna et al. 2007; Whyte et al. 2002; Williams et al. 2009; Dumit 2012). These researchers explore societal rates of pharmaceutical prescription, analyze the history of particular medicines and examine the emergence of whole new therapeutic classes (like antidepressants, "lifestyle" drugs, etc.). Given their focus on much wider societal developments, however, they in turn have not yet explored the specific area of security policy and medical countermeasures in any detail, even though this too is now an area of explicit government investment, as well as one marked by quite a unique set of challenges and dynamics. From both directions, there is thus an urgent need to shed greater light on the role that pharmaceuticals now play in security policy and to put this world of medical countermeasures under the proverbial magnifying glass.

Achieving such an improved understanding of the world of medical countermeasures is far from straightforward and requires navigating a number of formidable obstacles of its own. First and foremost, the processes of developing, acquiring, and rolling out new medical countermeasures are extraordinarily complex. Pharmaceuticals are widely considered to be some of the most complicated products in the world. The life cycle of any new medical countermeasure will also unfold over many years as it passes through multiple phases characterized by a fluctuating mix of challenges, risks, stakeholders, and policy tensions. Simply capturing that extraordinary complexity presents a major research challenge in and of itself. This book attempts to tame some of that overwhelming complexity by focusing on just one medical countermeasure. That should allow sufficient space to do justice to the many inherent complexities and tensions involved in the quest to secure populations pharmaceutically.

But which medical countermeasure would form the best research subject for such an extended and in-depth study? Although there are several to choose from, this book analyzes what is arguably the world's most prominent medical countermeasure: the antiviral drug oseltamivir (brand name Tamiflu). Among recent medical countermeasures, Tamiflu towers head and shoulders above all others because so many governments around the world identified it as a first line of defense against pandemic flu. Tamiflu is certainly not the only antiviral medication that governments have stockpiled, but it has rapidly established itself as the preferred medical countermeasure for pandemic preparedness. Following advice from the World Health Organization, 95 governments around the world built such Tamiflu stockpiles over the past decade (Reddy 2010: ii35). Around 350 million treatment courses, or 3.5 billion doses, were supplied to governments worldwide between 2004 and 2009 alone (Reddy 2010: ii35). To the best of the author's knowledge, that makes Tamiflu one of, if not *the* most widely acquired medical countermeasure of the twenty-first century. For this reason alone, Tamiflu suggests itself almost naturally for a deeper exploration of the world of medical countermeasures.

Compared to most other medical countermeasures, moreover, Tamiflu also has a number of subtler advantages as an object of further research. First, there is the comparative ease of access to information about the antiviral. Much information about medical countermeasures understandably remains classified or is deemed commercially sensitive—making medical countermeasures much more difficult to research than many other types of medicines used in more routine health-care settings. For example, even the composition and location of the Strategic National Stockpile in the United States remains classified for security reasons. Tamiflu is exceptional among the pantheon of recent medical countermeasures because of the amount of public scrutiny it has received. The antiviral attracted widespread media coverage during the pandemic scares of 2005 (H5N1) and 2009 (H1N1). That temporarily transformed Tamiflu into a household name in many countries—much like Prozac and Viagra in earlier years. Tamiflu has also provoked a lot of public controversy around its effectiveness against pandemic flu, even over its cost to the public purse. In the course of these public controversies, government agencies and the relevant pharmaceutical companies have had to place a substantial amount of information about Tamiflu into the public domain.

All of this means that there is now more information on Tamiflu openly available than there is for any other comparable medical countermeasure. In fact, the research challenge for Tamiflu has become the great availability of information. A search for Tamiflu on Google generates more than 2.5 million results! The sheer mass of information that is available about a drug whose story is not yet finished represents a daunting research challenge, but at least in ensures that there is plenty of information that can be easily accessed for the purposes of this study. Indeed, it makes Tamiflu one of the few medical countermeasures that can be extensively studied mostly through recourse to publicly available sources.

Tamiflu also has a second advantage over most other medical countermeasures: it is one of the most widely *deployed* medical countermeasures of recent years. Many other medical countermeasures have been developed and stockpiled over the past decade, but they now linger in warehouses and have never had to be distributed (fortunately!). Tamiflu, by contrast, was widely deployed to populations during the H1N1 influenza pandemic of 2009–2010. Over one million treatment courses of Tamiflu were distributed among the civilian population in England by the National Pandemic Flu Service alone. In the United States, it also formed a large part of the 12.5 million antiviral regimens that were deployed during the 2009 H1N1 pandemic (Nicholson et al. 2016: 8). By that point in time, more than 50 million people had taken Tamiflu around the world (Roche 2007: 12). Unlike many other medical countermeasures, therefore, Tamiflu has already been widely administered to the public during a pandemic. That fact will allow for the exploration of several additional but equally critical issues that emerge around the rolling out and mass distribution of medical countermeasures to populations during an actual emergency. Here, in other words, the choice of Tamiflu as the object of study will generate a much more comprehensive and complete picture of the many different challenges involved in securing populations pharmaceutically.

Tamiflu also suggests itself for a final reason. We will shortly see that when it comes to flu, we are not just dealing with one problem but simultaneously with two very different ones: there is the problem of *seasonal* flu affecting millions of people each year, but there is also the much more sporadic threat of *pandemic* flu. While the former is more of a routine medical and public health challenge, the latter is a quintessential example of a dreaded global health security threat against which governments now wish to better protect their populations. This Janus-faced nature of the flu problem has allowed Tamiflu to enjoy two very different lives. In the first half of its life, Tamiflu was mostly a fairly conventional pharmaceutical product aimed principally at the seasonal flu market. During that period, it confronted many of the same issues and challenges faced by other pharmaceutical products. However, Tamiflu then underwent a profound transformation, as it was suddenly reinvented and reborn as a medical countermeasure against pandemic flu in the second half of its life. At that point, a number of new challenges began to emerge, challenges that differ from those usually associated with more conventional pharmaceutical use.

Tamiflu's radical transformation over time from a more routine therapy to a medical countermeasure makes it a particularly fascinating product to analyze for the purposes of this study. It means that the two lives of Tamiflu—effectively the "before" and "after"—can be usefully compared and contrasted. We can first see how the process of pharmaceutical development unfolded normally in the first half of its life, when commercial logics largely dominated the process. We can then also trace how its appropriation by security logics in the second half of its life begins to change key political dynamics and generates a complex array of new challenges and tensions that arise when practicing security with pharmaceutical defenses. For all of these reasons, then, Tamiflu has been chosen to form the empirical basis for this in-depth study into the world of medical countermeasures. The only question that remains is *how* to best tell its fascinating story.

Learning from the Life of a Medical Countermeasure

This book tells the story of Tamiflu—somewhat unconventionally and experimentally—through what might be broadly called a "life-course" approach. Although not a formal theory per se, such life-course approaches have already been used in a variety of other disciplines and usually consist of at least two key elements. The first is that they take a *temporal* approach—looking at the relationship between events and processes over the course of a person's life span. This could include, for instance, studying how early childhood experiences may shape later decisions about marriage, employment, crime, the likelihood of acquiring a disease, and so forth. Second, life-course approaches also tend to take a *social* perspective, looking at individual lives within the context of their wider structural, social, cultural and economic environments. That aspect usually also renders life-course studies highly multidisciplinary in nature, as they effectively use a person's life as a lens through which to explore the wider interconnections between history, sociology, demography, psychology, health, economics, and so forth.

Adopting such a life-course approach to also study Tamiflu is slightly unconventional in that these approaches are usually reserved for the study of living things—like individuals or families—and not for material objects like a pharmaceutical product. The intellectual justification for taking a risk and breaking with this convention comes principally from medical anthropologists. They have already shown, in the aptly titled volume *Social Lives of Medicines*, that medicines too enjoy complex social lives that go well beyond their chemical structure and biological effects (Whyte et al. 2002: 3). If that is true, then it should be possible (and indeed permissible) to also use a life-course approach to study a medical countermeasure like Tamiflu. In practical terms, this simply means that the book will retrospectively shadow Tamiflu as it passed through each key stage of its "life"—from its birth and initial scientific inception, via its regulatory approval and government acquisition, all the way through to its stockpiling and eventual distribution during a pandemic. Each of the chapters that follow is dedicated to exploring one of these critical stages of its "life" in more detail.

Superficially, such a life-course approach shares many characteristics of a more traditional, in-depth case-study design that is also widely used in many other studies of pharmaceuticals. Indeed, there is a whole genre of books now dedicated to studying the stories of particular medicines like

Prozac (Healy 2004), Taxol (Goodman and Walsh 2001), and Viagra, and even entire classes of medicines—like antidepressants (Healy 1997) or statins (Kendrick 2007; Li 2009). That said, there are also some crucial aspects of the life-course approach that differentiate it from these more conventional case-study designs. Three axioms in particular guide the life-cycle approach used in this book.

First, the life-course approach seeks to show that the development and use of medical countermeasures is a complex social process that passes through several distinct phases. Methodologically, it is important to study these phases separately, because each of them involve a distinct constellation of actors, risks, and policy challenges. That is not a feature of medical countermeasures alone, as similar examples can also be found in other areas of social enquiry. In international relations, for example, scholars have long studied how new international norms, such as human rights, are initially developed in the international system, then become appropriated by governments and are eventually internalized by states. There scholars have developed a life-cycle model to study such processes of norm diffusion through multiple stages—from initial norm emergence through a period of norm cascading to an eventual stage of norm internalization by states (Finnemore and Sikkink 1998). The problems, challenges, and issues that arise during such processes of norm diffusion are not static over time but depend on what phase of the life cycle the norm is passing through.

The development of medical countermeasures similarly goes through a number of such distinct phases. There is the initial phase when a new product is scientifically developed, which is usually followed by clinical trials to analyze the effectiveness, safety, and proper dosage of the new product. There is then a regulatory approval phase, which (for successful products) is usually followed by government acquisition—often for a stockpile, where further considerations must be given to how such products are distributed and ultimately administered. More than just a heuristic device, then, this life-course approach posits that it is methodologically critical to focus on each of these phases individually because each stage presents a particular—and also different—set of policy challenges from all the other stages, involves a different mix of stakeholders and power dynamics, and has different potentials for causing policy tensions and/or public controversy.

Second, a life-course approach also attempts to explore the complex interdependencies that exist between—and indeed traverse—these different stages of the life cycle. Decisions and events in one of these phases can have potentially profound ramifications on other stages later in the life cycle, making the sequence of events an important factor to consider as well. In addition to breaking the story down into the constituent components of the life cycle, the life-course approach thus seeks to improve understanding of the often subtle interdependencies that can exist between the different stages of the life cycle. Again, this is not a feature unique to medical countermeasures. Scholars in development studies, for example, have identified the existence of such interdependencies through value chain analysis. Focusing on other products like food, clothing, or automobile parts, they analyze the whole global cycle of organization, production, and development of products—from inception to use and recycling (Kaplinsky 2000). In so doing, they have found that events or developments in one area of production can have significant implications for other phases and producers in the value chain.

Such interdependencies also exist across the whole spectrum of medical countermeasure development. The prospect and size of a potential government acquisition of a new medical countermeasure, for example, may influence commercial decisions made by companies at the outset about whether a drug candidate should be taken through clinical trials and developed. Similarly, excessive uncertainty about how to obtain regulatory approval for a product might deter companies from moving forward with particular products in earlier stages of the process. Even the likely eventual method of administration—whether by pill, injection, or other means—can influence many factors in the development processes. All of this means that the life-cycle approach is about more than just breaking down the complex process of medical countermeasure development and acquisition into its constitutive stages; it also entails identifying the nature and extent of these complex interdependencies. The approach remains open, in that way, to considering how the use or appropriation of a drug at a particular time may be intimately bound up with its earlier development process as well as expectations about its later use and utility.

Finally, and as a direct result of the two aforementioned considerations, the life-course approach also tries to deepen our understanding of recent policy developments in this area, especially why some governments would even resort to the design of new pharmaceutical regimes for medical countermeasures. Taking such a life-course approach will show that, in order to be effective, government policy must be able to address *all* of the many different stages involved, as well as the complex matrix of interdependencies that exist over the course of the entire life cycle. The need for such a more holistic policy approach has already being recognized in other areas, such as the economy. There, some economists are now deploying a life-cycle approach to understand the impact of government policy on economic behavior. Rather than focusing solely on one particular point in time, economists are trying to take into account individuals' income and saving patterns over the course of their entire lifetime and to shape policy with such a longer temporal horizon in mind.

In the security sphere, governments that are serious about developing new medical countermeasures have similarly had to take a more holistic approach to meet the many practical challenges involved. Through a prolonged process of trial and error, they have discovered that there is no single policy intervention that could function as a "magic bullet" to stimulate new medical countermeasure development. Governments that are intent on acquiring new pharmaceutical defenses have instead had to develop a wider suite of policy interventions that remain sensitive to these multiple phases in the product's life cycle. Here, the life-course approach can also help to explain why the government response, especially in the United States, has taken the shape that it has, culminating in a wide-ranging and new medical countermeasure "enterprise" that today includes the many different actors that are involved with a medical countermeasure over the course of its life cycle.

In the end, then, the life-course approach adopted here in relation to Tamiflu should also ensure that there are many more generalizable insights that can emerge from such a study. On the one hand, the empirical focus of this book is very much on the antiviral Tamiflu—for reasons that have already been explored. When it comes to drawing wider conclusions from the study, it will therefore be necessary to bear in mind that there are also significant differences between Tamiflu and other antivirals, between different classes of medical countermeasures (such as vaccines), and indeed between different kinds of health security threats. That said, the life-course approach taken here can also produce more generalizable insights because all new medical countermeasures will share a number of features. These include the fact that their development passes through several different stages, that they demonstrate extensive interdependencies between these various phases, and that they require a broader approach to their development that remains sensitive to these various stages and interdependencies.

By looking more closely at the fascinating life of Tamiflu, this book thus seeks to uncover the major challenges involved in developing new medical countermeasures more generally. The book identifies 10 such challenges in the chapters that follow—showing how these challenges also extend far beyond merely designing a few new pharmaceutical products. Even once a new medical countermeasure is successfully developed, there is still a lot of additional work that governments have to undertake in order to ensure that such products can be used effectively to protect their populations. The book further shows why some governments are already responding to many of these wider challenges by taking the extraordinary step of creating whole new pharmaceutical regimes designed specifically for medical countermeasures. Finally, the book also delineates what it would take for governments to move toward a position where they could actually make lifesaving pharmaceutical defenses rapidly available to people in response to future outbreaks. With these points in mind, examination of the experimental journey into the life of Tamiflu can begin.

THE DEVELOPMENT CHALLENGES

2

Discovering a Virus's Achilles Heel

Flu Fighting at the Molecular Scale

The best place to start the story of Tamiflu is undoubtedly at the very beginning of its life—with its birth. Tamiflu was developed in the 1990s as part of a new class of antiviral medicines for influenza called neuraminidase inhibitors. I will explain how these medicines are intended to work shortly. The key thing to note for the time being is that Tamiflu was not actually the first such neuraminidase inhibitor to be developed. That distinction went to another drug called Relenza. Tamiflu is only the second because it was developed as a direct commercial rival to Relenza. In fact, the whole birth of Tamiflu is inextricably bound up with the development of Relenza immediately before it. This chapter therefore initially explores how Relenza was developed as the world's first neuraminidase inhibitor to address the problem of flu—and out of the direct shadow of which Tamiflu would soon be born.

Revisiting this story of Relenza reveals that pharmaceutical companies developed neuraminidase inhibitors through a fairly conventional process of commercial drug development. That conventional process usually consists of private-sector companies marrying a scientific discovery to an intense process of commercial development, taking the innovative discovery from the "bench" to the "bedside." In the case of neuraminidase inhibitors, the decoding of the precise molecular structure of one of the influenza virus's key surface proteins allowed a new drug target to be identified. Based on that scientific understanding, it was then possible to design and synthesize an artificial new molecule that could interfere with the processes of viral replication taking place inside the human body, and that could form the basis for a new pharmaceutical intervention. Scientific advances in molecular biology had effectively opened up new avenues of commercial exploitation for pharmaceutical companies.

In addition to such scientific advances, however, the conventional process of new drug development also relies heavily upon the existence of a commercial market that the medicine can then be sold to. That market is crucial for companies to be able to recoup the significant up-front investment costs that are usually involved. A major reason why this commercial drug development process worked successfully in the case of Relenza is that such a lucrative market did indeed exist in the case of flu. However, that commercial market was not *pandemic* flu; rather, it was the closely related problem of *seasonal* flu, which spurred on the initial development of neuraminidase inhibitors. Companies were primarily interested in the commercial potential of neuraminidase inhibitors to address the problem of seasonal flu affecting tens of millions of people around the world every year. Neuraminidase inhibitors, it turns out upon closer inspection, were born very much as *accidental* medical countermeasures. They are largely the fortuitous byproduct of fairly conventional commercial efforts to address the parallel problem of seasonal flu.

What is more, it actually seems rather unlikely that neuraminidase inhibitors would ever have been commercially developed without this sizable parallel market in seasonal flu and solely to address the threat of pandemic flu. Taken on its own, that pandemic flu market is simply too uncertain and too unpredictable to justify the costly up-front commercial investment that is required. Nobody knows for certain if and when such a pandemic will occur or indeed what exactly it would look like, even if it does. Herein also lies the main reason why this conventional model for commercial drug development usually does not work very well for medical countermeasures in general. When it comes to most other health security threats, such a parallel market that could drive the commercial drug development process forward simply does not exist in the same way that it does for flu, and flu marks much more of an exception than the general rule in this regard. Without the promise of such a lucrative commercial market, most pharmaceutical companies simply fail to detect sufficient commercial potential in the whole area of health security and tend to steer a wide birth around medical countermeasures when deciding which products to prioritize and develop. When it comes to medical countermeasures in general, the conventional political economy of commercial pharmaceutical development thus becomes profoundly disrupted.

Some of the very earliest experiences with the birth of neuraminidase inhibitors thus already reveal two quite formidable—and also much more general—challenges that will confront any government wishing to acquire new medical countermeasures from the outset. First, there will be difficult *scientific* challenges that will need to be overcome before any new medical countermeasure can be successfully developed. Second, there will also be significant *economic* challenges, unless governments can find other ways to incentivize pharmaceutical companies to take on the commercial development costs associated with new medical countermeasures.

The Pandemic Flu Threat

Most people will have first encountered neuraminidase inhibitors like Relenza and Tamiflu in the context of pandemic flu. Perhaps they heard about them through the extensive media coverage they attracted during the international outbreaks of deadly human cases of H5N1 ("bird flu") and H1N1 ("swine flu") infection. Perhaps they read about then when, one by one, governments around the world rushed to build vast stockpiles of the drugs at a cost of billions of dollars. Or perhaps they even took the antiviral medicines during the 2009–2010 H1N1 pandemic, as millions of people around the world were urged to do by their governments. In either case, many people's first encounter with neuraminidase inhibitors would have been as a medical countermeasure against pandemic flu.

What exactly is pandemic flu? A flu pandemic is simply an epidemic of a new influenza virus spreading on a worldwide scale and infecting a large proportion of the human population. Influenza viruses are constantly circulating and have many natural hosts. Besides human beings, influenza viruses can also infect pigs, ducks, chickens, ferrets, and even horses. In fact, the very existence of influenza viruses was first discovered in pigs (in 1931). Some 20 years later aquatic birds were then determined to be natural hosts of influenza viruses (Klenk 2012). That said, influenza viruses can and do cause infections in human beings, which tend to manifest themselves in the onset of respiratory disease.

From the perspective of human health, probably the most significant aspect of influenza viruses is their inherent genetic instability. Many other viruses that cause human disease, such as measles, mumps, and smallpox, are genetically comparatively stable. Once people have been vaccinated and their bodies have developed antibodies, immunity can be quite long lasting. Influenza viruses, by contrast, have a comparatively high mutation rate and are constantly changing as they circulate (Klenk 2012). Influenza viruses are fast-moving targets in that sense.

There are two different ways in which new influenza viruses can emerge: through antigenic *drift* and antigenic *shift*. Antigenic drift is a more gradual process. It is usually behind the seasonal evolution of flu viruses that occurs from one year to the next. This process tends to be associated with minor changes in the structure of the viral proteins (Varghese et al. 1983: 35). Antigenic shift, by contrast, is a much more substantial and abrupt reassortment process. Entire gene segments can become replaced, potentially leading to increased human vulnerability to the resulting new virus (MacKellar 2007: 431). Such reassortment events can also occur in animals (such as pigs) that are susceptible to both human and avian influenza viruses and can thus serve as mixing vessels (MacKellar 2007: 431–432).

When such substantially novel influenza viruses are introduced into the human population, new pandemics can arise. That has happened on at least three separate occasions in the twentieth century alone. The Spanish flu of 1918–1919 killed more than an estimated 20 million people, with some estimates even putting the worldwide figure as high as 50 million (CDC 2005). Two subsequent but comparatively "lesser" flu pandemics of 1957 and 1968 killed an estimated one million people each (MacKellar 2007: 431). After further analysis of the 1918 (H1N1) virus, it is now thought that the 1918 pandemic was caused by an avian flu virus. The virus probably adapted to human beings without first passing through an intermediary animal host. The pandemics of 1957 (H2N2) and 1968 (H3N2), by contrast, were likely caused by a reassortment of genetic materials (shift). Historians have also identified older, globalized epidemics (pandemics) that occurred during the nineteenth century—such as the Russian flu of 1889–1893 (Laver and Garman 2002: 1309). Influenza pandemics have thus occurred repeatedly throughout history.

The episodic recurrence of such influenza pandemics leads many experts to believe that new flu pandemics occur roughly once every couple of decades. The exact timing and extent of future pandemics cannot be predicted with any degree of certainty. When they do occur, however, new influenza pandemics are often distinguished by comparatively higher "attack" rates—that is, the number of people experiencing clinical symptoms of infection. The viruses responsible for the 1918–1919 and 1957–1958 pandemics, for instance, had estimated attack rates of around 25 percent, compared to around 10 percent in a normal flu season in the United States (MacKellar 2007: 430–431). Such elevated attack rates can also generate a substantially higher burden of disease and mortality and may cause more widespread social and economic disruption.

There can be other significant differences between pandemic flu and seasonal flu. For instance, pandemic flu can occur at any time of year and can come in multiple waves. It can affect people of any age—rather than predominantly killing those who are either very old or very young. In addition to the direct mortality and morbidity associated with influenza pandemics, they also tend to produce much wider economic and social disruption. They can affect travel, trade, and critical infrastructure and can require the closure of schools and so forth. That is why the identification of lethal human infections with novel influenza viruses generates such international concern. There is always the specter that it might mark the beginning of the next human pandemic.

Precisely such concern also formed the backdrop against which public health officials raised alarm in 1997 over new human infections with a highly pathogenic strain of avian flu in Hong Kong (*MMWR Weekly* 1997). The H5N1 viruses were killing thousands of birds at the time, but they could also infect people coming into close contact with infected animals. It was the first known instance of human infection with this avian H5N1 virus (WHO 2011b). Although the officially reported number of human cases was still fairly low (18 in total), 6 of the cases proved fatal. That made the virus comparatively lethal. With the last influenza pandemic having occurred several decades earlier, experts became concerned that this could mark the beginning of a "long overdue" new human influenza pandemic. Control measures were quickly introduced in Hong Kong, and the initial outbreak was contained. Then things went quiet for several years.

In 2003, however, new human infections with the potentially deadly H5N1 virus suddenly reappeared, again in Hong Kong. This time the news was accompanied by reports of other human infections also occurring much more widely across other geographic areas in Southeast Asia and beyond. Tracking this alarming spread of H5N1, countries began to draw up much more extensive pandemic preparedness plans. The World Health Organization warned that a new pandemic infecting roughly 25 percent of the world population (a figure derived from previous pandemics) could affect more than 1.5 billion people and cause enormous social disruption because of a rapid surge in illnesses and deaths (WHO 2007: 47). In the United States, the CDC also warned that in the absence of any control measures (vaccination or drugs) a "medium-level" pandemic would cause 89,000 to 207,000 deaths, 314,000 to 734,000 hospitalizations, 18 million to 42 million outpatient visits, and another 20 million to 47 million people being sick in the United States alone. It further warned of economic consequences: "Between 15% and 35% of the population could be affected by an influenza pandemic, and the economic impact could range between $71.3 and $166.5 billion" (CDC 2005).

Confronted with the specter of such scenarios, many governments began to prepare in earnest for the arrival of a potentially catastrophic new human flu pandemic. The pandemic flu threat rapidly rose to the top of government agendas and was even added as a new threat to the national security strategies of several countries. High-level simulation exercises were carried out to test cross-government levels of preparedness. New government strategies on pandemic flu were set out. Wide-ranging international diplomatic initiatives on pandemic flu were also launched, and the threat was extensively discussed at a high level in a plethora of regional and international organizations. Pandemic preparedness became a new political buzzword on many people's minds. If it did materialize, such a flu pandemic would represent precisely the kind of global health security threat against which governments would like to better protect their populations in the twenty-first century.

How to Respond? Preparing for the Next Pandemic

What could governments actually do to strengthen the protection of their populations against this threat lurking at their door? If the lethal H5N1 virus evolved further and become readily transmissible between human beings, governments around the world would have a serious challenge on their hands. One option, of course, would then be to resort to more traditional public health interventions. There are many of these to choose from—like emphasizing personal hygiene, dispensing face masks, setting up quarantines, introducing travel restrictions, restricting mass gatherings, and so forth. Plans for introducing several of these measures were considered by governments, and additional evidence on their likely effectiveness was also gathered. But in the event of a highly transmissible virus, would such actions really be able to stop a burgeoning pandemic in its tracks? Or would they at best delay it for a short while? With so many urban places characterized by high population density, with so many different flows of livestock and people involved in international trade, it would likely prove very difficult to contain an outbreak in all but the best-case scenarios. No doubt it would be safer—and more reassuring—for governments to also have a medicine or vaccine readily at hand to protect their populations.

Surely such a safe and effective pharmaceutical intervention exists for flu that governments could easily deploy for the purposes of their pandemic preparedness planning. After all, there have been so many advances in medicine and pharmacology during the course of the past century alone. It is certainly true that many new medicines were developed in the twentieth century. Since the late 1920s, for instance, doctors have gradually seen the development and introduction of more than 80 different antibiotics to treat a range of bacterial infections. When it comes to influenza, however, the therapeutic landscape is markedly different, and there are actually far fewer medical options available than people might think.

One reason for this is that viruses, not bacteria, cause influenza. Viruses tend to be physically much smaller than bacteria. They also replicate *inside* human cells. That makes them much more difficult to target pharmaceutically, especially without also destroying their human host cells in the process. In fact, the very first antiviral medication (as opposed to antibiotic therapy) only became available in the 1960s, and over the next 25 years only four additional ones were developed (Dolan and Moukheibe 2003). Not until the AIDS pandemic would the pharmaceutical landscape of antivirals become radically transformed, which then stimulated the development of 23 new drugs in a space of just 15 years (Dolan and Moukheibe 2003). Developing safe and effective antiviral medications for flu thus remains very challenging, even today.

Why is it so challenging? A big part of the challenge has to do with how the human body responds to influenza viruses. The immune system normally "defends" itself against new microorganisms by producing specialized cells that destroy these tiny microbial attackers. The downside of this mechanism is that it takes some time for the process to unfold. In the meantime, the infection could already have progressed far enough to cause a range of unpleasant symptoms. But there is also an upside. Once this process has run its course, the body will generally be well protected against any future "invasion" of that same virus. This is because the next time around it will be able to produce the correct antibodies much more rapidly. That is also the reason why people usually only get diseases like measles once and are protected thereafter. On top of that, there are ways for people to get ahead of the curve by using preventive vaccines, which can stimulate the body into producing relevant antibodies in advance of an infection. Once a new virus enters the body, the immune system will then recognize the pathogen and can fight off the infection before it causes much harm.

When it comes to influenza, however, things are not quite as straightforward. Because influenza viruses are constantly mutating, the surface of the virus can look different from one year to the next (Schneider 2001). This means the immune system does not recognize and cannot efficiently fight off the new infection. The result is that the process of influenza infection can start all over again, leading to the recurrent problem of seasonal flu affecting so many people around the world year after year. From the perspective of the human immune system, the flu virus is a constantly shifting target, and so the system struggles more. It is simply a more complex challenge.

That very same problem also makes the use of medical interventions much more difficult in the case of flu. As we have just seen, vaccines usually work through the advance stimulation of the human immune system (prompting it to create new antibodies). This means vaccines usually have to be virus-specific in order to be effective. However, as the flu viruses keep changing from season to season, it is possible for the circulating influenza viruses to differ significantly from those included in the widely used flu vaccines. In that case, the latter will not offer much protection. With influenza forming such a constantly changing and fast-moving target, it is hard to predict exactly which of the many circulating strains will come to dominate during the next flu season. On top of this, there is also the problem that vaccine manufacturers still need a considerable lead time (spanning many months) to mass-produce seasonal flu vaccines.

At the moment, then, the best that influenza experts can do is to take a highly educated guess as to which strand of flu virus might be circulating in the next flu season. That is precisely what they do twice a year—once for the Northern Hemisphere, and once for the Southern Hemisphere. The processes of choosing the "right" viruses for the next vaccines are a finely tuned mix of science and art. Working with these recommendations, industry then begins the process of mass-producing the vaccine to ensure that the supplies are available in time for the flu season. Depending on how good the match turns out to be in the end, the process of seasonal flu vaccination is more successful in some years than in others. In any case, however, it is a process that must be repeated every year. It's a cumbersome and costly method, and many people of course also prefer not to be vaccinated. The ever-changing nature of influenza viruses thus complicates the use of medical interventions to manage the challenge they pose.

All of these issues are only exacerbated in the case of pandemic flu. It is, by definition, not possible to know in advance exactly what form a new pandemic influenza virus might take, making it is extremely difficult to develop an effective preventative vaccine *prior* to any flu pandemic occurring. That uncertainty alone creates a huge obstacle for a vaccine-based strategy for protecting populations against pandemic flu—though some prepandemic vaccines have recently been developed. How can an advance vaccine be developed against a flu virus when it is not known exactly what such a pandemic virus will look like?

Why, then, can governments not simply wait for a new pandemic flu virus to emerge and then quickly mass-produce a new vaccine based on that exact virus? Here the catch is, once again, the long lead time it takes time to mass-produce a vaccine. In the current model of vaccine production, it takes at least six to nine months to mass-produce a new pandemic vaccine, and that assumes that the process goes smoothly. Flu vaccines are traditionally also grown in eggs, and there may not be sufficient eggs available to meet pandemic demand for vaccine. So it would be several months, perhaps even a year, before a steady supply of pandemic flu vaccines specifically matched to the new strain would become available. In the meantime, countries would have to endure the full-blown effects of a pandemic for many months, without the availability of a protective vaccine for their populations.

There is also another catch. The scenario described above pertains to countries that possess their own vaccine manufacturing base. Most countries around the world, however, do not even possess their own domestic vaccine production capabilities. Once a pandemic vaccine does finally become available, there will not be nearly enough supply to meet global demand. That in turn raises nightmarish humanitarian scenarios around unequal global access to vaccines and around who in the world will be left unprotected from a lethal virus. There are thus several significant problems with relying on vaccines to protect populations against the threat of pandemic flu, ranging from their underlying mechanism of action to the technical challenges of developing new vaccines, as well as the limits of the current international political economy of vaccine production.

When it comes to pandemic influenza, then, governments are actually left confronting a quite unsavory and thorny political scenario. In the event of a new flu pandemic, they would initially have to let the virus run its course for many months while they wait for a virus-specific vaccine to gradually become available—provided, that is, they even have production capacity or are at least able to secure orders from elsewhere. This long period of delay could have devastating social, economic, political, and public health ramifications. During this period, governments would also run the political risk of being seen as weak, even negligent, in their core duty to protect the welfare of their populations. All the while, the virus could wreak immense human and socioeconomic havoc. It is clearly not a very desirable scenario for governments or indeed their people.

Are there not any other pharmaceutical interventions besides vaccines that governments could possibly opt for instead? The only other pharmaceutical option to protect populations against flu are antiviral medications. They differ from vaccines in that they do not work by priming the human immune system against a specific virus in advance of infection. Instead, antiviral medications seek to interrupt the process of viral replication taking place inside the human body, thereby buying valuable time for the human immune system to do its work. Antivirals thus offer the prospect of a very different approach from the vaccine-based strategies.

The problem with antivirals, however, is that there simply are not many types of influenza antivirals on the market. Notable examples from the past include amantadine and rimantadine. Developed in the 1960s, they represented the first class of influenza antivirals. They may superficially appear to be a more appealing option when compared to vaccines. One particularly attractive feature, for instance, is that they could work across a wide range of influenza viruses—unlike vaccines, which need to be virus-specific. In practice, however, these early influenza antivirals proved only modestly effective from a clinical point of view. They were also associated with several side effects, and viruses tended to become resistant to them very rapidly (Schneider 2001; von Itzstein 2007: 967). There would thus be significant issues with governments relying upon their widespread use during a pandemic.

The bottom line with regard to pharmaceutical interventions for pandemic flu is therefore actually this: all the medical advances of the twentieth century notwithstanding, the best that most people could immediately hope for in terms of medical interventions would be symptom-relief medication. A wide range of such over-the-counter products is already on offer in many countries. These may make people feel better by relieving some of the unpleasant symptoms of flu, but they do not combat the underlying virus infection. Upon reflection, it is not a particularly impressive or reassuring state of affairs—not for individual patients, and not for governments wishing to protect their populations against a future flu pandemic that many experts expect will eventually occur.

In the absence of such pharmaceutical interventions, the only other option is for governments to fall back upon their more traditional public health measures. These essentially seek to reduce the human spread of the virus by curtailing the movement of people. They can entail a variety of measures—like school closures, canceling public events, quarantine, isolation, temperature screening at airports, and so forth. Yet these measures, too, clearly have a number of drawbacks. Their introduction does not tend to be very popular politically, as they entail infringing upon the free movement of citizens. There are also questions about how effective they would be in practice. And they would of course result in the shutting down of many systems of circulation that are vital to the overall welfare of the population, such as trade, travel, education, and so forth. These measures may end up saving lives, but from an economic and social point of view, the interventions would be nearly as bad as the pandemic itself. In this scenario, too, there would be immense socioeconomic disruption. The "cure," in short, would not be that much better than the "poison." When it comes to confronting the specter of pandemic flu, there are simply very few attractive policy options for any government wishing to effectively protect its population.

A New Molecular Dawn: The Scientific Birth
of Neuraminidase Inhibitors

The limited therapeutic landscape for flu would only begin to change in the late 1990s with the development of a second generation of antiviral medications called neuraminidase inhibitors. A much-improved scientific understanding of the molecular processes involved in viral replication had made their development possible. After the first human influenza virus was isolated in 1933, scientists began to understand that viruses cannot replicate on their own. To do so, they first have to insert themselves into other cells. They can then "hijack" those cells in order to make more copies of themselves. The newly formed virus particles subsequently leave the host cell again, destroying the cell in the process. Once released, the newly formed viruses can then also go on to infect further cells, repeating this cycle over and over again and causing disease in the human body (Schneider 2001).

Over the course of the twentieth century, scientists gradually refined their knowledge of all of these molecular processes unfolding inside the human body during an influenza infection. One such scientist was George Hirst, who is widely regarded today as a historic pioneer in molecular virology. Working at the famous Rockefeller Institute in New York in the 1940s, Hirst suspected that influenza viruses possess a crucial enzyme that destroys virus receptors on host cells (Laver et al. 2000: 180). It was a critical hypothesis, as it was later confirmed that such an enzyme—called neuraminidase—does indeed exist. As the newly formed viruses leave the host cell, they become attached to a sticky coating of sialic acid found on the surface of the host cell. In order to unstick themselves they therefore have to rely on the work of this critical enzyme called neuraminidase. Metaphorically, the neuraminidase acts like a pair of scissors that cuts newly formed virus particles free from the surface of their host cells, allowing these new virus particles to then go on to infect yet more cells, thus extending into a wider infection. Without necessarily knowing it, many will already be familiar with this neuraminidase because it is widely identified by the "N" designation in the international virus classifications commonly used in the scientific literature and also frequently reported in the media for naming influenza viruses—like H5N1, H1N1, H7N9, etc. (where the H refers to the other surface protein called hemagglutinin, which allows viruses to stick to the surface of cells lining the respiratory tract).

All of this begs the question of what would happen to influenza viruses without the proper functioning of this critical neuraminidase? In that case, the new viruses would not be destroyed, but they would likely remain stuck on the surface of the host cell, unable to free themselves. Being stuck, they could not easily go on to infect other cells, as would be necessary for causing a wider and more severe infection in the body. Therefore, if there could be a pharmaceutical way to disrupt or inhibit the proper functioning of this crucial neuraminidase enzyme, that could mark an exciting entry point for a new type of antiviral medication—at least in theory.

That highly attractive prospect moved a big step closer in the 1970s and 1980s, when the precise molecular structure of the neuraminidase enzyme was first decoded. The Australian scientist Professor Graeme Laver had found a way of spinning neuraminidase into a crystalline form (using a centrifuge). Laver was working for the Australian National University in Canberra at the time. By his own admission, creating such a crystalline form of neuraminidase was largely a matter of serendipity. In an email to one of his students he later recalled how the idea of trying to crystallize neuraminidase came to him in March 1977, while he was on a long flight from Europe back to Australia. He was adamant that his discovery was essentially one of "sheer luck and not at all intentional" (Laver n.d.). In fact, initially Laver did not really know what he should do with the new crystals. He did not realize at the time that having the neuraminidase in such a crystal form, rather than in its normal amorphous form, would soon open up critical new possibilities for studying it scientifically (Jack 2006).

Laver was later introduced to Peter Colman, who was working in Melbourne at the protein chemistry division of the Australian research organization called the Commonwealth Scientific and Industrial Research Organization (CSIRO). A number of scientists at the time were beginning to map the precise chemical structures of biological molecules through a new technique called X-ray crystallography. For the process to work properly, however, scientists first needed a crystal of the molecules they wished to study. That crystal would then be placed in a beam of X-rays. Analysis of the resulting diffraction patterns would allow the relative positions of the atoms and molecules to be determined. Having the neuraminidase enzyme in its crystallized form (thanks to Laver), Colman could now use that very same technique to also "solve" the neuraminidase enzyme's crystal structure. He did so and then published the findings in *Nature* in 1983

(Varghese et al. 1983). By 1983 scientists were thus able—for the first time in history—to map the spatial arrangement of the thousands of atoms that make up the neuraminidase molecule.

Decoding these precise molecular structures yielded yet another critical discovery, perhaps the most pivotal one of all. The surface of influenza neuraminidase can change from one influenza virus to another. Yet the scientists also managed to find a crucial site that appeared to remain constant across most influenza viruses, a deep cleft or pocket-like cavity. This may sound like a lot of scientific detail, but this static site could effectively turn out to be the influenza viruses' Achilles heel. If this site remained very stable, even as influenza viruses constantly changed, it could be a valuable site that a new type of drug could target (Schneider 2001; Webster 2010: 230). With this new knowledge about its precise molecular structure, it might now be possible to engage in a project of rational drug design by deliberately designing a new synthetic molecule to work upon this newly identified target (Laver and Garman 2002: 1312). The refined scientific understanding of the molecular structure and processes involved in influenza infection had suddenly opened up the possibility of a new therapeutic approach.

To take this project forward, Laver and his colleagues next set up a new biotechnology company in Australia called Biota Holdings. CSIRO and the university did not have the funds to support the commercial development of the new drug target. So Biota Holdings purchased the patents and then sought funds to develop the drug at the Victoria College of Pharmacy in collaboration with Mark von Itzstein (O'Neill 1989). A team of researchers led by von Itzstein studied the crucial cleft and then used computer simulations to design a new molecule that would "plug in" to it (Jack 2006). In essence, that is how the world's first neuraminidase inhibitor was born. Von Itzstein published the exciting discovery in the prestigious scientific journal *Nature* in 1993. It promised to be a major breakthrough.

To be clear, even if it worked as intended, this new molecule would not actually "cure" people of the flu. It would not even destroy the viruses already inside the human body. But the idea was that it could help to suppress the process of viral replication in the human body. In theory, that would buy valuable time for the natural immune system to respond to the (reduced) infection, provided the therapy was started in the early stages of infection. It promised to be a major advance in the therapeutic landscape for influenza. Laver had made the crystals; Colman had solved the molecular structure and discovered the site; von Itzstein had made the new drug. All three therefore shared the 1996 Australia Prize for their contributions to this critical development. On paper at least, neuraminidase inhibitors heralded the prospect of doing something that human evolution could not—finding a way of keeping the influenza virus in check. A series of scientific breakthroughs now heralded the prospect of a very new way of protecting people against the flu.

Nor is it hard to see the potential attraction of this new antiviral from the perspective of governments also trying to better protect their populations against the threat of pandemic flu. A whole new way of managing the influenza threat pharmaceutically had suddenly become possible. Crucially, these new antivirals would not have to be virus-specific in the same way that vaccines had to be. Because the scientists had identified a static site, there was a good chance that neuraminidase inhibitors would work across a broad cross section of influenza viruses, including future ones that might cause a pandemic. This meant that neuraminidase inhibitors could probably be administered almost immediately after the outbreak of a new influenza pandemic, in contrast to the long lead time of many months needed for new pandemic vaccines to become available. Provided such antivirals were readily at hand in sufficient quantities, neuraminidase inhibitors could effectively form a new first line of defense against pandemic flu and could buy governments valuable time until pandemic vaccines became more widely available. Neuraminidase could finally give government planners the option of responding to an anticipated flu pandemic pharmaceutically, without first having to wait many months and without resorting to much more intrusive public health measures. Before any of these potential benefits could accrue, however, there was still a lot of commercial drug development work that would need to be carried out first.

From Bench to Bedside: The Commercial Lure of the Seasonal Flu Market

No matter how ingenious the scientific discovery, taking a promising new drug candidate from the "bench" to the "beside" is a complicated and costly process. It involves carrying out large-scale clinical trials, gaining regulatory approval, building commercial production facilities, developing marketing strategies, and so forth. Somebody has to have the expertise to carry out these tasks as well as the funds to take on the considerable commercial risk involved. Clearly that company could not be Biota. As a new and small biotechnology company, it had neither the skills nor the funds nor the experience to do all of these things on its own. In order to move the new molecule forward to the next stage of its commercial development, the company would need the help of a much larger and more experienced pharmaceutical company.

Fortunately, Biota found one such company that was interested, and in 1990 Biota licensed the new compound to the UK-based pharmaceutical company Glaxo Wellcome. As a large and well-established pharmaceutical company, Glaxo Wellcome possessed the requisite funds and expertise in drug commercialization that Biota lacked. In an interview about the new neuraminidase inhibitor with the Australian Broadcasting Corporation in 1999, Laver recalled just how crucial it had been to find that partner: "You wouldn't believe the number of knock-backs we had and it only took off when one of the big drug companies took it up and then all the other big drug companies wanted to be in it too" (Laver 1999). Asked whether he was surprised that the compound was licensed to a UK-based rather than an Australian company, Laver tellingly replied: "Surprise? . . . No, because we know it's effective and we know that there's a huge market for it and to develop these drugs, taking them from the lab to the clinical trials to the community literally costs hundreds of millions of dollars. And, no. I mean, there's no company in Australia big enough for it" (Laver 1999).

With the benefit of hindsight, then, it is clear that Glaxo Wellcome's decision to take on the new drug candidate was absolutely critical for transforming it into a product that could eventually be prescribed to patients and stockpiled by governments against the threat of pandemic flu. Biota would not have been able to undertake this work on its own. Without a partner like Glaxo Wellcome, the new drug candidate would likely have simply lingered on or fizzled out with no one willing to take it forward. It would have gone down in history as a laudable scientific discovery but not much more than that. With a single stroke, Glaxo Wellcome's decision seemed to change all of that.

So why did Glaxo Wellcome decide to take on this new product? The company decided to do so mostly on quite conventional commercial grounds. In fact, its decision at the time appears to have had very little if anything to do with health security considerations about pandemic flu. Instead, the company was mostly interested in the lucrative market for *seasonal* flu. Why seasonal flu? To the casual observer seasonal flu may not seem like a particularly significant public health problem, especially when compared to the more menacing specter of pandemic flu. It might not appear worthy of sustained interest by pharmaceutical companies seeking to generate high-revenue producing "blockbuster" drugs. The symptoms of flu are unpleasant, to be sure; they include fever, cough, sore throat, myalgia and headache. Yet for adults who are otherwise healthy, seasonal flu is usually also a self-limiting illness. When left untreated, it tends to run its course in a matter of one to two weeks. One could therefore be forgiven for wondering why any large pharmaceutical company would want to invest immense sums of money into developing a new treatment for seasonal flu. That is especially true when one also considers the fact that there are already so many over-the-counter products readily available for relieving or reducing many of the flu's unpleasant symptoms.

In reality, however, the seasonal flu landscape is a little more complicated than this simplistic picture suggests. Even when flu is not life threatening, the symptoms are sufficiently unpleasant that many people might be willing to pay significant sums of money each year on a wide range of symptom-relief medications. That market would represent a sizable commercial opportunity for any company that could develop an effective, safe, and easy-to-take pharmaceutical "fix." At the time that companies were developing neuraminidase inhibitors, estimates indicated that each year there were around 100 million people suffering from seasonal flu in the world's major pharmaceutical markets such as the United States, Japan, and Europe (Schneider 2001). For those with sufficient disposable income, a new flu treatment could be marketed as a way for preventing the onset of the unpleasant symptoms of flu. That was a potentially hugely attractive commercial market.

The large number of people who are affected by flu every year could also provide a new drug with an additional public health market. The sheer volume and scale of annual influenza infections generates a substantial public health and economic burden in many societies around the world. The CDC, which is charged with protecting public health and controlling disease in the United States, estimates that every year—on average—between 5 and

20 percent of the population becomes infected with the flu in the United States, leading to more than 200,000 annual hospitalizations linked to flu-related complications (CDC 2012). A potential new influenza therapy might thus also be considered by governments as part of their wider public health strategies. It is, after all, precisely because of this burden that many governments already make seasonal flu shots available for many people. Here a new antiviral treatment held out the prospect of also tapping into a significant public health market, broadening the commercial opportunities further still.

Finally, it is important to bear in mind that there are also circumstances in which an influenza infection can kill—especially in persons with a number of other underlying medical risk factors. Those at risk from flu complications include groups like older people, young children, pregnant women, and people with certain underlying health conditions. Between 1976 and 2006, annual estimates of flu-related deaths range from 3,000 to 49,000, depending on the severity of the flu season (CDC 2012). There was thus a reasonable prospect that a new antiviral might also be used preventatively in places like nursing homes for the elderly. That, in turn, could represent yet another commercial market.

When one considers all of these possibilities, then, there is actually a potentially very sizable, lucrative, and recurring commercial market of people and institutions that might be willing to pay for a new influenza treatment. This predictable and potentially highly profitable commercial market for a common illness affecting millions of people a year—*every* year—is what ultimately prompted a large pharmaceutical company like Glaxo Wellcome to enter the proverbial "ring" and invest its extensive resources and expertise in taking Biota's new molecule forward. So the molecular discovery was further developed and eventually turned into a new pharmaceutical product that could obtain regulatory approval and be prescribed to patients. The name they gave this new product in the end was Relenza, which reportedly derives its trademark name from RELief of influ-ENZA (Garfield 2009). All of this also means, however, that the major driver for the commercial development of the world's first neuraminidase inhibitors was *seasonal* flu, not pandemic flu. Upon closer inspection it turns out that neuraminidase inhibitors were very much born as *accidental* medical countermeasures; they are largely the fortuitous byproduct of fairly conventional commercial efforts to address the parallel problem of seasonal flu.

Where Is the Market for Medical Countermeasures?

The fact that the world's first neuraminidase inhibitor was largely developed with seasonal flu in mind—and not for pandemic flu—is highly significant for the wider quest to develop new medical countermeasures. It suggests that pharmaceutical development tends to be driven by strict commercial logics and not by security considerations. Governments may well be keen to acquire new medical countermeasures to better protect their populations and economies against an array of biological threats like pandemic flu. Most pharmaceutical development, however, is carried out by large pharmaceutical companies that are driven by commercial considerations and market forces. Indeed, we have just seen that the main reason why a large pharmaceutical company took a neuraminidase inhibitor like Relenza forward was because of the sizable commercial market for seasonal flu. To put that point another way, the fact that we have at least some medical countermeasures against pandemic flu available today (in the form of neuraminidase inhibitors) is largely due to an accident of history. It is essentially explained by the Janus-faced nature of flu.

If that is true, however, it immediately begs another question: What would have happened to this exciting new molecule without the existence of that parallel commercial market for seasonal flu? Would a large pharmaceutical company like Glaxo Wellcome still have taken on its risky commercial development solely on the basis of the pandemic flu threat? It is impossible to be certain about such a counterfactual scenario, but it does seem rather unlikely. The threat of pandemic flu on its own would probably have proved too unpredictable and diffuse to justify the level of commercial investment needed. As Angus Nicoll put it at the time in his capacity as the head of the influenza program at the European Centre for Disease Prevention and Control (ECDC), when it comes to pandemic flu we just "don't know when one is going to happen, where it will start or what it will be like" (Nicoll and Sprenger 2011: 191). There is just too much uncertainty around the threat of pandemic flu in terms of when (or indeed if) it will arise, how large it will be, and exactly what it will look like. It is very difficult to construct a persuasive commercial business model around such a high degree of uncertainty.

That same fundamental uncertainty also plagues most other health security threats. Consider, for example, the threat of bioterrorism. It too remains highly unpredictable and deeply uncertain. Will such an attack ever occur? What agent would be used? How many people would likely be affected? Where would it occur? All of that uncertainty again makes it very difficult to construct a viable business case for developing a costly new medical countermeasure. How can a large commercial pharmaceutical company, existing in a competitive environment and with shareholders to satisfy, construct a commercial business case for developing a new drug against a threat for which it is not known *when* it will materialize, *if* it will materialize, and—even if it does materialize—*who* and *how many* people it will affect? Overall, the cost of new medical countermeasure development simply remains too high compared to the low frequency and massive uncertainty around health security threats. In many ways, the market for medical countermeasures is the exact opposite of what most commercially operating pharmaceutical companies would be looking for in an attractive business case to take a new product forward.

Moving from the development of more routine pharmaceuticals to the world of security and medical countermeasures thus alters the overall commercial equation for new drug development considerably. The conventional political economy of pharmaceutical development that worked so well—but essentially accidently—in the case of flu, is unlikely to work when applied to most other health security threats. Unlike flu, these other biological threats simply do not have a parallel commercial market to drive the costly drug development process forward. When it comes to the world of medical countermeasures more generally, the conventional political economy of pharmaceutical development is therefore profoundly disrupted, and it remains unclear who will take the development of such products forward, especially given the fact that almost all drug development nowadays is carried out by large commercial pharmaceutical companies.

Instead, a considerable gap begins to open up between the growing political demand for new pharmaceutical defenses expressed by governments on the one hand and the lack of commercial drivers that pharmaceutical companies are looking for in order to develop such products on the other. Precisely that gap also helps to explain why, in practice, it has actually proved very difficult for governments to persuade (especially large) pharmaceutical companies to become more actively involved in the quest to develop new medical countermeasures. The increased political desire for developing novel medical countermeasures is simply not very well aligned with the research and development priorities of large pharmaceutical companies, most of which avoid the area of medical countermeasures. In the end, governments are thus left confronting a quite protracted economic challenge about how to persuade commercially operating pharmaceutical companies to develop new medical countermeasures in the absence of an underlying commercial market to sell those products into.

Revisiting these very earliest stages in the life of neuraminidase inhibitors, then, already reveals two major challenges confronting efforts to develop new medical countermeasures more generally—perhaps the two most formidable of all. The first is *scientific*. As with many new types of medicines, there are considerable scientific challenges that must be overcome before a new medical countermeasure can actually be designed. In the case of flu, our increased scientific understanding of the molecular processes involved in influenza virus replication revealed the way in which the surface proteins of the virus can mutate, possibly leading to new pandemic threats in the future. The subsequent decoding of the exact molecular structures of some of those surface proteins (especially neuraminidase) then led to the identification of a new drug target and eventually even the scientific design of an artificial new molecule to interfere with the process of viral replication. Even at that stage, however, the development of Relenza still experienced a number of setbacks along the way, and serendipity also played a pivotal role in its discovery. The task of developing new drugs is scientifically and technologically so complex that many promising drug candidates never see the light of day. John Rex, vice president and medical director for infection at Astra-Zeneca, put its plainly: "Most new or in-development pharmaceutical products fail" (quoted in Wizemann et al. 2010: 18).

There are several different points along the way where a promising new drug candidate can suddenly transform into a "no-go." The three most significant factors impeding successful drug development are usually a failure in efficacy (the drug ends up not working as intended), a failure in safety (accounting for about two-thirds of failures), and failure in commercial considerations (e.g., cost to bring the product to market, perceived profitability of the product) (Wizemann et al. 2010: 5). The scientific challenges involved in new drug development cannot therefore be underestimated. Indeed, two industry experts explain: "We have so few drugs to show for so long and such expensive research not because we don't try hard enough, not because we are 'idiots,' but because it's extraordinarily hard to find effective, safe new drugs" (Bartfai and Lees 2006: 15). Expectations about the future development of new medical countermeasures will need to be tailored to that underlying reality. Their scientific development will likely be a slow and at times painstaking enterprise, with a number of setbacks along the way to be expected. It also means that the option of generating a novel countermeasure quickly in response to an unfolding crisis still remains remote in many areas at present (Cole 2013: 27).

That said, all of this does also point to at least one longer-term strategy that governments could adopt in relation to medical countermeasures: investing in scientific research. Molecular biology played a key role for the discovery of neuraminidase inhibitors—by refining our understanding of the molecular processes involved viral replication, by decoding the precise molecular structures of key elements of the virus, and also by identifying new molecular targets that could form new sites of pharmaceutical intervention. Extrapolating from that experience, public investment in science could also lead to other fundamental discoveries in the future that could then form the promising basis for new medicines and vaccines, albeit perhaps not in a very linear manner or along the path originally anticipated. Supporting basic science would thus mark one potentially quite significant way in which government can still influence the process of medical countermeasure development over the long run.

In addition to these scientific challenges, however, governments wishing to encourage the development of new medical countermeasures will also confront a second, economic obstacle. New drug development is usually a commercial process profoundly shaped by market forces and logics. It is also a very risky and expensive one. Conventional commercial drug development thus tends to be driven by private companies lured by the promise of a sizable, recurrent, and predictable market to offset these costs and risks. That is exactly what happened in case of Relenza. A large and experienced pharmaceutical company decided to invest in bringing the product to market largely because of the lucrative commercial market for seasonal flu. So the conventional political economy of pharmaceutical development worked successfully in that case, in the sense that Relenza was eventually brought to market.

Beyond flu, however, such parallel commercial markets do not exist for most other health security threats, making it much more difficult for companies to compile a viable business case justifying commercial investment in medical countermeasures. In the case of more widespread diseases, such as diabetes or cancer, a pharmaceutical company can usually calculate (or at least reasonably estimate) levels of demand, the price they can charge for their new product, the cost of development, the degree of market competition, and so forth (Matheny et al. 2007: 229). For health security threats, by contrast, no company can be sure when—or even if—a particular threat will materialize, how large the threat might be, and whether the threat is likely to repeat itself. Once a new product is developed, moreover, there will likely only be a handful of government buyers, perhaps even as few as one. The fact that medical countermeasures are aimed at rarer and more unpredictable security threats thus complicates matters considerably and begins to alter the underlying commercial equation for pharmaceutical companies. For most medical countermeasures, the conventional political economy of new drug development quickly falters because there is no parallel commercial market that companies can sell into. Most large pharmaceutical companies will simply steer a wide birth around the whole area of health security as a result. From the very outset, then, developing new medical countermeasures to protect populations involves confronting a formidable mixture of both scientific and economic challenges.

3

The Pill Always Wins

Gilead Sciences, Roche, and the Birth

of Tamiflu

With the commercial development of Relenza already well under way, what point was there in trying to develop a second neuraminidase inhibitor—to eventually become Tamiflu? The answer reveals another key consideration of pharmaceutical development: a medicine's method of administration. Relenza may have earned the distinction of being the world's first neuraminidase inhibitor, but it still suffered from at least one serious drawback. Patients had to use a fairly complicated, breath-activated inhalation device to administer a dry powder into their lungs. It would be much easier for patients if they could simply swallow a pill or capsule. Even though Relenza had a head start and would likely come to market first, a rival product with an easier method of administration could still catch up and quickly gain market share. In the long run, such a rival product could conceivably even overtake Relenza as the market leader for neuraminidase inhibitors. The birth of Tamiflu is the result of exactly that commercial wager.

This chapter explores the scientific and commercial development of Tamiflu as a direct competitor to Relenza. Looking in more depth at the birth of Tamiflu will reveal striking parallels with the story of Relenza. Like Relenza, Tamiflu was developed with a commercial eye to the lucrative seasonal flu market—and not primarily as a medical countermeasure against pandemic flu. As with Relenza, the scientific ability to determine and model the precise molecular structure of the viral neuraminidase was key. As with Relenza, the innovative molecule forming the basis for Tamiflu was initially developed by a small biotechnology company, in this case Gilead Sciences. And as with Relenza, the new compound was subsequently licensed for further commercial development to a much larger and more established pharmaceutical company, in this case Roche. The companies involved were different, and the method of administration was different, but the underlying pattern of molecular discovery and commercial drug development was very similar for both products.

This emerging pattern of pharmaceutical development points to a highly significant division of labor between smaller and larger pharmaceutical companies in the overall process of new drug development. Smaller companies tend to focus on initial innovation, and larger companies then specialize in later-stage development, when costs can rise dramatically. That division of labor is critical from the perspective of governments wishing to encourage the development of new medical countermeasures. It means that even if large pharmaceutical companies mostly eschew the area of medical countermeasures, there is still the possibility that smaller companies might be much more willing partners in this quest. Smaller pharmaceutical companies usually have lower opportunity costs, are often keener to access government funding as a way of stabilizing their more precarious financial position, and can also see other nonfinancial benefits from partnering with the government. Governments wishing to encourage the development of new medical countermeasures could thus try to form closer partnerships with such smaller or medium-sized pharmaceutical companies instead. That in fact is the strategy that most government efforts to develop new medical countermeasures have taken over the past decade—especially in the United States.

Yet going down that route of working primarily with smaller companies then immediately gives rise to another challenge: Who will subsequently carry out all the late-stage development work? This work—which includes conducting large-scale clinical trials, planning mass-production processes, gaining regulatory approval, and so forth—is vital for successfully transforming a new compound or molecule into a viable pharmaceutical product. In the conventional model of drug development this work is mostly carried out by the larger pharmaceutical companies because the smaller ones usually do not possess the requisite resources and expertise to do so. Once governments form successful partnerships with smaller companies, they will therefore still have to figure out a way of carrying out these vital later-stage development tasks. Making sure that promising new products do not perish in what the industry calls the developmental "valley of death", and that this late-stage development work is completed successfully, is thus a third major challenge that arises in the quest to develop of new medical countermeasures more generally. It is also the reason why the US government eventually decided to establish a whole new institution dedicated to helping pharmaceutical companies with carrying out such advanced development tasks—the Biomedical Advanced Research and Development Authority.

Gilead Sciences, Michael Riordan, and . . . Donald Rumsfeld

Scientific advances in molecular biology have so far taken us to Relenza and the development of the world's first neuraminidase inhibitor. To get to the birth of Tamiflu, we also need to take into account the complex ecology of venture capital and biotechnology startups simmering in California in the early 1990s. Michael Riordan is the key protagonist in that story. He set up a new biotechnology company called Oligogen in 1987. Aged only 29 at the time, Riordan possessed quite impressive academic credentials, having graduated with a medical degree from Johns Hopkins in 1984 and an MBA from Harvard in 1986.

When he set up his new company, Riordan had just finished working for the capital venture company Menlo Ventures. The company was named after its geographical location in Menlo Park, south of San Francisco. Menlo Ventures essentially raised pools of money that it was looking to invest in new or early-stage companies, and Riordan's role there mostly involved managing the company's medical investments. He had essentially been tasked with using his scientific knowledge and contacts to spot new companies that could prove to be good investment opportunities. At one point, he told me during an interview for this book, he was even speaking to Apple cofounder Steve Jobs about an opportunity in the field of computer graphics (Riordan 2013b).

Yet Riordan also harbored deep entrepreneurial ambitions to set up his own company one day. He was particularly interested in the rapidly evolving field of nucleotide chemistry, the study of the molecular building blocks of DNA and RNA. He spent a lot of time getting to know the academic leaders in the field. He would even fly out to Japan during his holidays to meet scientists who had made significant progress in that field. Because the venture capital business is so competitive, Riordan was worried that somebody might scoop his idea. So he initially kept his thoughts for a new company under wraps. As his plans firmed up, however, he eventually informed

Menlo Ventures about them. He even explored the possibility that they might invest in the new venture themselves. Following successful negotiations, Riordan initially secured $2 million from Menlo for his new company and later also raised other investments of $10 million.

Riordan founded his new company in June of 1987, but it would take him until late summer of that year to find a suitable geographic site for its location. Riordan recalls being torn between staying in the San Francisco Bay Area or heading further south to San Diego, also home to a burgeoning biotech industry. As most of the people that he wanted to hire for his new company were already living in the Bay Area, Riordan finally decided to set up his new company there. He started searching up and down the San Francisco Peninsula for a suitable site and eventually managed to find a fitting laboratory space in a company (Kevex Corporation) where Glenn Seaborg had been chairman of the board. Seaborg was a famous American chemist and Nobel laureate who codiscovered several new elements, including plutonium. The site was located in Foster City, just south of San Francisco. With the site secured, Riordan now went about buying up a number of used laboratory benches, furniture, and other materials to equip the new site.

Riordan initially named his new company Oligogen, even though he never intended that to be its final name. He really wanted to call his new company Gilead Sciences instead—after the ancient site of a healing willow tree. Riordan first came across the Gilead name during medical school, where he read the play *Balm in Gilead* by Lanford Wilson. He explains: "I wondered where the word came from, and found out that a willow tree species from the ancient region of Gilead had been found in modern times to contain acetylsalicylic acid, or aspirin. So the willow extract from Gilead was one of the first genuine therapeutics" (Riordan 2013a). He could not use that name from the outset, however, because a nonprofit organization in California was already using Gilead in its name. Riordan would first have to ensure that there would be no trademark issues. So he established contact with the organization and donated $1,000 in return for being able to use the name. Now the road was clear for renaming his new company Gilead Sciences, which is the name it retains to this day. By this stage Riordan had secured both a good location for the company and its desired name.

Yet Riordan also needed good scientists to form the backbone of his new company. He soon managed to assemble what can only be described as quite a stellar team of scientists. Many of those who joined the new company would go on to receive high scientific and commercial acclaim. Scientists advising the company in these early days include Harold Varmus, who received the Nobel Prize a year after becoming an advisor at Gilead, and who also went on become director of the National Institutes of Health. Jack Szostak, recipient of the Nobel Prize for Physiology or Medicine in 2009, was another Gilead advisor (Riordan 2013b). Riordan also successfully recruited Gordon Moore, who later became the cofounder of Intel Corporation (Riordan 2013b).

Even with a name, a site, and such a high-caliber cadre of scientists in place, however, Riordan's business model still contained one glaring weakness. Riordan had very little hands-on experience with the actual day-to-day running of a new biotechnology company. To remedy this gap Riordan tried to persuade other people with more extensive industry experience to sit on the company's board. Riordan first asked DuBose Montgomery, with whom he had earlier worked at Menlo, to join the board. Montgomery agreed, and went on to serve on Gilead's board for 10 years (serving as Chairman for 6 of those years). Together Riordan and Montgomery set about recruiting other influential business people to serve on the new company's board. They next recruited Benno Schmidt, an influential lawyer widely credited with having coined the term "venture capital."

Without question, however, the most surprising person on Riordan's "hit list" was Donald Rumsfeld—the same Donald Rumsfeld who later became secretary of defense in the George W. Bush administration. Most people are unaware that prior to this influential political role, Rumsfeld had an extensive career in the pharmaceutical industry. Rumsfeld served as chief executive officer of G. D. Searle (a worldwide pharmaceutical company) from 1977 to 1985. During that time, he was even twice recognized as the Outstanding Chief Executive Officer by the pharmaceutical industry (in 1980 and 1981). As Riordan explained,

> And then the next person I recruited to the board was Don Rumsfeld, who I had been tracking for some time because he was one of the few people who had experience in leading a pharmaceutical company. . . . And so he had been on my hit list and I started keeping a file on him—back in the days when you had to keep paper files instead of computer files. And so I figured out some people who might be able to introduce me to him. I kept calling him and trying to meet with him

and he finally said yes, and I flew out to Southern California where he was giving a speech and that was the first time we talked. . . . And eventually—within a few months or six months, I don't remember exactly how long—he said yes. So that was another big plus for the company; he also agreed to invest some of his personal money in a round of financing, I think the next one that came up. So he was the first sort of outside nonpure investor director. (Riordan 2013b)

Following Riordan's successful recruitment efforts, Rumsfeld joined Gilead as a director in 1988. Riordan recalls that Rumsfeld was particularly helpful at facilitating links and introductions to other senior figures in the pharmaceutical industry (Riordan 2013b).

Besides Rumsfeld, there were also other political heavyweights serving on the Gilead board. Another prominent board member with strong political connections was George P. Shultz (from 1996 to 2005)—a former US secretary of state for the Reagan administration who had also served as secretary of the treasury, secretary of labor, and director of the Office of Management and Budget (Gilead Sciences 2010). Gayle Wilson, who was California's first lady from 1991 to 1999 and married to former California governor and senator Pete Wilson, was another (Gilead 2010b). Gilead was rapidly developing a very strong track record of attracting influential and well-connected people to its board.

That said, the Gilead team did not always get the people they wanted. One notable person who did not join was Condoleezza Rice, even though she had been personally approached by Rumsfeld. According to papers located in his archives, Rumsfeld went to considerable lengths to persuade Rice to join the board. On 9 November 1998, for example, Rumsfeld wrote to George Shultz:

> At the right moment, we ought to have a woman on the Gilead Board. I don't know anyone who would be better than Condi Rice. I know that everyone in the world is already after her. And I suspect there will be even more after her in the coming period. Why don't you have lunch with her and talk to her a bit about Gilead. The fact that it meets in Foster City and that it only meets four times a year ought to be attractive. I think that if we decide to go after her, we'd better get ourselves in the queue before she makes any public decisions about her future. The minute she does it, it is going to be a long line. Please let me know what you think. (Rumsfeld 1998)

Rumsfeld later followed up his efforts with a direct message to Rice. On 29 March 1999 he wrote to her again:

> Dear Condi:
>   When are you going to call me up and say, "Gee, Don, I would be delighted to join the Gilead Board. I think that is just a wonderful idea! Those are good folks, it is an interesting business, it is nearby, it only meets four times a year, so the answer is yes!" Patiently,
>   Signed Don (Rumsfeld 1999)

Rumsfeld was ultimately unsuccessful in this matter, though of course he would later go on to work very closely with Rice when she became secretary of state and national security advisor in the George W. Bush administration. Even without her involvement, however, the board was certainly a politically influential collection of people. As for Rumsfeld, he went on to eventually replace Riordan as chairman of the Gilead board in 1997. With a strong board now in place, Gilead Sciences quickly began to grow—so much so that it would soon have to move to a new and larger site in Foster City, where it remains headquartered to this day.

Gilead Sciences has since gone on to evolve into a large and highly profitable company. Yet one of the most striking things in looking back at those early days of the company is just how precarious an undertaking the whole endeavor was initially. Even with a prestigious array of scientists and businesspeople on board, Riordan recalls "just how close the company was to death on a few occasions. Looking back people don't understand, the first decade was pretty close to the edge. . . . It was touch and go for a long time" (Riordan 2013b). The overriding question of how to make money

> was a preoccupation of mine every second of the day for eight years. We are not making any money, we had some revenue from contracts and collaborations. . . . The good news is that at the time there were a lot of institutional investors who are willing to make that bet. But they cut, they came and went. So, when you're not making money you don't know if you're going to be able to raise money tomorrow, because the marketing conditions fluctuate. So I was worried about this all the time; this was the main concern of my life. (Riordan 2013b)

Riordan recalls that on several occasions he felt as though he was looking at the cliff and was even considered doing some kind of deal with a big pharmaceutical company just to keep the company on its feet (Riordan 2013b).

His experiences reflect the fact that smaller pharmaceutical companies often live a much more precarious existence compared to their larger and more established counterparts.

That fundamental difference between small and large pharmaceutical companies is potentially also highly pertinent for governments wishing to encourage the development of new medical countermeasures. It means that even though large pharmaceutical companies will largely eschew the area of medical countermeasures, smaller companies may be much more interested in partnering with governments as a way of accessing vital funds and gaining some stability. That, in fact, is one of the strategies that Riordan himself initially pursued for Gilead Sciences during those early and very precarious years. Gilead, for example, signed an agreement with the Department of Defense's Defense Advanced Research Projects Agency over potential treatments against malaria and dengue fever.

Why did Gilead decide to enter into this agreement with the government at the time? In his interview, Riordan recalls being interested in the deal for several reasons. One was that it involved vital funding that the young company so desperately needed. Beyond the funding, Gilead might also be able to apply the lessons and technologies derived from the project for other commercial applications. That could benefit the company further down the line. As a respected government agency, moreover, the contract also provided external validation for a new and young company still trying to establish itself commercially (Riordan 2013b). These early and quite uncertain days in the history of Gilead thus also suggest more generally that smaller and younger pharmaceutical companies might be much more amenable to government partnerships. For governments interested in developing new medical countermeasures, a more nuanced strategy might well consist of specifically targeting and working with such smaller companies.

GS4104: The Discovery of a Neuraminidase Inhibitor in Capsule Form

How, then, did Gilead Sciences eventually get involved with Tamiflu? If one had to pin down Gilead's inspiration for developing Tamiflu to a specific date, it would probably have to be 14 October 1992. That was the day Gilead's lead for research and development at the time, Norbert Bischofberger, attended the major annual Interscience Conference on Antimicrobial Agents and Chemotherapy in Los Angeles. At the conference, Bischofberger chanced upon a poster presentation by Mark von Itzstein and his fellow researchers from Monash University in Parkville, Australia. The poster presentation detailed how the Australian team of researchers were working on developing the world's first neuraminidase inhibitor for influenza (Schneider 2001). The poster showed that the team managed to synthesize a new molecule, called GG167, which stopped the proliferation of influenza viruses in mice (Schneider 2001). It seemed that the scientists working in Australia had found a new molecule that successfully "plugged" the cleft of the neuraminidase. He was looking, of course, at the molecule that would later become the basis for Relenza.

Bischofberger was very interested in influenza because Gilead was already working on a number of other influenza agents at the time. The work formed part of the company's wider focus on antiviral development during those early days. The crucial findings of the Australian research team would not be published in *Nature* until the following year, but standing there and looking directly at the poster presentation at the conference, Bischofberger immediately realized that he was looking at something quite extraordinary. If correct, the new molecule could herald nothing less than the birth of a whole new class of antiviral drugs that worked by targeting viruses' neuraminidases—with a potentially enormous international market of annual flu sufferers (Laver et al. 2000: 183). The scientists from Australia might just have found the equivalent of the Holy Grail in influenza research.

As much as Bischofberger admired the scientific discovery staring him in the face, he also detected at least one crucial drawback with the new compound. The GG167 molecule—as it was still called at the time—did not move from the mice's stomachs into their blood stream. This meant that, in all likelihood, the drug would not work if swallowed; it would have to be inhaled. Biota and Glaxo (who were developing the compound commercially) actually thought that the inhalation delivery model would be preferable in the case of influenza (Schneider 2001). That is because the affected human cells were mostly located in the throat and the lungs, making an inhalational drug an obvious choice.

Bischofberger was not convinced, however. All his prior experience in the pharmaceutical industry led him to wager that, given a choice between inhaling a medicine and swallowing it, most people would prefer swallowing. That view was also shared by Gilead's senior director at the time, Dr. Choung Kim: "We had a flu program before . . . but we were looking at a different target. One reason we switched was because the Glaxo compound was not orally bioavailable. I've been in the drug-development business for 25 years, working on many anti-bacterial drugs in both injectable, inhalant and pill form. In the end, the pill is always the big winner" (quoted in Garfield 2009). All other things held equal, a pill is the easiest and most convenient form of administering a medicine and is thus likely to be favored by most doctors and patients alike.

Their hunch proved correct. Relenza would indeed have to be inhaled. The "diskhaler" eventually designed to administer Relenza was even more complicated than the common asthma inhalers still widely used today, which are familiar to many readers. The inhalation process required patients to modify their breathing to use the device properly and to follow a fairly complex set of instructions (Clinical Development Scientist 2015). It would usually also require patients to first receive detailed medical instruction in how to use the device properly. The process would take more than 10 steps, and patients also needed to remain mindful of additional instructions about how to properly hold, inspect, and replenish the device. All of that could pose particular challenges for administering the new drug to high-risk groups for influenza. The elderly, children, and those with underlying respiratory conditions might all struggle to use the device properly.

Beyond the immediate administration of the drug, moreover, there are also many other factors that could favor a pill or capsule. The latter might also have a longer shelf life. An orally administered agent could conceivably also be clinically more effective. That is because the activity of the medicine would not necessarily be restricted to the lungs but could also work in other areas of the body where the influenza virus might be replicating (Riordan 2013b). Although Relenza marked the first in a new class of medicines, its method of administration meant that it was still far from ideal.

Betting on the comparative attractions of a pill, Gilead quickly decided to throw its hat into the ring and entered the race to develop a Relenza rival in pill or capsule form. Kim recalls in an interview for the *Financial Times* how "there was time pressure for everything. We were losing money, and concerned if the company would make it. It was always clear to us that flu was a commercially interesting disease" (quoted in Jack 2006). And time was only one of many pressures, because Gilead Sciences was not the only company thinking about such a product.

Several other pharmaceutical companies also wanted to accomplish the same thing. The Australian scientist Graeme Laver, who had found a way of spinning neuraminidase into a crystalline form, was reportedly already selling his crystals to nearly a dozen other pharmaceutical companies interested in developing a pill-based neuraminidase inhibitor. That list of companies included formidable pharmaceutical "giants" like Pfizer, Abbott, and Eli Lilly (Jack 2006). International competition to find an orally available neuraminidase inhibitor would likely be intense. So, putting his proverbial money where his mouth was, Bischofberger returned to Foster City, and within a short time assembled a team of around ten people at Gilead to develop a neuraminidase inhibitor that could be orally administered (Schneider 2001). Other key members of the team included chemists such as Choung Kim and Swami Swaminathan.

How would they go about designing a rival product to Relenza? The use of three-dimensional computer modeling would prove critical in their quest to develop a promising new molecule. Under Riordan's leadership, Gilead Sciences had invested substantially in computing technology. That technology now enabled them to generate complex three-dimensional models of the molecular structure of the neuraminidase. Riordan recalls that with the aid of the computer models, it was "like gamers, you know, [who] have 3-D—you know shooter things. So this was, you could go in and you could say this atom is here, this atom is here, this atom is here. You could also measure the precise distances to get the hydrophobic modelling. . . . I think it is also the precision; you can build a model and say, "Well, I've got a greasy group here; I've got a polar group here but exactly where it is, the exact distances. . . ." I think that precision and the three-dimensional viewpoint [is key]" (Riordan 2013b). The computer models gave Gilead scientists a much clearer understanding and visualization of the molecular structure of neuraminidase and where there might be ways to design new compounds to interact with it.

With the help of such models the team could then also design new "virtual" molecules to see how they might attach to the neuraminidase. Riordan recalls that the scientists were literally hunched around the computer, intensely studying the model. "And they could also put in hypothetically other molecules that they could just make with the software and put them in the active site. And then they can look around in a 3-D way, look around the other parts, adjacent areas to the active site." (Riordan 2013b). Computer modeling thus proved doubly pivotal to the work of new drug discovery, both in terms of getting a better sense of the precise molecular structures of influenza viruses and in trialing designs for new molecules in a virtual environment.

Eventually Gilead scientists found a different approach to blocking the functioning of neuraminidase from the way that zanamivir (Relenza) did. Riordan continues:

> And so they looked at the molecular model on the computer with great level of detail and they saw that there was a pocket that hadn't been appreciated before, that was adjacent to the active site; that pocket was hydrophobic or sort of greasy. They constructed variance of sialic acid or benzoic acid inhibitor of the active side that carried the hydrophobic group right in that precise location, so it would stick into the pocket. In water, hydrophobic or greasy things like to stick together—that's the point. They put a greasy structure that matched the greasy pocket. (Riordan 2013b)

As with Relenza, the ability to decode and virtually model the precise molecular structure of the neuraminidase had led to the discovery of a new potential drug target. So the team went about developing a new synthetic molecule to exploit this pocket.

By all accounts it was painstaking work conducted by a multidisciplinary team of scientists. They would first try to design virtual molecules that met their requirements. Whenever a promising lead would emerge, the chemists would try to synthesize it in the lab, and biologists would also test it in the test tube (Schneider 2001). After testing more than 600 substances in this way, a new molecule that seemed to fit the criteria, GS4071, composed of 44 atoms, was finally discovered at the end of 1995 (Schneider 2001). As with the rival Biota molecule before it, however, the excitement was short lived, and disappointment soon followed. Further testing on mice again failed to demonstrate absorption through the intestines. Although it was a new molecule, the drug essentially still suffered the same problem as Relenza and would need to be inhaled.

Fortunately, and with a little bit of further tweaking, such absorption was eventually made possible, giving rise to yet another new molecule, GS4104. The new molecule was effectively a "masked" form of the drug and seemed to work in both mice and ferrets (Schneider 2001). Crucially, it could to do what Relenza could not, that is, pass through the intestines into the blood stream. There it would then become metabolized to GS4071 and would then be able to reach the lungs and other parts of the body (Jack 2006). The discovery of this new molecule was a major breakthrough. The goal of designing a different neuraminidase inhibitor that could be orally administered had finally been achieved.

The next step now would be to file for a patent in order to protect their new molecule. Obtaining the patent and making sure it was "watertight" would be absolutely pivotal for transforming the discovery into a commercial success. Riordan recalls having long conversations with patent lawyers at the time. Because the field was so competitive, they knew that if the patent for their new product was not rock solid, it would be rapidly "attacked" by competitors (Riordan 2013b). Yet once they secured the patent in 1996, Gilead Sciences had effectively won the race to develop the world's first orally available neuraminidase inhibitor. It would go on to become known as oseltamivir—or by its brand name, Tamiflu. Graeme Laver, who had first crystallized the neuraminidase, vividly recalled the day he found out about the discovery and the Gilead patent on oseltamivir. He had just been trying to sell his crystals to a research team at the pharmaceutical giant Pfizer and described how "the tears streamed down their faces when they handed me the patent and said: 'We've been beaten'" (Jack 2006).

In many ways, then, the story of the discovery of Tamiflu is a textbook success story of "rational" drug design. That is, the new drug was not discovered accidentally but was deliberately designed to meet a specific set of requirements. In the early days of pharmacology, therapeutic drugs were usually derived from medicinal plants. Aspirin is a good example. As we have already seen, it came from the bark of the willow tree and formed the basis for the name of Gilead Sciences. Sometimes new medicines were also discovered by chance while conducting other research—what is referred to as "drug serendipity" (Takenaka 2001). Penicillin, some types of antidepressants, and even Viagra are prominent examples of new drugs that were essentially discovered in that way.

However, that is not how neuraminidase inhibitors like Relenza and Tamiflu were developed. Their development resulted from a very different approach taken from the 1960s onward. The 1960s had witnessed a huge breakthrough in our scientific understanding of the molecular dynamics surrounding biological processes—including cellular receptors, ion channels, and enzymes. The improved understanding of these molecular processes meant that new drug discovery could become a much more rational and scientific enterprise (Takenaka 2001). With the help of computers and bioinformatics it became possible to compare three-dimensional protein structures and to develop new drug targets at molecular scale (Takenaka 2001). The discovery of Tamiflu was very much a part of this wider trajectory in drug development. Indeed, Riordan recalls, the discovery of Tamiflu "was a pretty rare instance at that time to be able to do a real molecular fit based upon a computational structure" (Riordan 2013b). The rise of new molecular knowledge and visualization techniques had thus been vital for the development of this new class of antivirals. As with Relenza before it, moreover, this scientific innovation had again been achieved by a comparatively small and young biotechnology company.

Enter Roche: Gilead Sciences Partners with Big Pharma

With the patent secured, the next big challenge facing Gilead Sciences was how to bring the new drug to market. As with Relenza, that would require a whole different skill set. This new product would likely be aimed very widely at the general population, and there was also a desire to market it internationally. It would therefore be necessary to carry out extensive clinical trials in multiple countries. Running such clinical trials would also require access to substantial funds—hundreds of millions of dollars in fact—as well as considerable experience. Even once the clinical trials were completed, moreover, the new drug would then still need to obtain regulatory approval in many different countries, and there would also be a need for substantial international marketing efforts to promote the new product in a potentially global marketplace.

As a new and comparatively small start-up company still trying to find its feet, Gilead Sciences possessed neither the skills nor the experience nor the funds to do these things on its own. Gilead had highly competent scientists to be sure, but at that stage it did not yet have much expertise in the later stages of commercial drug development (Clinical Development Scientist 2015). Gilead did harbor aspirations to develop its own products in the future, but it was aiming more for the clinical market than for the general population market (Riordan 2013b). At the time, Gilead was also developing several other products that were a greater priority for the company— including new products for HIV/AIDS and hepatitis B. Gilead realized, moreover, that commercialization of the product would require global marketing and primary-care sales efforts to ensure the product reached the patients

(Gilead Sciences 2016). For these next stages of developing the new influenza antiviral Gilead would thus be looking to license the compound to a large pharmaceutical company with much greater expertise in these areas.

In January 1996, much as Biota had done before it with Relenza, Gilead Sciences thus began to negotiate with several large pharmaceutical companies about licensing its newly developed molecule, GS4104. One of the companies Gilead approached was the Swiss pharmaceutical giant Roche. Roche was a natural choice because it was already in discussions with Gilead about a number of other compounds. Roche also had plenty of technical experience in drug development and in bringing antivirals to market at its site in Welwyn Garden City north of London (Ward 2015). Roche was even trying to establish itself as the market leader in antivirals at the time (Schneider 2001). This meant Roche was already running clinical development programs for several other products against hepatitis and HIV and was interested in respiratory viruses and herpes. Roche quickly undertook a series of risk and cost calculations for the new neuraminidase inhibitor. It reportedly calculated that people suffering from the flu would be willing to pay up to $50 for a course of the medicine (Schneider 2001). Based on these calculations, Roche decided it was interested in striking a deal with Gilead over the new compound.

Although Roche was not the only company interested in the compound, it had at least one thing working in its favor. The new compound was pretty complicated to make, and there were challenges in producing large quantities of it. Yet Roche routinely conducted its toxicology studies in marmosets—a species of small monkeys not much larger than rats. This meant that only small quantities of the drug would initially be required for Roche to proceed, and things could therefore progress more quickly (Ward 2015). Another critical factor in making the deal go Roche's way was interpersonal. Franz Humer, who previously was Glaxo's negotiator with Biota over Relenza, had recently switched companies and now worked for Roche. Humer would later rise to the position of chairman and executive at Roche (Jack 2006). Riordan recalls that after a meeting between the two in Switzerland, Humer was interested in the product (Riordan 2013b). Roche apparently shared Gilead's view that its product could still win the race because the pill would ultimately win out over Relenza (Clinical Development Scientist 2015; Schlatter 1999). Finally, Roche also possessed expertise in diagnostics, and it was thought at the time that diagnostics would play a key role in the development and commercialization of the product (Gilead Sciences 2016).

Roche thus set out to develop a business model for the new neuraminidase inhibitor formed around three primary axes: (1) seasonal treatment, whereby people suffering symptoms would take the drug; (2) prophylaxis, which would consist of giving the drug to people in care homes when flu is in the area, as well as other high-risk groups such as those who are immune compromised or have asthma, cancer patients, etc.; and (3) pandemic preparedness. Seasonal flu was the primary strategy, and the aspiration was even to make it available as an over-the-counter product (Clinical Development Scientist 2015).

There were no standard formulae for the deal that was about to be brokered between Gilead Sciences and Roche, but there were some key elements that would have be considered. These elements included stipulating who would pay for clinical development, who would organize it, what timelines would be required, what the benchmarks would be, setting the royalty rate, deciding whether manufacturing would be shared or exclusive to one party, and so forth (Riordan 2013b). There would also have to be a lot of due diligence over the patent to make sure it was solid before Roche could sign on the proverbial dotted line. Overall, however, Riordan recalls that the negotiations proceeded quite quickly because it was a clearly distinguished molecule and because it was a big priority for the organization (Riordan 2013b). On the Gilead side the negotiations were led by then CEO John Martin (Gilead Sciences 2016). On the Roche side, Franz Humer personally approved the acquisition of the molecule from Gilead (Clinical Development Scientist 2015).

Under the terms of the agreement, Roche received the sole and exclusive rights to Gilead's neuraminidase inhibitors, including the lead product candidate, GS4104. In return, Gilead received $10 million and additional provisions for up to $40 million upon future achievement of developmental and regulatory milestones. Roche was to carry all research and development costs and to pay Gilead "undisclosed" royalties on the net sales of any products resulting from the collaboration (Gilead Press Release 30/9/96). Ownership of the patent would remain with Gilead until its expiration in 2016. The precise terms of this licensing arrangement would become highly significant years later when fears about pandemic flu began to reverberate around the world and the companies found themselves in dispute with one another.

Gilead and Roche officially announced on 30 September 1996 that they had entered into a new partnership. "This collaboration," Humer said at the time, "marks another milestone in Hoffmann-La Roche's clear leadership strategy in the field of antivirals. . . . We recently have introduced the first proteinase inhibitor worldwide, and we continue to pursue an extensive in-house research and development program in this field of therapy. Partnering with Gilead complements this strategy extremely well' (Gilead Press Release 30/9/96). All of this also meant that—just as with Relenza before it—the late-stage development for Tamiflu would again be carried out by a larger and more established pharmaceutical company.

"Beat Glaxo!": Roche's Race to Get GS4104 through Clinical Trials

With the Gilead-Roche licensing agreement in place, the race was on to see whether Roche could actually get to market faster than Glaxo, which was already testing its product in human subjects. To set the right tone for what was about to follow, everyone attending the first meeting between the Gilead and Roche teams after completing the licensing deal was handed a T-shirt with "Beat Glaxo" printed on it. Reto Schneider has extensively chronicled the story of that intense race (Schneider 2001). There were some important things that needed to be figured out quite quickly, such as whether the molecule would prove effective in humans, how to produce larger quantities of it, and so forth (Schneider 2001). Without delay, Penny Ward and Renata Crome thus took charge of the human testing at Roche (Schneider 2001).

From the outset, the Roche team encountered a number of challenges—especially in conducting the clinical trials for the new compound. First, they had to know more about influenza and exactly how it moves. For many other diseases, one can identify specialist clinics attended by people suffering from a particular condition whom one could recruit as participants for clinical trials. But with a highly mobile target like influenza, it was much more difficult to find a regular tranche of such people. Roche could try to set up a trial site in one city, only to later discover that flu would not be prevalent there that year. Flu, one clinical development scientist explains, moves in mysterious ways, so the company had to create twice the number of usual trial sites to account for the fact that some of these sites would not work out (Clinical Development Scientist 2015).

To address this challenge Roche even began to carry out its own flu surveillance. Armed with this additional surveillance information, the company could then quickly move resources to geographic areas where it found the flu to be circulating. Time was a critical factor. Patients would need to be enrolled in the trial within 24 hours of the onset of symptoms. Flu also only stays around for a short time—usually around six weeks. Roche thus set up the pharmaceutical equivalent of a war room, furnished with maps and all. A further challenge was that Roche did not yet have large quantities of the drug on hand, so it could not deploy drugs to all sites. Instead, the company would have to wait until getting confirmation that influenza was circulating and then quickly move the drug into the affected area. Those were all costs that Roche initially carried as part of its development program.

As if all of these challenges were not daunting enough, the pressure on Roche was compounded by the company's desire to go to market for the 2000 flu season. That would give the team just three years. To put that into perspective, carrying out phases 1 through 3 of clinical trials would normally take around seven years (Schneider 2001). Phase 1 tests the compound on otherwise healthy humans—to gauge optimal dosages and to test for unexpected side effects. This testing commenced on 11 March 1997, when the first human being (of an initial group of eight persons) ingested 10 milligrams of GS4104 (Schneider 2001). The trial was designed to determine the safety, tolerability, and absorption of GS4104 in humans and reportedly went well (Gilead Press Release 11/3/1997). A critical milestone in the drug development process had been passed, and Roche made a further payment to Gilead now that this milestone had been reached (Schneider 2001).

After safe dosages were established, there was still some uncertainty about exactly where to set the bar for assessing the drug's effectiveness. Investing so much money into the acquisition and clinical trials for the drug, Roche wanted to maximize the chances of successfully securing regulatory approval following the clinical trials. For the first generation of influenza antivirals (like amantadin and rimantadin), the FDA had set the benchmark for approval at a reduction in duration of symptoms of at least one day (Schneider 2001). But to reduce uncertainty further, Penny Ward decided to invite many international flu experts into a hotel near London's Heathrow Airport with the aim of agreeing on a set of influenza symptoms. When the discussion became too drawn out for her liking, Ward recalls, she simply threatened the room full of distinguished influenza scientists that they would not be allowed to leave the room and break up for lunch until they had agreed (Ward 2015). The threat apparently worked, as Ward remembers how they then agreed on a short list in only a few minutes (Ward 2015).

On 29 May 1997 Gilead and Roche then also jointly announced the start of phase 2, human testing of GS4104 in the United States. Those phase 2 trials sought to evaluate the effectiveness of the drug in patients actually affected by influenza and to determine side effects and risks (Gilead Press Release 29/5/1997). The timing was not ideal, as this was not the prime time for flu to present itself. Ward therefore followed the common practice of deliberately infecting 117 people with the flu virus (A/Texas/36/91) by inserting cotton swabs into both nostrils (Schneider 2001). Those taking the drug subsequently reported the cessation of symptoms after 53 hours, whereas it normally took 95 hours (Schneider 2001). Yet another crucial milestone in the complex process of drug development had been achieved.

Phase 3 trials would mark the next crucial stage. These are the largest of the trials and usually also last the longest. The drugs are often tested on patients in different parts of the world and serve to test the efficacy and safety on a much larger scale of patients. To move on to phase 3 trials, however, Roche would first need to produce larger quantities of the drug. Fortunately, its chemists had been able to produce 20 kilograms of the new compound by November (Schneider 2001). Again, however, the phase 3 trials would prove challenging because there are no specialized flu clinics that can be targeted to identify suitable recruits and because of the difficulty of recruiting only those who actually have the flu rather than just the common cold (Schneider 2001).

To make matters worse, toward the end of 1997 it was becoming clear that the flu season was proving to be comparatively mild that year. This, of course, was good news for people who might suffer from the flu, but it was not particularly helpful for Roche when it was urgently trying to conduct a large-scale clinical trial in its race to develop a new antiviral flu medication. There would be very few cases of flu until February 1998 (Schneider 2001), by which time Gilead and Roche were still actively recruiting volunteers for their human trials in the United States. Pulling out all the stops, they launched a public campaign, even asking people experiencing flu-like symptoms to immediately call 1-888-I-GOT-FLU (1-888-446-8358) (Gilead Press Release 12/2/1998). Still, it would prove very difficult to find a sufficiently large number of recruits, though they did manage to recruit 1,355 in total (Schneider 2001).

By this point in time it was becoming clear that Roche would not be able to complete the clinical trials in one season alone. To minimize any further delay, the company decided that it would shift its attention to the Southern Hemisphere. This seemed preferable to delaying things for a whole year and waiting for the next flu season to arrive. Yet in making this decision the company had not anticipated just how difficult it would prove to secure approval for running clinical trials in the Southern Hemisphere. The relevant countries had long lead times for obtaining official approval, and different countries also had different requirements, while the company had a window of only about six weeks (Clinical Development Scientist 2015). With the benefit of hindsight, one clinical development scientist recalls, it would probably have been more effective for Roche to simply double the number of sites in the better recruiting countries like Germany, France, Spain, and the United Kingdom (Clinical Development Scientist 2015). If it had done so, it might have been able to complete the trials in one season.

Nevertheless, on 30 June 1998 Gilead could finally announce the preliminary results of four phase 2 and 3 clinical trials testing the efficacy and safety of GS4104. The trials had enrolled over 2,900 people during the 1997–1998 Northern Hemisphere flu season. According to the press release issued at the time, the trials went well and showed statistically significant effects (Gilead Press Release 30/6/98). Another critical hurdle had been overcome, and Roche would soon be able to file for official regulatory approval. In the end, it had taken Roche just 2 years and 10 months to go from acquiring the drug from Gilead to filing for its regulatory approval. By this stage Glaxo had already filed for regulatory approval of Relenza, but overall Roche had been faster than Glaxo, which had taken around four years to reach that point. Roche, in other words, had managed to narrow the gap considerably, meaning that both companies ended up filing for regulatory approval for their rival products in the same year (Clinical Development Scientist 2015).

With GS4104 rapidly approaching submission for regulatory approval, the time was now approaching to find an appropriate name for the new drug. The World Health Organization approved "oseltamivir" as the international nonproprietary name for the antiviral (Schneider 2001). Yet as late as February 1999, Roche was still searching for a brand name for the new product. From an initial list of more than 1,000 possible names, 50 had been subjected to market analysis, which, among other things, tests name associations with pharmacists in different countries and languages (Schneider

2001). When Roche did finally settle on a name, however, another company reportedly objected that it was too close to its name. Roche would instead have to settle on its backup choice, Tamiflu (Schneider 2001). According to Roche, the name is derived from the international nonproprietary name oseltamivir and the merging of "tami" and "flu" (Rollerhagen and Braxton 2016: 10). By March 1999 Roche was finally ready to submit Tamiflu for regulatory approval to the FDA in the United States.

In revisiting the birth of Tamiflu, it is striking just how many similarities there are with the commercial development of its immediate predecessor drug, Relenza. Tamiflu too was initially developed as a commercial product with an eye firmly on the lucrative seasonal flu market, not primarily as a medical countermeasure against pandemic flu. Again, the ability to precisely map (and model) the molecular structure of the neuraminidase was key. Again, a small biotechnology company first developed the new molecule that formed the basis for the new drug, in this case Gilead Sciences. And again, the new molecule was then licensed for further commercial development to a large and established pharmaceutical company, in this case Roche. Although the companies involved and the method of administration ultimately differed, the underlying pattern of molecular discovery and commercial drug development was very similar for both products.

That underlying pattern also reveals the very different roles that small and large pharmaceutical companies ultimately play in the overall commercial drug development process. Those roles can be broadly distinguished between an "upstream" and "downstream" division of labor. Smaller companies tend to work "upstream" by initially discovering and developing innovative new molecules and then licensing promising compounds to larger pharmaceutical companies to do the "downstream" work of taking them through clinical trials, obtaining regulatory approval, and eventually bringing them to market.

These crucial differences between small and large pharmaceutical companies are highly significant from the perspective of governments interested in encouraging the commercial development of new medical countermeasures. We have already seen that large pharmaceutical companies are unlikely government partners in the quest to develop new medical countermeasures because they do not see sufficient commercial potential in this area. For them, it is not just a matter of absolute cost but—in a competitive marketplace—also one of opportunity cost. Large pharmaceutical companies (especially publicly listed ones) have a fiduciary duty to shareholders to ensure good returns on their research and development priorities (Wizemann et al. 2010: 127). Given that development costs for new drugs are roughly similar for pharmaceutical companies, it makes commercial sense to focus on those that will achieve the largest sales (Bartfai and Lees 2013: 107–108). Devoting resources to medical countermeasure development would mean that pharmaceutical companies are not channeling their resources to the commercially most rewarding areas, which could be to a company's detriment in the long run. Large pharmaceutical companies are thus unlikely partners for governments in the quest to develop new medical countermeasures.

Yet this still leaves open the possibility that governments could instead partner with smaller pharmaceutical companies. Compared to their larger counterparts, smaller companies tend to be leaner organizations, operate at lower cost during the early stages of drug discovery, and are often more willing to take on risk and explore unproven opportunities (Drugdevelopment-technology.com 2012). They can also find themselves in a much more precarious financial position, as we have just seen in the case of Gilead Sciences. For such smaller companies, government contracts can be a vital way of raising income and for gaining wider credibility for their new commercial venture. These were also some the very same reasons that Gilead Sciences decided to enter into such government contracts during its early days. Even though large pharmaceutical companies tend to eschew the area of medical countermeasures, it may still be possible for governments to build a more targeted medical countermeasure strategy around extensive engagement with smaller and medium-sized companies. That, in fact, is the course that the US government has largely adopted over the past decade.

Taking that route of focusing on smaller companies, however, then immediately generates another critical challenge. Who will subsequently complete the costlier and risky work of late-stage drug development usually carried out by the larger companies? Without the involvement of those larger pharmaceutical companies, even promising new compounds would simply remain stuck in the development pipeline because there is no one willing to take them forward through late-stage development. Even when governments can successfully engage smaller biotechnology companies in the development of new medical countermeasures, that pivotal late-stage piece of the development puzzle will still need to be addressed. That is why late-stage development is a third major challenge to emerge around the development of new medical countermeasures more generally. It is not just a question of designing a promising new compound but of accomplishing the riskier and costlier downstream work of late-stage development as well.

In order to address that formidable challenge, the US government has already created a new institution dedicated specifically to meeting this challenge in the development pipeline for medical countermeasures. The government effectively moved in to fill this gap itself and began to provide smaller pharmaceutical companies with specialist advice and assistance in those areas of advanced drug development that are traditionally carried out by the larger pharmaceutical companies. The new institution the government set up for that purpose in 2006 is called the Biomedical Advanced Research and Development Authority, which today provides pharmaceutical companies with a wide array of advice and assistance as part of what it calls its "National Countermeasure Response Infrastructure" (Nicholson et al. 2016: 118). In the absence of more extensive engagement on medical countermeasures by "big pharma," the government has effectively had to step in and share the development risks associated with medical countermeasure development. As one BARDA official put it, the institution's role is essentially to act as a virtual pharmaceutical company (Nicholson et al. 2016: 17).

More generally, then, all of these early experiences with neuraminidase inhibitors like Relenza and Tamiflu also suggest that there are actually several different challenges involved in the initial development of new medical countermeasures. Government efforts to procure such products face not just one but at least a trio of interconnected challenges: *scientific* challenges, *economic* challenges, and *late-stage development* challenges. Given the extensive nature of these challenges, the successful development of any new medical countermeasure would mark a formidable achievement in and of itself. Yet even once such a medical countermeasure is successfully developed, there is still a whole second set of challenges that then quickly comes into play. These additional "acquisition" challenges revolve around how governments subsequently acquire any newly developed medical countermeasure as part of their health security strategies and transform it into an effective medical countermeasure capability that could be readily deployed to the population in a future emergency.

II THE ACQUISITION CHALLENGES

4

What a Difference a Day Makes

The Margin Call for Regulatory Agencies

Once a new medicine is successfully developed, it still has to secure marketing approval from the regulatory agencies before it can be prescribed and sold to people. Those regulatory bodies will first want to be satisfied that the new drug is safe and effective. Filing for regulatory approval therefore usually marks the next stage in the life of a new medicine. At this point, pharmaceutical companies must provide regulators with detailed evidence that their new molecules work effectively inside the human body and not just in a laboratory setting. Generating that evidence is a complicated process because pharmaceutical products operate at such tiny scale and thus well beyond the perception of the naked human eye. The most common way that pharmaceutical companies visualize these effects is by carrying out extensive human clinical trials.

This chapter explores how regulatory agencies evaluated such clinical trial data for Tamiflu in the world's major pharmaceutical markets—like the United States, Japan, and Europe. A cursory glance at these regulatory processes initially paints a fairly uneventful picture, pointing to a series of successful approval applications obtained from regulators in many countries around the world. Digging a little bit deeper, however, reveals that some of these crucial regulatory decisions—especially in the United States—were colored by prior difficulties experienced with the approval of Relenza. In the case of Relenza, US regulators had encountered a number of problems, and the decision about whether or not to grant regulatory approval hung in the balance. Considerations about the role that neuraminidase inhibitors might play in a future flu pandemic helped to eventually tip the balance in favor of approval. Yet the balance was tipped even though there was no reliable data about how effective the antiviral would actually be in a future pandemic; all the clinical trials had been conducted for *seasonal* flu. In fact, it would have been nearly impossible to generate such clinical trial data for pandemic flu because nobody could know in advance exactly what such a new pandemic flu virus would look like.

All of the nuanced difficulties encountered during the regulatory approval processes for neuraminidase inhibitors reveal that additional challenges can still arise once a new medical countermeasure has been successfully developed. Such challenges revolve around the official processes through which governments would subsequently acquire any new product and convert it into a workable medical countermeasure capability that could be reliably used during a future emergency. Obtaining regulatory approval is one of the additional challenges to emerge at this stage, for the simple reason that any new medical countermeasure must first be shown to be safe and effective before it can be acquired by governments as part of their health security strategies. After all, it would be very difficult for a government to deploy a medical countermeasure that does not have regulatory approval.

Yet obtaining such regulatory approval can also be much more difficult for medical countermeasures than for many other pharmaceutical products. Regulators usually make these commercially critical decisions about the official approval of new pharmaceutical products on the basis of multiple clinical trials carried out with human subjects. There can be major practical and ethical obstacles to carrying out such clinical trials for medical countermeasures because of the exceptional dangerousness (and often also rarity) of the pathogens involved. Companies cannot just deliberately infect large numbers of people with lethal pathogens (such as smallpox or plague) simply to satisfy the regulatory requirement to conduct large-scale clinical trials. So how can a company even contemplate investing in the development of a new medical countermeasure if it does not know how it could run the clinical trials required for obtaining regulatory approval further down the line? Increased difficulties and uncertainties around obtaining regulatory approval thus represent a fourth major challenge facing new medical countermeasures in general.

Regulatory Approval for Tamiflu in the World's Major Markets

Before any new medicine comes to market, regulatory agencies first need to discharge their duty of protecting the population from unsafe or ineffective products. When making such decisions about marketing approval, regulators often operate in a context of considerable public scrutiny. On the one hand, they want to discharge their duties thoroughly and ensure that they get their decisions right. At the same time, they also do not wish to be seen as preventing effective new therapies from coming to market as quickly as possible. Regulators have to strike a difficult balance here.

From the perspective of pharmaceutical companies, clearing this regulatory approval stage is of the upmost commercial importance. The companies will usually have already invested considerable sums of money just to get the novel drug to this point. If regulatory approval is turned down, the companies will not be able to recoup their research and development costs, nor will they be able to make any profits from the product. A successful outcome is therefore critical for companies. "Because drug review consummates the conversion of idea into product," Daniel Carpenter explains, "the process of drug review is accompanied by widespread anxiety and massive scrutiny. It is shot through with subtle politics, with battles over nuance and detail" (Carpenter 2010: 467).

That said, a successful outcome is not the only commercial consideration for many pharmaceutical companies. Timing is another pivotal factor. We have already seen that most pharmaceutical companies protect their investment in new drugs through patents. Those patents, in turn, are time limited and will eventually expire. When that happens, and a drug comes off patent, it effectively becomes a generic drug. Other pharmaceutical companies can then produce and sell the drug as well—translating into more competition and, generally speaking, significantly lower profit margins than when the drug is still under patent. From a commercial point of view, every single day the drug is under patent but has not yet been approved by the regulator is therefore one day less that companies will have to sell the product under more lucrative monopoly conditions. That is why pharmaceutical companies do not just wish for a successful outcome; they also want the process to go quickly and often push politically for these regulatory approval processes to be accelerated. Success *and* timing are therefore twin factors to consider for pharmaceutical companies when trying to secure regulatory approval for new drugs.

How did the regulatory approval process unfold in the case of Tamiflu? The world's first ever regulatory approval for Tamiflu was granted to Roche in its home country of Switzerland. Roche and Gilead jointly announced on

24 September 1999 that the Swiss regulatory authority—then called the Interkantonale Kontrollstelle für Heilmittel (but replaced in 2002 by Swissmedic)—had approved Tamiflu for the treatment of influenza. The new drug would be available in Switzerland beginning on 1 October 1999. It was a very good start for the new product. The companies were also expecting more good news to follow soon, as Tamiflu had been granted priority review status by the regulators in the United States and Canada. In an industry where every day counts, and for a seasonal condition like influenza, this meant that there was every prospect of still securing a decision in time for the 1999–2000 flu season in the Northern Hemisphere (Gilead Press Release 24/9/1999). All eyes were therefore now firmly on the much bigger market of the United States and the FDA.

The Holy Grail of Drug Approval: Triple Success for Tamiflu at the FDA

Approval by the US Food and Drug Administration is the most prized in the world according to many industry analysts. The FDA is responsible for ensuring that new drugs (and vaccines) are safe and effective, and it carries out research on the treatment of disease outbreaks and diagnostic tools. Although it is just one of many drug regulators around the world, the FDA approval possesses particular significance because of the sheer size of the US pharmaceutical market, which is the most profitable pharmaceutical market in the world and does not have explicit price controls (Carpenter 2010: 1–2). From the perspective of pharmaceutical companies, the FDA is effectively the gatekeeper to the lucrative US pharmaceutical market.

The FDA's significance also extends beyond the US market, however. Securing FDA approval has a strong international signaling function as well. If the FDA approves a new drug, it is likely that many more regulators around the world will similarly approve the drug. That is because most other regulatory agencies simply do not possess the same capacity as the FDA in terms of budget and manpower. The organization has (especially since the 1970s) employed more scientists and trained personnel than all other similar agencies in the world combined (Carpenter 2010: 21). Other regulatory agencies around the world will therefore look to FDA decisions informally in order to guide their own decision making. That is also why FDA approval matters not just for access to the US market but more broadly for access to many other international markets as well.

So what happened when Tamiflu was submitted to the FDA for regulatory approval? A cursory review of the FDA approval processes for Tamiflu paints a fairly uneventful picture. In fact, the sequence of events leading up to FDA approval for Tamiflu can be quickly summarized. A month after the Swiss approval, on 27 October 1999, the FDA approved Tamiflu for "the treatment of uncomplicated acute illness due to influenza infection in adults who have been symptomatic for no more than 2 days" (FDA 1999b). This marketing approval process unfolded rapidly according to the priority review procedure—within six months—following Roche's initial application for FDA approval on 29 April 1999.

The benchmark for FDA approval is that a new drug has to be better than a placebo (or inactive substance)—but usually does not have to be better than already existing drugs. The FDA authorization documentation accepted as evidence for such efficacy two placebo-controlled and double-blind clinical studies (one carried out inside and one outside of the United States). The trials for Tamiflu used a self-assessment system of symptoms for patients who had begun treatment with the drug (75 mg twice daily for five days) within 40 hours of the onset of symptoms. Patients had then been asked to subjectively score the severity of a range of influenza-related symptoms. Overall, these trials showed a 1.3-day reduction in the median time to improvement in influenza-infected subjects who had received Tamiflu compared to subjects receiving placebo (FDA 1999b: 4). With the positive decision by the FDA, a major regulatory hurdle had been overcome. Tamiflu could now be marketed and sold in the lucrative US market—and all in time for the influenza season in the United States.

Keen to secure the widest possible market for its new drug, Roche submitted another application to the FDA on 22 May 2000. The additional application was for using the drug in the *prophylaxis* (or prevention) of influenza. If successful, it would allow the drug to be marketed not just to people who were already suffering from influenza infection; it could then also be given preventatively to close contacts—like family members—who might become infected because of close proximity to somebody suffering from flu. If such a prophylactic effect could be demonstrated, it could enlarge the potential market for the product in the United States significantly. Again, the FDA processed this application quite quickly—within six months—and FDA approval was granted on 17 November 2000 (FDA 2000).

While this second application was still pending, Roche also tried to expand the Tamiflu market in yet a third direction—this time for the treatment of influenza in children. On 16 June 2000, while they were still awaiting the result of the prophylaxis application, Roche and Gilead jointly announced that they had submitted a further Tamiflu application to FDA "for the treatment of acute illness due to influenza in children 1 year and older" (Gilead Press Release 16/6/2000). If successful, this additional indication would also give Tamiflu another competitive edge over its competitor product Relenza, which did not have marketing approval for children. Again, this third application was processed by FDA within six months, and again the application proved successful. On 14 December 2000 Roche and Gilead announced that they had received marketing approval for the pediatric use of Tamiflu—in a liquid suspension form—for children over the age of 1 who had been symptomatic for no more than two days (Gilead Press Release 14/12/2000).

By this stage, Tamiflu had successfully crossed the most difficult hurdle and achieved what is widely considered in the industry as the "holy grail" of new drug development—marketing approval by the Food and Drug Administration in the world's most lucrative pharmaceutical market. Roche had made three applications and achieved three successes. Those favorable FDA decisions, moreover, came in conjunction with a flurry of other approvals granted by regulators in other international markets like Canada (23 December 1999), Russia (10 July 2000), Australia (13 September 2000) and more than two dozen additional countries (EMEA 2005a). There was every chance now that Roche and Gilead could recoup their upfront investment costs in developing Tamiflu and achieve handsome commercial rewards from their new product. Roche was reportedly anticipating that the drug would generate a turnover over of 400–800 million Swiss Francs over the next five years and that Tamiflu would become one of company's top five products (Schlatter 1999). Yet Tamiflu's overall commercial fate would ultimately also hinge upon the world's two other major pharmaceutical markets at the time: Japan and Europe.

Japan: Another Pivotal Market Secured

Japan was another crucial market because the Japanese government traditionally took the burden of influenza very seriously. According to Penny Ward, who worked on Tamiflu for Roche, there are a number of possible explanations for this strong emphasis on influenza in Japan. These include the high density of the Japanese public transport systems, the fact that there is close contact with poultry in many rural areas, and the fact that Japan's workforce is concentrated in large cities. For these reasons, the management of seasonal influenza has long been a priority in Japan. In fact, Japan remains the only nation in the world to vaccinate its entire population against influenza every year (Ward 2015).

Roche and Gilead were clearly aware of the commercial significance of the Japanese market. In a press release issued at the time, they pointed out that "in Japan, influenza can affect between 5 to 10 percent of its 125 million inhabitants in a normal year, and this number can increase significantly during severe epidemics. Over a three-month period in 1999, more than 1,200 people died in Japan as a result of influenza and its complications" (Gilead Press Release 12/12/2000). Japan could thus become another potentially very significant market for Tamiflu in addition to the lucrative US market. On 2 August 2000 Roche and Gilead announced that Roche had submitted Tamiflu to the Japanese Ministry for Health and Welfare for regulatory approval for influenza virus infection in adults. The application was both for treatment and prophylaxis. As in the United States, the application was dealt with under priority review (Gilead Press Release 2/8/2000).

Penelope Ward recalls that, generally speaking, the Japanese approval process can be quite demanding, and the regulators tend to raise many scientific questions. While this was not unusual in the case of Tamiflu, it meant there was quite a bit of back and forth between the regulator and Roche in order to explain or reconcile potential inconsistencies (Ward 2015). In the end, however, Tamiflu received fairly rapid approval by the Japanese regulators as well. Gilead and Roche announced the successful approval for treatment of influenza in Japan on 12 December 2000 (Gilead Press Release 12/12/2000). It marked another commercially significant milestone for Tamiflu. The companies could not have known it at the time, but Japan would soon become the world's largest consumer of Tamiflu and would continue to be for many years to come.

To Sneeze . . . or to Vomit? A Bumpy Ride
by the European Regulator
What about the European market? The process of regulatory approval in Europe differs in key respects from the approval processes in the

United States and Japan. In the European Union, pharmaceutical companies seeking new drug approval have the option of going through a consolidated process that simultaneously grants them authorization in all member states of the European Union. That saves the companies from having to apply separately for regulatory approval in each EU member state. It is known as the "centralized procedure" and is coordinated by the European Medicines Agency (EMA). Roche opted for this centralized procedure and submitted its Tamiflu application several months prior to submitting its FDA application in the United States.

One of the most notable features of the European regulatory system is that the committee conducting the scientific review of new drug applications proceeds by initially forming not just one but two separate teams of experts. The two teams are led by a rapporteur and a corapporteur, respectively. The two teams work in parallel—but also largely independently from one another—to produce their initial reports. Both reports are then shared with the committee for discussion, and committee members feed their views into the discussion. The system means that the two reports can occasionally generate quite different assessments, although in practice they are usually complementary.

Following receipt of Roche's Tamiflu application, the Committee for Medicinal Products for Human Use follows this procedure and designates two members as the leaders in charge of coordinating the scientific evaluation of the new drug—a rapporteur and a corapporteur. After the reports are discussed by the committee, a list of consolidated questions about the application is compiled for the manufacturer. The list can easily exceed 100 questions, as was the case with Tamiflu (Kurki 2015). The company submitting the application then has an opportunity to respond to the questions. If, having considered the company's responses, the committee feels that there are still some unresolved issues, a second round of questions can ensue. It is even possible to have a third round if by that stage there are still unresolved questions. This review period can last up to 210 days, albeit with pauses allowed for some criteria. The rapporteur is then obliged to merge the reports and comments. Where there are differences, the committee has to decide where it stands. It can do this either by majority vote or by consensus. In either case, however, the committee's view is technically just an opinion. The final decision about whether to grant marketing authority to a drug formally rests with the European Commission (NAO 2013: 13–18).

Yet there is also a less well known, and more peculiar, aspect to the European regulatory procedure that prevailed when Tamiflu was being considered. The probable committee opinion would be communicated to the manufacturer in advance. Where a committee was likely to view an application unfavorably, the company would then be given the option of withdrawing its application. A key ramification of opting for withdrawal is that all the data relating to the application are subsequently covered by a confidentiality agreement. None of the information about that application, in other words, ends up going into the public domain. As Cristina Sampaio, the corapporteur for the Tamiflu application, explained in an interview, it was to the advantage of the company at that time to avoid a negative opinion by withdrawing its dossier, and the materials and issues around the application would then be prevented from becoming public (Sampaio 2015).

That is exactly what happened with Roche's initial Tamiflu application in Europe; the company eventually decided to withdraw it. Given the confidentiality implications of that decision, it has proved quite challenging to gain greater insight into what exactly happened during this initial application. Did the European regulator spot something that the other regulators had missed? Were they looking at different data? Had they possibly uncovered signals of different side effects in the data? It is impossible to know. When asked directly about this initial application, representatives of the EMA said they were still bound by confidentiality requirements. They confirmed that "this is material that is not in the public domain," that "these materials have to be still considered as confidential," and that "we cannot disclose the content and the reasoning behind the withdrawal" (EMA Officer 2013).

What we do know, however, is that the rapporteur during this initial application process came from the United Kingdom and that the corapporteur came from Portugal. Ward, who was still working for Roche on Tamiflu at the time, recalls a number of issues that emerged during the initial application. Indeed, Tamiflu presented one of those comparatively few cases where the two independent teams of experts differed and had a difficult time reaching a consolidated opinion. While the teams agreed on effectiveness, the team led by Portugal raised questions about preclinical information, which suggested that there was a possibility that the product could have an impact on a cardiovascular finding that had not been satisfied by the response Roche gave. Ward also recalls Roche being asked a question about influenza B virus, which was not very prevalent at the time they conducted clinical trials (Ward 2015).

Probably the biggest obstacle, however, emerged when it became clear that the corapporteur from Portugal also had another issue with Tamiflu: How would it be paid for? The Portuguese corapporteur, Ward (2015) recalls, felt very passionately that affordability should be an important consideration in the approval process, and it therefore wanted cost-utility considerations to be included in addition to safety and efficacy. Ward thinks that one possible explanation for this might be that Portugal is among the poorest countries in the region; the Portuguese corapporteur could see this product potentially causing high public demand and possibly breaking the country's health-care system and being unaffordable there. In her recollection, Roche thus found itself facing two opposing camps on the committee, with some representatives on the committee largely agreeing that they wanted to approve the product and several southern European representatives who felt that it was an expensive product and remained unsure of any real utility (Ward 2015).

In the end, Roche decided to exercise its option to withdraw the Tamiflu application. With so much back and forth with the European regulator, while at the same time also having to respond to the many enquiries from the Japanese regulator, Roche had to make some pragmatic choices. The company had limited time and resources to deal with all of these questions, and it was quickly coming up against the limits of what it could manage. Sensing that its chances were better in Japan, the company put its efforts into that process instead, with the aim of coming back to the European market later (Ward 2015). On 26 May 2000 Roche and Gilead thus announced that it had "decided to withdraw the European application for the antiviral Tamiflu (oseltamivir) for the treatment of influenza in order to have more time to submit further data" (Gilead Press Release 26/5/2000). That decision would also give Roche extra time to amalgamate the data with the data on prophylactic and pediatric use, to address the cardiac question, and eventually go back and ask the EMA to reconsider the application (Ward 2015).

That is exactly what the company ended up doing. Roche later resubmitted the Tamiflu application to the European Agency for the Evaluation of Medicinal Products (EMEA) on 9 February 2001—again through the centralized procedure (EMEA 2005a). Some of those closely involved in the process the second time around recall that overall there was still not a lot of excitement about the drug but that it was recognized that this was an area of high unmet medical need, and eventually the decision by the committee was unanimous (Kurki 2015). Committee for Proprietary Medicinal Products (CPMP) thus issued a positive recommendation for the granting of marketing approval to Tamiflu on 21 March 2002, and the European Commission then adopted the corresponding decision on 20 June 2002. Albeit with some "delay" in gaining European approval, Roche had now achieved marketing approval in the world's major pharmaceutical markets.

The differing ways in which the respective regulatory processes played out in the United States, Japan, and the European Union point to significant divergences in how marketing approval is approached by countries around the world. Cristina Sampaio, who was the corapporteur in both the first and second Tamiflu applications in Europe, explains a key difference between the United States and Europe at the time. At the FDA, a great value was placed on statistical significance. All other things held equal, if one could show that there was a statistically significant difference from the effect of a placebo (an inactive substance), even if it was small, the FDA would be inclined to approve the medicine and let the market decide if it would become a success or not (Sampaio 2015). Among European regulators, by contrast, less emphasis was placed on market forces, as governments pay for a lot of the medicines. Greater consideration was therefore given by Europeans to the clinical relevance of a product rather than statistical significance alone.

The issue with Tamiflu in particular was that there seemed to be a trade-off between a modest reduction in the duration of symptoms and the antiviral's most common side effects, like nausea and vomiting. It was, Sampaio recalls jokingly, akin to the question of whether people would rather sneeze or vomit. That underlying difference in attitude and approach can also help to explain why there are sometimes differences in the conclusions that European and American regulators can come to on the same drug (Sampaio 2015). All of that said, there is also much more to the Tamiflu regulatory approval story—especially in the United States—than initially meets the eye.

The Fallout from the Relenza Backstory in the United States

At first glance, the FDA approval process for Tamiflu appears to have proceeded quite smoothly. Roche submitted three applications and achieved three successes. Yet there is also a crucial backstory to these applications that is not widely known. That backstory pertains to Tamiflu's immediate predecessor and competitor drug, Relenza. Because Glaxo's Relenza was slightly ahead of Tamiflu in the development race, it would also have to pass through the relevant FDA approval processes first. Only a few months prior to considering the Tamiflu application, FDA therefore had to first process the Relenza (zanamivir) application.

That FDA approval process for Relenza turned out to be anything but smooth. In fact, it was so fraught with difficulties that it put considerable strain on a number of professional and personal relationships within the agency. Things got so heated at the FDA in the case of Relenza that some of those involved in the application ended up moving to other divisions, leaving the agency altogether, or even becoming whistle-blowers. Indeed, in conducting the interviews for this book, it was striking how those involved with the Relenza application at the FDA seemed to recall the events as if they had only occurred yesterday—even though this process took place more than a decade ago. Crucially, those events would also prove critical for understanding how the regulatory approval process for Tamiflu was subsequently handled by the FDA.

The Relenza Advisory Committee

Because Relenza was the first of a new class of antivirals (neuraminidase inhibitors), it became the subject of an independent scientific Antiviral Drugs Advisory Committee meeting. Such advisory committees are made up of independent scientific experts in the field. The experts gather in a room and listen to presentations by both the industry and the FDA. After further discussion, they then provide an independent recommendation as to whether the new drug should be approved or not. In the case of Relenza, the committee was made up of antiviral experts and pulmonary experts—because this was a new kind of antiviral medication, and because influenza principally affects the respiratory system.

The independent advisory committee for Relenza met on 24 February 1999 in Gaithersburg, Maryland, at the Gaithersburg Holiday Inn. More than 200 people were in attendance, and the meeting started punctually at 8.30 a.m. After an initial welcome and introductions, the meeting commenced—as many such gatherings do—with formal procedures for acknowledging any conflicts of interest that any panel members might have. Much of the rest of the morning was then taken up with presentations about Relenza by industry representatives. They would make their presentations, would answer questions, would observe proceedings, and so forth but would not of course be allowed to vote on the final recommendation of the committee.

The meeting took a critical turn in the afternoon, however, when it was the FDA's turn to make its presentations. Then its statistical reviewer, Mike Elashoff, took to the floor. Members of the FDA usually go to considerable lengths to prepare for these advisory committee meetings. Extensive discussion and preparations—even dress rehearsals—will often take place before the actual meeting. FDA officials are usually also very precise and considered communicators, taking great care with the words they chose. That is because the officials involved are aware that there will be an official transcript of the meeting. Views expressed there by the agency need to be defensible even under close subsequent scrutiny.

In line with FDA practice, Elashoff had been given access to the detailed clinical trial data for Relenza. He had been pouring over the data for several months, trying to replicate the findings by the drug sponsor and performing a range of statistical sensitivity analyses on the data. Based on his own extensive analysis, Elashoff raised two major concerns in his presentation. First, he noted that "the largest treatment effect was seen in the smallest study, while the smallest treatment effect was seen in the largest study, and that study was as large as the other two studies put together" (FDA 1999a: 81). Three clinical trials for Relenza had been submitted to the regulator for consideration—one from North America, one from Europe, and one from the Southern Hemisphere. The study from North America was the largest, and yet it was by far the weakest in showing any effect, according to Elashoff. So there was considerable variability as to whether and how much of an effect the three different clinical trials indicated.

The second concern that Elashoff raised would subsequently generate a lot of further discussion within the agency: "It was the North American study, arguably the most relevant study for us, that was the one with the smallest treatment effect and the non-significant p value" (FDA 1999a: 81). It was, in other words, not just a question of the size of the study relative to the two other studies; there was also a slightly more sensitive political question as to whether the FDA—as the regulator within the United States— should consider a study carried out on the North American population as more relevant in its discussion than the other two trials that were conducted in Europe and the Southern Hemisphere. The degree to which that consideration should have proved so controversial illustrates very well the scrutiny that the testimony of FDA officials can receive—especially when large and politically influential pharmaceutical companies are involved.

Elashoff's presentation also raised a string of other issues with the data. Looking at the issue of symptom "rebound," for example, he found that symptoms would often reappear a day or two after patients had already been scored as "alleviated" for the purposes of the studies. Elashoff found that there were a lot of patients (up to 30 percent) whose symptoms reappeared after 48 hours but that these were not "counted" in the industry analysis because the patients had already been counted as alleviated at that point (FDA 1999a: 82). He also raised some wider statistical considerations: "When you summarize the treatment effects using a median, that can exaggerate small differences since the endpoint is very discrete, alleviation occurring in half-a-day units . . . so, we have a situation where a very similar analysis to the primary analysis, one that uses the same criteria, but analyzes the data slightly differently, finds noticeably different results. The European and southern hemisphere studies are still statistically significant, although with smaller treatment effects, but the North American study is not really even close to clinical or statistical significance anymore" (FDA 1999a: 84). Elashoff's use of a wider variety of statistical techniques to examine the same data produced results that were much less clear cut than the analysis presented by industry.

Evidently, this was not the kind of additional statistical scrutiny that the pharmaceutical company was anticipating—or hoping to hear—from a Harvard-trained statistician. Worse still, Elashoff was not finished yet. He went on to shed further light for the committee on how to interpret the data from a statistical point of view: "A difference of, say, 7 days versus 5 days in the European study sounds impressive, like 2 days less of flu, but the reality even in the best study was one of continued gradual improvement. So, at day 5, for example, patients on zanamivir weren't feeling too much different from patients on placebo even though these zanamivir patients might have been considered alleviated while the patients on placebo might not have been considered alleviated" (FDA 1999a: 90). By this point the presentation's overall direction was clear for all to see, even long before Elashoff finally concluded that "these significant between-study differences in treatment effect, combined with a lack of a proven explanation for the difference, do not allow us to calculate an overall treatment effect and apply that to North America. And even if we ignore the lack of significance in North America, the observed treatment effects were on the order of a fraction of a day or a fraction of a single point in symptom scores" (FDA 1999a: 95). For a company that had invested considerable sums to get its new and hopefully "blockbuster" product to this stage, Elashoff's presentation was a distressing turn of events.

By many accounts Elashoff's presentation turned out to be a "game changer." That can be seen in the way his presentation was referenced repeatedly throughout subsequent deliberations of the committee. It was also invoked by several committee members when giving the rationale for their votes toward the end of the meeting. Committee member John Hamilton, for example, concluded:

> Dr. Elashoff's presentation brought into sharp focus, for me at least, an issue that has been bothering me throughout the morning, and that is the reliance on this primary endpoint, time to primary endpoint. Flu doesn't just stop in one day, and a difference in one day between the placebo and the active drug treatment is said to be significant in the sense that it reduces global misery somehow and that it translates into a more productive, let's call it, work force. It seems to me looking at the graphs and tables and figures that you showed, the disease doesn't end at the time of the primary endpoint. It lingers. It goes on and on, and so to imagine that that translates into a more productive citizen I find that to be something of a leap of faith. (FDA 1999a: 120)

The subsequent discussion certainly showed appreciation for the original design of the drug, but it also appeared that committee members were generally not convinced by the data for Relenza. As one voting member summed it up poignantly at the time using a baseball metaphor, "This is maybe a base hit, but it's not a home run" (FDA 1999a: 186). Overall, the committee thus voted 13-4 *against* the view that safety and efficacy had been established (FDA 1999a: 223–224). The drug had mostly gone down on efficacy, and it looked like things might now be slipping away for Glaxo's Relenza.

The Repercussions at FDA

The unfavorable recommendation by the advisory committee now also put senior FDA management in a difficult position vis-à-vis Glaxo. On

2 March 1999 James Palmer, then senior vice president and director of the Group Medical, Regulatory and Product Strategy organization at Glaxo Wellcome, wrote a lengthy letter to the FDA. Palmer explained in his letter that the company's "chief frustration is that the multiple procedural deficiencies of this hearing, exemplified most acutely by a new 'surprise' primary endpoint analysis by the reviewing statistician, are inconsistent with our many years of constructive and open interaction on the development and registration of important, new antiviral drugs" (Palmer 1999: 1). The exhaustive 17-page letter goes on to catalog a list of complaints too long to replicate here.

A few choice points from the letter are worth highlighting, however. The first is that the letter explicitly invokes the political will of Congress in order to express the company's deep disquiet about the decision. Palmer points out that the division's "sudden reversal is completely at odds with the will of Congress that drug development and approval proceed swiftly and surely on the basis of reliable communication between sponsors and FDA. Congress expressed its will by enacting section 119 of the Food and Drug Modernization Act of 1997, which provides for generally binding agreements between sponsors and FDA on the design and size of pivotal effectiveness trials" (Palmer 1999: 5). Just as striking is the way in which—even after the events of this advisory committee meeting—the company appeared undeterred by the outcome and simply rearticulated its goal of bringing the new drug to market. In closing his letter, Palmer thus notes that "my personal goal and our corporate goal is still to have Relenza available as a therapeutic option for the treatment of influenza as it emerges in the 1999–2000 seasons. I look forward to meeting with you to discuss the way forward" (Palmer 1999: 17).

Needless to say, all of this also created a rather big headache for senior managers at the FDA. Mike Elashoff recalls:

> From their point of view, it was a big hassle for them to have to deal with something like this, and so the decisions that they made were things basically designed to minimize hassles in the future. Now, for example, if they tried to fire me . . . that would have been a big hassle for them, so the things that they did were first reassign the Tamiflu review, and second tell me I wasn't allowed to deal with any more advisory committees. So because then I wouldn't be at least publicly making any more controversy for them. (Elashoff 2012)

The events of the advisory committee meeting would indeed have serious personal ramifications for Elashoff. Describing his perceived treatment in the days and weeks after the meeting, Elashoff recalls how "it was a very personally difficult time for me after the advisory committee" and that "the underlying message they had was we are not going to fire you but you need to leave. . . . It won't be pleasant for you either personally or professionally until you do" (Elashoff 2012).

Elashoff initially switched divisions at the FDA. Yet he recalls soon witnessing some of these same issues there as well. He remembers talking to other reviewers who shared similar concerns about some of the reviews they were doing and was disturbed to discover that this seemed to be a more pervasive issue: "Because, if you think [about it], there is enormous impact that FDA review process has on public health, and to think that that is flawed. If you think that FAA is not inspecting airplanes properly, that's a disturbing thought" (Elashoff 2012). Eventually Elashoff decided to leave the FDA.

Yet that is not the end of the story. Elashoff believes that the immense difficulties experienced with the Relenza application also colored the subsequent application process for Tamiflu that followed only a few months later. In the immediate aftermath of the Relenza advisory committee decision, for example, Elashoff was removed from the Tamiflu brief. "Originally," Elashoff explains, "I was going to be the reviewer of Tamiflu as well. I had all the boxes and documents in my office already," but "it was said someone else will do the Tamiflu review and so then someone took the boxes out of my office" (Elashoff 2012). The statistical review was passed on to a colleague. Reflecting on whether his colleague was aware of the wider issues, Elashoff replies: "He understood the situation extremely clearly and knew what they wanted him to do." In fact, according to Elashoff, the implications of the actions for others at FDA were clear: "Nobody wanted something to happen to them like what happened to me. So . . . the lesson was pretty well understood by everyone of don't do a range of different analyses on Tamiflu, just stick to what was originally proposed. It is not going to go to advisory committee, just kind of do basic reviews, say what the company did looks fine, and then move on past this" (Elashoff 2012). By the time the boxes of Tamiflu data were actually removed from his office, Elashoff had already had a chance to look at some of the Tamiflu data. His recollection was that Tamiflu "looked modestly better"—an effect of around a day rather than just hours as in the case of Relenza: "I guess I [would] put it this way: if you got the flu and didn't know whether you were taking placebo, Tamiflu or Relenza—I don't think you'd be able to tell" (Elashoff 2012). In either case, the FDA's decision to replace the statistical reviewer for Tamiflu was one way in which the Relenza backstory also began to slowly feed into the Tamiflu application as well.

Perhaps the most crucial consequence of the whole Relenza episode, however, was that when it then came to processing the Tamiflu application, it was eventually decided *not* to take it to an advisory committee in the way that Relenza had. Elashoff recalls that "the original plan [on Tamiflu] was that that would be an advisory committee too. Because . . . these were basically two new compounds in what was a high-profile area. . . . But subsequent to the Relenza advisory committee they decided not to take Tamiflu to the advisory committee" (Elashoff 2012). Asked whether he thinks Tamiflu might have gone the same way as Relenza if it had gone first, Elashoff replies:

> It's entirely possible. . . . Yes, I mean Relenza just looked so bad; I mean Tamiflu looks marginal as opposed to bad. So, it certainly would have gone to the advisory committee, and it may well have been more of a balanced opinion rather than a negative opinion from the advisory committee; and that would have caused less debate all around or less problems all around. . . . But no, they didn't want a repeat of that [Relenza episode] happening. They wanted to be able to make the approval decision without the advisory committee, which, when they are reviewing, is much more of a wild card opposed to Relenza than they were previously. (Elashoff 2012)

So there would be no independent scientific advisory committee meeting for Tamiflu as there had been for Relenza.

When approached to corroborate this course of events, an FDA reviewer closely involved in these issues, but who did not wish to be named, disputed this interpretation, explaining:

> Tamiflu clearly won on all the endpoints for both treatment and prophylaxis and was tested in both community (elder care facilities) and household settings. It was the second drug in its class and there were no controversial issues so there was no need for an advisory committee meeting. Advisory committee meetings are not cheap or easy to set up so they are not routine in all drug re-

views. They are supposed to be called only when there is actually some doubt about the efficacy or safety of the product. There was a period earlier in the AIDS epidemic when almost every anti-viral went to advisory committee meetings even when efficacy was pretty clear just as part of making knowledge of the new drug publically widespread. We mostly don't do that anymore. (FDA Reviewer 2015)

According to other people involved in the Tamiflu application process, however, it appears that such a meeting had indeed been planned but was canceled shortly before it was due to take place (Influenza Scientist 2014).

In fact, at least one former Roche employee interviewed for this book vividly recalls practicing and rehearsing in depth for the Tamiflu advisory committee that was planned for the autumn of 1999. The employee remembers being "petrified" and practicing—even being filmed—over the summer, but was then advised a week before it was scheduled to happen that the FDA had determined that no advisory board was needed (Clinical Development Scientist 2015). Overall, however, the former employee also recalls not being particularly worried about the ultimate outcome, because Roche felt it had demonstrated what it had agreed to demonstrate and that the evidence was overwhelming (Clinical Development Scientist 2015). In either case, the FDA approval process for Tamiflu, which looked so uneventful on the surface, had taken place in the shadow of a particularly acrimonious experience at the FDA around the regulatory approval of Relenza immediately prior to it.

Playing the Pandemic Card: A Final Twist in the Relenza Debacle

What happened with the Relenza application in the end, especially following the unfavorable recommendation by the advisory committee? After further deliberations, senior managers at the FDA decided *not* to follow the recommendation of the advisory committee and approved Relenza nevertheless. This option was available to them because the decision by the advisory committee is, strictly speaking, only a recommendation; it is not binding. While it is relatively rare for such recommendations to be overturned, there are precedents (Moynihan and Cassels 2005: 163).

What could possibly have tipped the balance back in favor of approval? In a final significant twist in the story, part of the justification for ultimately approving Relenza—despite the negative recommendation of the advisory committee—was the parallel concern about pandemic flu. Glaxo Wellcome had invoked such health security issues in its letter to the FDA in the immediate aftermath of the advisory committee hearing. Writing to the FDA on behalf of Glaxo Wellcome, Palmer reminded the FDA:

> In 1998, the Centers for Disease Control (as part of a collaborative effort with the Department of Health and Human Services and FDA) requested that Glaxo Wellcome construct a plan to provide zanamivir [Relenza] in the event of a future pandemic. In response to this request, we have prepared such a plan, including information on scale up of manufacturing, accumulation of sufficient inventory of the drug, and operational distribution through the world. In view of the negative recommendation from the Antiviral Drugs Advisory Committee and the absence of a commercial platform in parallel with this humanitarian effort, we cannot implement these plans for the United States. We are continuing to implement pandemic preparedness plans for other countries. (Palmer 1999: 7)

The implications are concerning: not approving this drug would likely also undermine the pandemic preparedness of the United States. It is a striking example of how a large pharmaceutical company could invoke government concerns about health security in the context of an ongoing regulatory approval process for one of its new commercial products.

Looking in more detail at the final FDA documentation produced in approving Relenza reveals that such pandemic considerations did prove critical in justifying the eventual decision to approve the drug in the end. The document acknowledges that on efficacy the seasonal studies "are not immediately compelling and can be interpreted in multiple ways" and that "the basic decision on whether the drug is approvable for influenza treatment using currently available information can be argued in either direction, and a rationale can be constructed either for non-approval or for approval" (FDA 1999c: 140). Regulatory approval for Relenza was, in other words, a pretty marginal call, and things were very much hanging in the balance.

Yet wider considerations about the threat of a flu pandemic would eventually help tip the scales in favor of approval. As the Relenza review goes on to point out, "A rationale for making therapeutic options available has been recognized even where benefit to the average patient may be small, as a small average benefit could translate into potentially important impact at population level, especially in the setting of widespread epidemic or pandemic influenza activity" (FDA 1999c: 147–148). Indeed, "On the basis of study results showing treatment effects (albeit modest and variable) in numerous studies, a safety profile that has shown few causes for concern from a reasonably extensive database, and the prospect of expanding the useable treatment options for a widespread disease with pandemic potential where even a small average benefit may carry substantial public health importance, the overall conclusion was that this application could be considered to provide adequate evidence for approvability in the context of the understandings reached regarding label language and phase 4 commitments" (FDA 1999c: 153). Referencing months of intensive discussions within the agency, the document concludes that approval could be justified (FDA 1999c: 152). Health security considerations about pandemic flu had, in the end, seeped into the approval processes for neuraminidase inhibitors, even though the applications for regulatory approval were—strictly speaking—only for seasonal flu, and on the basis of clinical trials also carried out only with people suffering from seasonal flu. In a context where regulators would have to make a difficult marginal call, health security considerations helped to eventually tip the balance in favor of a positive recommendation.

Nor was this kind of pandemic logic confined to the US approval process. In Europe, such pandemic considerations similarly formed part of the backdrop of regulatory decision making on Tamiflu. This was confirmed in interviews carried out with the European regulators: "You can imagine from our regulatory perspective, and you can see in the benefit risk consideration, that the potential utility of this drug in the context of a pandemic, or a drift in the circulating viruses even in seasonal context, is considered as an important aspect, as an important potential benefit of Tamiflu. So clearly it was considered" (EMA Officer 2013). For the European approval process, these pandemic considerations are also explicitly included in the publicly available European public assessment reports: "On the basis of current knowledge, neuraminidase inhibitors will not play a major role during typical influenza seasons. However, they might have a significant role in case of a pandemic or a drift in circulating influenza strains after the selection of the vaccine strains" (EMEA 2005b: 24). In the case of neuraminidase inhibitors, where regulatory processes for seasonal influenza hung in a delicate balance on more than one occasion, and where regulators would have to make a difficult margin call, pandemic considerations strengthened the case for an otherwise marginal decision to become a favorable one.

There is just one—rather significant—problem with applying such reasoning. The regulators actually have strikingly little data about the efficacy that such products would have in the case of a future pandemic flu. It is not really possible to generate such data through clinical trials. One former FDA official, Paul Flyer, explains the problem here with exemplary clarity: "The primary concern with pandemic flu is the potential for increased morbidity and death relative to seasonal flu. It is difficult, if not impossible, to study a treatment for pandemic flu because an outbreak cannot be predicted and it may be considered unethical to randomize people during an outbreak" (Flyer 2013). There are, in other words, both practical and ethical reasons why such clinical trial data cannot be generated for pandemic flu. How can one run clinical trials for a threat whose precise shape and extent cannot be known in advance? Even once a pandemic arrives, the need to randomize the trials so as to exclude bias would mean withholding the medicine from some trial participants—raising a number of ethical issues. All of this suggests that there really could be no strong evidence base available at the time that these products would actually be effective against a future flu pandemic.

In the end, claims that neuraminidase inhibitors could also play a useful role in a future *pandemic* were—at the time—really a matter of extrapolation and conjecture based on data principally derived from *seasonal* flu. As Flyer goes on to explain,

> The question then becomes whether or not data from seasonal flu outbreaks could be used to approve products for the treatment of pandemic flu. One would like to extrapolate the data from seasonal flu to pandemic flu by reasoning that it may be harder for the body to suppress the virus associated with pandemic flu, and antiviral treatment can help suppress the virus until the patient is able to suppress the virus on its own. Though this seems to be a logical possibility, we don't have any evidence that I am aware of that in fact the currently approved products will reduce the morbidity and mortality associated with pandemic flu. From a public health perspective and regulatory perspective, is it better to allow pharmaceutical companies to promote the use of currently approved products based upon extrapolation or to require data before a product can be promoted? The regulators are likely to be placed in the awkward posi-

tion of having limited or no clinical evidence to prepare for pandemic flu while possibly being called upon to make approval decisions or make recommendations in the absence of adequate human clinical data. (Flyer 2013)

The bottom line is that when it comes to the threat of pandemic flu (as opposed to seasonal flu) there are no clinical trial data available because there are significant practical as well as ethical obstacles to generating such data for pandemic flu. The likely effects of such antivirals in a pandemic have to be inferred or extrapolated instead, raising a number of complex issues.

Nor is this a problem confined to pandemic flu. It pertains to most other health security threats as well. There are so many threatening diseases— such as smallpox or plague—that may not occur naturally, may only occur in very small numbers, or that are extremely dangerous, even lethal. In such circumstances, it is much more difficult, if not impossible, to carry out properly powered human clinical trials. It would also not be acceptable to deliberately infect a large number of people with a lethal pathogen simply in order to generate such data. The whole question of whether pandemic considerations should influence the regulatory approval decisions about neuraminidase inhibitors thus also highlights a much bigger problem surrounding the development of new medical countermeasures more generally. How can such products ever hope to obtain regulatory approval if it is not possible to run proper human clinical trials? Pharmaceutical companies can hardly be expected to take on the costly development of new medical countermeasures if there is no reasonable prospect of obtaining regulatory approval further down the line. The question of how to obtain regulatory approval is thus an added complication that arises in developing medical countermeasures in general.

Special Rules for Medical Countermeasures

How are governments responding to this lacuna? On the one hand, governments want to encourage the development of new medical countermeasures in order to better protect their populations against future health emergencies. On the other hand, it is also the task of government to protect the public by properly regulating medicines to ensure that they are safe and effective. Should governments therefore give medical countermeasures special treatment when it comes to their regulatory approval? If so, how far should regulatory processes be adapted to allow more flexibility?

How far can existing procedures be stretched before they begin to pose a threat to people's safety?

Some governments have already begun to establish new and extraordinary legal frameworks governing the approval of medical countermeasures. The FDA, for example, developed a new procedure referred to as the "animal rule" in May 2002. The animal rule stipulates that rather than having to rely on extensive human clinical trials to demonstrate the effectiveness of a product, developers of medical countermeasures could use animal studies instead. This could be done in situations where the mechanisms of toxicity of the product are well understood, where the effect is established in more than one species of animal expected to be predictive for humans (in some cases one well-characterized animal model could be sufficient), and where the workings of the drug are sufficiently well understood to allow for the selection of an effective dose in humans (FDA 2002).

Crucially, the rule does not exempt the safety evaluation of products, which remain unchanged from existing requirements for new drugs. Even for new medical countermeasures, in other words, there would still need to be some smaller-scale clinical trials in humans (but in human beings who are not infected with the agent) to determine the safety of the product and to check for adverse effects. What is more, the rule also envisions further postmarketing studies that would then still be carried out to verify the product's clinical benefit and to further assess safety, once such studies become feasible and ethical (Wizemann et al. 2016: 35).

The US government has gradually been phasing in this new animal rule over the past decade. Regulators initially took a cautious approach, using the rule mostly to approve new indications for products that had already been approved for other indications. On 5 February 2003, for instance, the FDA approved the application of pyridostigmine bromide (PB) for prophylaxis against the lethal effects of Soman nerve agent poisoning. PB had already been approved in 1955 in the United States for the treatment of a rare neurological disorder called myasthenia gravis but was now being considered for a new indication (Aebersold 2012). It marked the first time the new animal rule was used.

The animal rule was again invoked in 2006, this time for an antidote treating patients with known or suspected cyanide poisoning called Cyanokit. Cyanokit too had already been granted marketing authorization by French authorities (in May 1996) on the basis of one prospective study and several retrospective studies in victims of smoke inhalation (Aebersold 2012). Following additional animal studies, the FDA again deployed the animal rule to approve Cyanokit in December 2006. The decision was based primarily on a single placebo-controlled study in dogs (Aebersold 2012). In 2015, the FDA then also used the animal rule to approve a new indication for BioThrax, an anthrax vaccine that had initially been approved by the FDA in 1970. It was the first vaccine ever to receive approval on the basis of the animal rule (FDA 2015). All these products were approved by the FDA for new indications using the animal rule, but all the products had previously already secured approval for other indications.

More recently, the animal rule has been utilized more boldly to approve newly developed medical countermeasures. In April 2012, for example, the FDA used the procedure to authorize Levaquin (levofloxacin)—an antibiotic manufactured by Johnson & Johnson intended to treat pneumonic plague. The approval was granted on the basis of tests carried out on African green monkeys that had been experimentally infected with pneumonic plague (Gaffney 2012). In December of the same year, the FDA also granted approval to GlaxoSmithKline's raxibacumab—a monoclonal antibody intended to treat inhalational anthrax. In this case, one study was performed on monkeys and three further ones on rabbits. These more recent examples mean that the animal rule has also enabled a number of new medical countermeasures to gain regulatory approval that was unlikely to have been achieved under more normal or routine procedures. It marks another significant way in which governments have begun to adjust their regulatory processes around pharmaceuticals in order to accommodate the particular needs of medical countermeasure development.

Exploring this next stage in the life of Tamiflu has revealed just how critical regulatory approval processes are for new medicines. Because pharmaceutical products operate at such a tiny scale, well beyond the limits of human perception, companies first have to provide regulators with extensive evidence that their new molecules work safely and effectively inside the human body. The clinical trials that need to be carried out for those purposes are very expensive, so companies will usually have already invested significant financial sums just to get a new product to this stage. Yet they will have no guarantee that regulatory approval will ultimately be granted unless the regulators are thoroughly satisfied that the product is both safe and effective. If the application for approval turns out to be unsuccessful, their initial financial investment will likely be lost.

There is thus already considerable commercial risk involved for pharmaceutical companies in taking any new products through clinical trials and to the stage of regulatory approval. The experience with neuraminidase inhibitors bears those risks out, as both of the sponsoring companies for Tamiflu and Relenza experienced a number of critical setbacks at this regulatory approval stage. In the case of Relenza, the drug initially received a negative recommendation from the advisory committee in the United States (although the drug was eventually approved by the FDA). In the case of Tamiflu, the European application ran into difficulties the first time around, leading to a delay of its launch there. Such setbacks would naturally also have commercial ramifications for all of the companies involved. Any additional uncertainty about such regulatory approval processes would therefore pose a significant deterrent for a commercially operating pharmaceutical company in deciding whether or not to take on the development of a new product.

Yet precisely those commercial risks around obtaining regulatory approval are also exacerbated when it comes to many medical countermeasures. Here too the security context complicates matters again, because it would be much more difficult to run such clinical trials for many of the threatening diseases against which governments would like to have new medical countermeasures available. Unlike influenza, those diseases may not be naturally occurring or may not occur naturally in large enough numbers to allow from properly powered clinical trials to be carried out. We have also seen that running such trials would raise considerable ethical reservations, because one would not want to deliberately infect a large number of people with a lethal disease just to run clinical trials or to withhold potentially lifesaving treatments from those who are infected, as would be necessary for a placebo-controlled trial. As two influenza experts explain, "A randomized controlled trial that recruited only patients with severe influenza, although feasible from a design perspective, could not ethically evaluate active treatment versus placebo treatment because oseltamivir treatment is the standard of care for patients with severe influenza virus infection" (Hurt and Kelly 2016). That is also why—even in the case of Tamiflu—it was only possible to conduct clinical trials for seasonal flu, but not for pandemic flu. When it comes to new medical countermeasures, visualizing and evidencing their effectiveness can be much more difficult than for many other pharmaceutical products destined for more routine clinical use.

Such elevated risks around regulatory approval thus form another—and fourth—major challenge that arises around medical countermeasures more generally. It also means that governments wishing to encourage the development of new medical countermeasures will not just have to contend with an initial set of scientific, economic, and late-stage development obstacles. They will also have to manage a whole second set of challenges that arise once a new medical countermeasure is developed and that revolve around how governments would subsequently turn such products into a meaningful medical countermeasure capability that could be deployed in a future emergency. Obtaining official regulatory approval is one of those additional challenges, because a government would first need to be sure that any new medical countermeasure is safe and effective before it can acquire it in large volumes to protect its population.

Some regulators have therefore also already begun to build greater flexibilities into their regulatory approval processes governing new medical countermeasures. In the European Union, there is now a procedure now for granting a marketing authorization under exceptional circumstances. This is intended for situations where an applicant is unable to provide comprehensive data on the efficacy and safety of the medicinal product under normal conditions of use because a disease is rare or collecting such information would go against medical ethics (Cavaleri 2016). The US government has introduced even greater flexibilities through the "animal rule." BARDA, moreover, has also developed a whole new Clinical Studies Network to assist companies working on medical countermeasures with performing clinical studies, as well as establishing a separate Nonclinical Development Network to help them with developing viable animal models that can stand up to regulatory rigor (Nicholson et al. 2016: 18). Overall, 23 medical countermeasures supported by BARDA have now cleared the hurdle of FDA approval in the United States (Hatchett 2016a).

5

Virtual Blockbuster

Bird Flu and the Pandemic of

Preparedness Planning

Once regulatory approval has been granted, the next stage in the life of a new medicine is usually taking the product to market. This is the point at which companies can begin to recoup the financial investment made in developing the new medicine. Yet even then significant commercial risks remain. The fact that a new medicine has been granted regulatory approval does not necessarily mean that it will become a commercial success. Licensure and adoption of a new medicine are not one and the same thing. This chapter therefore explores what happened to Tamiflu after it secured its marketing approvals and entered the marketplace. Would Tamiflu finally become the new blockbuster drug that Roche was hoping?

It would not—at least not initially. Once Tamiflu entered the marketplace, it quickly encountered a number of obstacles that prevented it from becoming the desired commercial success. Most countries ban direct-to-consumer marketing, making it very difficult for Roche to raise awareness of its new product among the potential customer base for Tamiflu. Some governments in key pharmaceutical markets also set up new institutions charged with scrutinizing novel medicines on cost-benefit grounds. Medicines would not just have to demonstrate that they are safe and effective; they would also have to represent good value for the money. All the while, parallel attempts by Roche to persuade governments to purchase Tamiflu for pandemic preparedness purposes largely fell on deaf ears during these early years. Several years after it obtained regulatory approval, the overall commercial performance of Tamiflu was proving quite disappointing for the company—especially when measured against the high initial expectations. Tamiflu was not likely to become a blockbuster product after all.

This unfavorable commercial picture only began to change in 2003. That year witnessed the unexpected reemergence of lethal human infections with highly pathogenic avian influenza viruses (H5N1) in Hong Kong. As deadly human infections with the H5N1 "bird flu" virus began to spread to other countries and eventually also moved closer to the borders of several high-income countries, government interest in Tamiflu suddenly peaked. With international concern about an imminent flu pandemic now skyrocketing, Tamiflu's first—and fairly unsuccessful—commercial life as an antiviral medication for seasonal flu faded into the background, as the antiviral rapidly transitioned into its second (and much more prosperous) life as the world's most prominent medical countermeasure against the looming pandemic flu threat. In a complete reversal of Tamiflu's commercial fortunes, there was suddenly a massive explosion in global demand for the drug—with governments, corporations, and individuals all clamoring to acquire scarce international supplies of the antiviral as the first line of defense against pandemic flu.

This sudden reversal in the global demand for Tamiflu reveals two further challenges surrounding medical countermeasures more generally. First, governments also have to carefully gauge their demand for such products to ensure that they have access to the right number of the right medical countermeasures at the right time in order to protect their populations. It may not be feasible for governments to simply wait until an emergency has occurred before trying to obtain them. That is because such medical countermeasures may need to be administered very rapidly, because governments may require a larger volume of such medical countermeasures than normal supply chains can quickly deliver, and because those existing supply chains may themselves become disrupted during an emergency. Again, the security context within which medical countermeasures would be used begins to complicate matters considerably.

In the case of Tamiflu, many governments have tried to address this challenge by creating new emergency stockpiles of the antiviral. Yet simply having warehouses stacked full of such medical countermeasures would also be fairly pointless without a parallel logistical strategy for rapidly distributing them to the population in the event they are urgently needed. Even once a pharmaceutical stockpile has been set up, governments must still give further thought to exactly how those medical countermeasures would then be distributed to individuals in a very short period of time—and possibly in a context where normal distribution channels have become disrupted because of the outbreak of a pandemic. In addition to the demand management challenge, there is thus also a second logistical challenge that emerges at this stage about how governments would go about mass distributing such stockpiled medical countermeasures to the population when a future emergency transpires.

These two additional challenges, moreover, again also show that developing an effective medical countermeasure capability is ultimately not just a narrow question of how governments can encourage pharmaceutical companies to develop a few new products. Governments will also need to do much more than that if they wish to secure their populations pharmaceutically. They will need to further ensure that they would have access to the right number of medical countermeasures at the right time. They will also need to put into place systems for quickly distributing them to the population during a future emergency.

Tamiflu on the Tightrope: Struggling for a Viable Commercial Market

Once regulatory approval for Tamiflu was secured, Roche still faced a number of hurdles before it could begin to make a profit from its new product. The biggest of these challenges was to figure out how the company would raise awareness about its new antiviral product among patients. After all, if doctors and patients did not know that this new product for treating the flu even existed, they could hardly prescribe and purchase it. What is more, people were generally not accustomed to going to their doctor to treat the flu. Popular wisdom dictated that adults who were otherwise healthy should stay at home, drink plenty of fluids, and rest in bed. Yet if Tamiflu were to work as intended, patients would have to begin treatment during the early onset of the illness. All of this meant that for Tamiflu to become a commercial success, Roche would first have to do nothing short of changing people's flu-related behavior and get them to actively seek out their doctors at the earliest signs of flu. Mathias Dick, product manager for Roche Pharma Switzerland at the time, succinctly summarized the challenge in the following terms: "For seventy years we had been telling people that the best thing to do for influenza was to stay in bed . . . yet now we had to convince them to go to see their doctor" (Schneider 2001). Provoking such behavior change was going to prove especially challenging in the world's major pharmaceutical markets.

The Ban on Direct-to-Consumer Marketing

The first hurdle that Roche confronted in turning Tamiflu into a commercial success was that the advertisement of medicines is heavily regulated in many of the world's pharmaceutical markets. That problem is illustrated very well by the case of Switzerland, where Tamiflu had received the world's first regulatory approval. Swiss law stipulated that new medicines would need to be prescription-only for the first five years after licensing. On top of that, the country also operated a ban on direct-to-consumer marketing for prescription medicines. How would Roche raise awareness of the drug among patients and doctors within the Swiss regulatory environment? Various ideas were floated and tried. Mathias Dick's team at Roche first developed credit card–sized leaflets explaining the difference between influenza and a common cold. The cards also provided a telephone number for queries and an Internet address. More than five million of the cards were distributed in Switzerland alone (Schneider 2001).

In parallel, Roche also developed a new poster campaign with messages along the lines of: "What do you know about influenza? Find out about it. Now. www.Tamiflu.ch" (Schneider 2001). The design of the new poster campaign was clever in that it did not explicitly mention the drug by name, but the name was clearly embedded in the website domain name: www.Tamiflu .ch (Baumgartner 2000). Roche's team also developed an informational campaign tour of 12 Swiss cities to make doctors and pharmacists aware of the new drug. The company even flew some Swiss journalists to a press conference in London, which provided them with background information on the health and economic threat posed by flu and how Tamiflu worked (Schneider 2001).

Unsurprisingly, perhaps, the Swiss authorities were not entirely pleased with all of those activities. In their opinion, some of the campaigns fell afoul of the relevant regulations. They therefore prohibited Roche from using the Tamiflu name in the Internet address that formed part of its advertisements, and eventually the domain name was changed to www.roche-grippe.ch (Baumgartner 2000). In this kind of regulatory context Roche was clearly going to struggle to turn Tamiflu into a significant commercial success.

Reflecting on the outlook at the time, and given that the success of the drug requires patients to change their flu behavior by rapidly going to their doctors, Roche's marketing team suspected it would take at least five to ten years for the drug to establish itself in the market (Schneider 2001).

The kinds of regulatory constraints Roche encountered in Switzerland would also feature in other European markets. Direct-to-consumer advertising of prescription medicines is prohibited throughout the European Union. In fact, direct-to-consumer marketing of prescription medicines is banned in most countries around the world—with the notable exceptions of the United States and New Zealand. Even in those two countries, where it was made legal in the late 1990s, the practice is controversial, and in both countries there have also been subsequent attempts to change the legislation in a way that would introduce a moratorium on advertising newly approved drugs (Magrini and Font 2007). In the United States, such advertising also remains subject to regulation by the Food and Drug Administration. From a strictly commercial point of view, the bans on direct-to-consumer marketing thus posed a significant hurdle to a more widespread promotion and adoption of Tamiflu.

That said, the United States was clearly one of the few countries in the world where Roche could unleash its full marketing prowess in a more unrestrained manner. Glaxo Wellcome was already heavily promoting its rival product Relenza there, even recruiting the celebrity Wayne Knight from the popular sitcom *Seinfeld* to play the role of an obnoxious houseguest called "influenza" (West 2000: 122). To quickly make up ground, Roche worked with the specialist company Edelman New York (West 200: 120). The US marketing campaign for Tamiflu would begin on 15 November 1999—only three weeks after the FDA had approved Tamiflu—and would include both television and print ads (West 2000: 120). All would feature a toll-free number, 1-800-I-GOT-FLU, and a website address, www.Tamiflu.com (West 2000: 121).

The campaign's most creative idea, however, was undoubtedly the use of the Tamiflu van. This van, or truck, featured a live actor on display in a glass-enclosed, fully furnished apartment (roughly 9 feet by 20 feet) mounted on the back of a truck. In plain view, the actor would get out of bed in his pajamas and undertake a number of mundane activities, such as eating breakfast and reading the newspaper. He would then go watch TV, work, play video games, and so forth, all inside this glass apartment without paying any attention to the bystanders who could clearly see everything he was doing. The punch line—printed across the side of the truck—was "One person in this town who can probably feel safe from the flu . . . For the rest of us flu sufferers, there's Tamiflu." The tour made its way through America's 71 largest flu markets using a total of 8 such mobile apartments (Bittar 2001).

As the creative marketing campaign began to bear fruit, Tamiflu went on to dominate the antiviral flu market, securing a 58 percent market share in the United States and achieving $41 million in sales from November 1999 through to April 2000, compared to Relenza's at $20 million (Bittar 2001). Coming to market second rather than first had not been such a disadvantage after all. One influenza scientist interviewed for this book recalls that the timing of the peak flu season around the Christmas vacation that year may also have played a role. Glaxo Wellcome had apparently shut down its computers because of fears about the millennium bug—meaning that they could not ship Relenza from France where it was being produced (but Relenza also later developed some issues with side effects) (Influenza Scientist 2014). In either case, the commercial situation with Tamiflu in the United States very much marked the exception rather than the rule—especially when compared with the wider international picture.

A Fourth Hurdle? NICE and the Rise of Cost-Benefit Analysis

Roche (and Glaxo) also faced another hurdle in trying to turn their new neuraminidase inhibitors into blockbuster products. In some of the world's key pharmaceutical markets, governments were in the process of setting up new institutions to further scrutinize new medicines on cost-benefit grounds. Many governments continue to be faced with spiraling health-care costs and have to make difficult decisions about how to allocate limited public resources. Because neuraminidase inhibitors seemed to reduce the duration of symptoms by "only" around one day, Relenza and Tamiflu were often considered to be borderline drugs in terms of their cost-effectiveness. Going back once more to Roche's home market, for example, Swiss health insurance funds were generally not willing to reimburse the costs of these new medicines and were demanding price reductions of 20 percent. They felt that the utility, effectiveness, and public health benefits did not justify the price and also that at those prices it would make more sense to just keep vaccinating (Schlatter 1999).

The battle between governments and pharmaceutical companies over cost-effectiveness came to a particularly dramatic head in the United Kingdom. There, the licensing of Relenza coincided with the creation of the new National Institute for Clinical Excellence (NICE). NICE is charged with advising the UK National Health Service on the clinical and cost effectiveness of drugs. The very first drug appraisal that the new organization ever carried out was on Relenza. In discussions with NICE, it was agreed that Relenza should be subject to a fast-track assessment prior to the 1999–2000 influenza season. Glaxo Wellcome accordingly made its Relenza submission to NICE on 1 September 1999. Everyone realized that the outcome would be crucial for all sides—for the company in terms of the future market for Relenza, as well as for NICE in terms of establishing itself as a credible new institution.

After conducting its review, NICE arrived at the one conclusion that the pharmaceutical companies had probably feared most. It advised that "health professionals should not prescribe zanamivir (Relenza) during the 1999/2000 influenza season" (NICE 1999: 2). NICE had sent a clear signal that cost-benefit analysis would become much more critical for governments moving forward and that pharmaceutical products that did not meet its threshold would henceforth have a much harder time.

Market analysts quickly pointed to the decision's wider commercial significance. According to Nigel Barnes, analyst at the wealth management firm Merrill Lynch, "If you look at the UK [which accounts for 6 percent of global drugs sales] in isolation, this decision would probably have minimal impact. . . . But it could have ramifications elsewhere, particularly in Europe where healthcare expenditure is under even greater focus" (quoted in Pilling 1999). From the commercial side, there was particular concern that NICE's decision could influence regulators in Japan, where a similar approval process was under way. Japan was the world's second biggest drug market at the time (Pilling 1999).

If Glaxo was shocked by this decision, so too was the wider UK-based pharmaceutical industry. The industry upset caused by the decision was so great, in fact, that the British Pharma Group—made up at the time of AstraZeneca, Glaxo Wellcome, and SmithKline Beecham—took the unusual step of writing a letter directly to the British prime minister, Tony Blair. The letter claimed that the companies were "appalled at the recommendation" and pointed to the "potentially devastating consequences for the future of the British-based pharmaceutical industry." The letter also expressed concern that NICE was now effectively operating as a "fourth hurdle" for new medicines: "Much damage has already been done by the signals sent out by NICE's recommendations on Relenza," it asserted, and "the landmark ruling on Relenza makes it crystal clear that our worst fears were fully justified" (McKillop 1999). NICE would not succumb to such political pressure by the industry, however. When it issued further guidance the following year (in November 2000), it again found that "for otherwise healthy adults with influenza, the use of zanamivir is not recommended" (NICE 2000: 1). By 2004 Glaxo would have only sold around £4 million worth of the drug (Jack 2006).

If the NICE assessments did not go well for Glaxo's Relenza (zanamivir), Tamiflu (oseltamivir) did not fare much better a couple of years later. NICE issued recommendations on oseltamivir in February and September 2003—looking separately at the questions of treatment and prophylactic use. The first only recommended use in "at risk" adults and children presenting with influenza-like illness and who could start therapy within 48 hours of the onset of symptoms (NICE 2003b: 1–2). The second did not recommend oseltamivir for seasonal prophylaxis of influenza but recommended postexposure prophylaxis for certain "at-risk" groups aged over 13 who were exposed to someone with influenza-like illness, who could begin prophylaxis within 48 hours, and who were not protected by a vaccine (NICE 2003a: 4).

In either case, greater government emphasis on cost-benefit considerations began to form a second "hurdle" to the widespread adoption of these new antiviral drugs—especially given the claimed reduction in symptom duration of around one day. The commercial developers of neuraminidase inhibitors were now effectively faced with a dual challenge. Even though they had developed a new drug and obtained regulatory approval, in most markets they could not advertise widely for their new product, and new agencies like NICE that were increasingly looking at cost-benefit issues were not recommending widespread adoption of the new medicine. Things were not going well. As one report in the *PharmaTimes* from 2003 noted, "Despite the fanfare hailing these products, they have not been the hoped-for success both firms had anticipated and Tamiflu generated just 97 million Swiss francs in 2001 (the last figures available) despite being made available in more than 40 countries around the world following concerns over their cost-effectiveness" (*PharmaTimes* 2003). It was becoming increasingly clear that neuraminidase inhibitors were unlikely to become the blockbuster products that the companies had initially hoped for.

Falling on Deaf Ears: Government Reluctance to Create Pandemic Stockpiles

With efforts on seasonal flu running into difficulties, Roche still had one last option left in its playbook to turn around Tamiflu's commercial fortunes. Given the dual nature of the flu challenge, the company could instead try to push the antiviral for *pandemic* flu. Thus, Roche also began to approach governments to see if they would be interested in acquiring the drug as part of their pandemic preparedness planning. Sales made directly to governments for such pandemic preparedness purposes would not require direct-to-consumer marketing. Nor would they be subject to the same kinds of cost-effectiveness evaluations increasingly conducted for seasonal use. Indeed, health security threats and pandemic flu (rather than seasonal flu) were generally seen to be beyond the remit of organizations like NICE. Given the large number of governments in Europe (and around the world), as well as the need to create sizable stockpiles to cover a significant proportion of the populations, pandemic preparedness could form a very different route toward commercial success for Roche to pursue.

However, most governments at the time did not take Roche's early attempts to warn about the specter of a renewed pandemic very seriously. In fact, they proved remarkably recalcitrant in *not* placing stockpiling orders during those early years. According to David Reddy, Roche's influenza pandemic team leader at the time, Roche was discussing pandemic preparedness plans with various governments, but, he said, "Our awareness campaigns had fallen on deaf ears. The threat was perceived as too elusive. The few orders that did come in were nothing we could not cope with" (quoted in Samii and van Wassenhove 2008: 1). Even though WHO was by this time recommending that governments make pandemic preparedness plans, and Roche was trying to convince governments to stockpile Tamiflu, most governments still had no pandemic preparedness plans in place (Samii and van Wassenhove 2008: 6). One former Roche employee even recalled, "I remember how some regulators almost ridiculed us and laughed at us saying a pandemic—what's that?—that's never going to happen" (Bergstrom 2013).

One country where Roche's argument about the need for government stockpiling strategy gained at least some traction was the United States. US preparations for a possible pandemic had begun to gather pace in August 1997. That year the CDC conducted an outbreak investigation on avian influenza (H5N1) infections occurring in poultry and humans in Hong Kong. It was the first time such infections had been detected in human beings, and a significant proportion of them proved lethal. In this context of escalating pandemic fears, the US government awarded a small contract to Ameri-Source/McKesson at the end of 2003. The contract was for $10.6 million to acquire 238,000 treatment courses of Tamiflu using funds from the Strategic National Stockpile (US Senate 2005: 20). In 2004 this was followed with another contract with Roche for $74 million to acquire 2.1 million treatment courses of Tamiflu, again using Strategic National Stockpile funds (US Senate 2005: 20).

That said, even the US Tamiflu stockpile was still quite small and would not make a huge difference to the overall profitability of the drug. Internationally, it also very much marked the exception rather than the rule. The overall commercial picture for Tamiflu therefore continued to look quite bleak by this point, and it did not seem likely that pandemic preparedness arguments would be able to offset the poor commercial performance of Tamiflu for seasonal flu. As Roche's Franz Humer, who had initially acquired the drug for Roche from Gilead, explained in an interview for the *Financial Times* at the time, "Our forecasts were more optimistic initially. . . . We had thought that doctors would prescribe and governments reimburse" (quoted in Jack 2006). By and large that assumption proved incorrect, with the notable exception of Japan, which agreed to reimburse health services for Tamiflu (Jack 2006). With low prescription figures, Tamiflu was not even on the list of the 20 most sold Roche medicines by 2003 (Vetterli 2009).

By this stage, then, Tamiflu was fast becoming a commercial flop—notwithstanding all of the investment Roche had put into acquiring the molecule from Gilead, developing it, setting up mass manufacturing facilities, carrying out the clinical trials necessary for regulatory approval, marketing it, and so forth. The whole Tamiflu experience was fast turning into a salutary reminder that acquiring regulatory approval alone is no guarantee of commercial success, and of just how careful pharmaceutical companies need to be in deciding which medicines to take forward. Even where there is a fairly clearly defined commercial market, there is still no certainty that commercial success will ensue. So Tamiflu's first life as a fairly conventional pharmaceutical product aimed at the seasonal flu market slowly started to fade into the background.

Tipping Point: Tamiflu as the First Line of Defense

The international picture around Tamiflu suddenly changed very dramatically through an unexpected turn of events in 2003. That year saw the surfacing of new reports about a type of highly pathogenic avian influenza—H5N1—sporadically infecting humans in Asia. The authorities in Hong Kong had first encountered such human infections with the H5N1 virus in 1997 but quickly took measures at the time to contain the initial outbreak—including the culling of many birds. The measures appeared successful, and things went quiet for several years. In 2003, however, human cases of lethal infection with H5N1 reemerged in the city. Further clusters were then also detected in Vietnam in February and March 2004. Those cases were particularly significant because human-to-human transmission could not be immediately ruled out, raising significant international concern about the possible onset of a new pandemic (WHO 2011a).

Over time, further human infections with the H5N1 virus were registered in other Asian countries and started moving closer to the borders of Europe. The advent of such lethal new cases of human infections with H5N1 in Asia, in conjunction with an H7N7 influenza outbreak in the Netherlands that caused a human fatality, would mark a crucial turning point in the history of Tamiflu. Suddenly the possibility of a new flu pandemic seemed much more palpable to politicians, and governments could see that they were likely to come under much more political pressure to ensure that they would be prepared for the possibility that these outbreaks could turn into a wider pandemic. What would governments do to protect their populations in that eventuality, and would they have taken the necessary precautions to ensure that they had access to antiviral medications and vaccines?

To make matters worse, a number of governments had recently appeared quite unprepared in the face of other unexpected crises. They would thus be keen to avoid a politically damaging repeat. In the United States, for instance, President George W. Bush's administration was still reeling from its botched handling of Hurricane Katrina and needed to better prepare for catastrophic events with a small probability but a high impact (Schulz 2005). French president Jacques Chirac similarly wanted to avoid a repetition of the political fallout from the excessive deaths of elderly people that had recently been caused by summer heat waves. In the United Kingdom the experience of a foot-and-mouth disease debacle still lingered (Jack 2009). With the spread of H5N1, all eyes would now be on governments once more to gauge how capable they would be at handling the next crisis—and it looked like that next crisis might well be a flu pandemic (Caduff 2015). In this context, the interests and priorities of many governments changed as they suddenly felt popular and political pressure not to be unprepared (Lakoff 2018).

Precisely that political realization ushered in Tamiflu's second life as a prominent medical countermeasure against pandemic flu. Moving forward, government considerations around the drug would be governed less by strict cost-benefit considerations and more by security logics and political imperatives that now moved into the foreground. Shifting out of the context of seasonal flu and into that of pandemic flu fundamentally transformed the financial arithmetic around Tamiflu. Given that a pandemic posed a potentially much more serious and disruptive economic threat than seasonal flu, even modest clinical benefits would be seen as desirable, especially when aggregated at population level. Rather than assessing the drug economically on strict cost-benefit grounds, the political logic now morphed into one of taking out "insurance" against the possibility of a potentially catastrophic threat. As one senior policy maker working on influenza in Europe explains, "The problem that comes with pandemics is that you are looking much more for an insurance policy approach than you are for value for money" (European Influenza Expert 2012). The threat of a pandemic was beginning to shift the government calculus toward using public funds to purchase significant quantities of Tamiflu, and the prospect of large-scale government stockpiles of Tamiflu began to open up politically. Government demand for Tamiflu began to rise sharply as a result. It rose so sharply, in fact, that there was now effectively an international run on the drug—with government demand rapidly outstripping what the commercial supply chains could generate.

Guidance issued by the World Health Organization in 2005 played a crucial role in this political process. WHO guidance was that some drugs available for the treatment and prevention of influenza could also be effective in treating the illnesses caused by avian influenza (WHO 2005: 48–51). While acknowledging several constraints, the guidance found that "antiviral drugs have important roles to play, both now and at the start of a pandemic" (WHO 2005: 49). Antivirals would be particularly crucial during the early phases of a pandemic, because vaccines will not yet be available at that stage: "Under pandemic conditions, their [antivirals'] importance is elevated during the first wave of infection when vaccines—unquestionably the most useful medical tool for reducing morbidity and mortality—are not yet available. In the absence of vaccines, antiviral drugs will be the only medical intervention for providing both protection against disease and therapeutic benefit in persons who are ill" (WHO 2005: 49). As the only medical intervention available in the early phases of a flu pandemic, antivirals would effectively come to constitute the first line of defense—at least for those countries that could secure access to them.

Yet how could governments ensure that they would have sufficient Tamiflu available to protect their populations? Governments would need access to sufficiently large quantities of the antiviral to cover significant proportions of their populations. They would also need to administer them very quickly to their citizens, because these pharmaceutical interventions had to be taken early on in the course of infection. Yet usage of the antiviral for seasonal flu was very low in most countries. This meant that existing supply chains were unlikely to be able to satisfy this surge of demand during such a pandemic (Nguyen-Van-Tam 2015). Nor could governments simply try to buy more stocks once a pandemic occurred, because many countries around the world would then all be chasing scarce global supplies of Tamiflu at the same time. There could thus be no guarantee that sufficient quantities of Tamiflu would actually be available in the global marketplace to fulfil a government order during a pandemic. If a government wanted to be prepared, special arrangements would have to be made. WHO accordingly advised governments that "stockpiling drugs in advance is presently the only way to ensure that sufficient supplies are available at the start of a pandemic" (WHO 2005: 51). Many governments decided to follow that advice and began to build such stockpiles to ensure that they would indeed have the right medical countermeasure available in the right quantities and at the right time.

How large should those new government stockpiles be? That question generated a lot uncertainty among influenza experts. Although WHO guidance did not provide a specific figure, its estimate that such a pandemic could affect around 25 percent of the population proved to be a widely adopted reference point for many pandemic preparedness planners (Jack 2006). In general terms, and reflecting on the European experience in particular, one senior European policy maker working on influenza described the process of deciding appropriate levels of stockpiling in the following terms: governments "would seek advice but eventually the decision is a central one, a political one"—not least because "we have to say, Look, there isn't an answer for that because it so much depends on the virus and the new virus that is emerging." (European Influenza Expert 2012). By and large, countries that decided to build Tamiflu stockpiles wanted to be able to cover a significant proportion of their population. So the first and foremost effect of shifting to a health security logic was to stimulate a rapid global rise in demand for Tamiflu as governments clamored to create pharmaceutical stockpiles for their populations.

Stockpiling Frenzy: H5N1 and the Pandemic of Preparedness Planning

Which governments were first out of the gate in what was quickly becoming a global race to stockpile Tamiflu? The first countries to stockpile tended to be high-income countries that were either in close geographic proximity to some of the human cases of H5N1 reported in Asia or that had already suffered earlier formative experiences with other infectious disease outbreaks. The Australian government, for example, began to build up a stockpile of antivirals as early as February 2004. In April 2004 it then placed a Tamiflu order to treat nearly 20 percent of the Australian population. According to Tony Abbott, then minister for health and aging, their order "virtually cornered the world anti-viral market for 12 months" (Abbott 2005).

Canada was another country to build an early stockpile. It announced a government purchase of Tamiflu in February 2005 to treat nearly one million people (Jack 2006). Canada's decision was likely linked to its earlier experiences with SARS in 2003, which had led to 438 suspected cases and 44 deaths (Jack 2006). Canada thus had relatively recent and firsthand experience with the impact of a new infectious disease outbreak, with WHO even issuing travel adversaries for people traveling to Canada at the time. Together with the United States and Australia, Canada formed part of the first wave of governments moving toward a policy of creating government stockpiles of Tamiflu.

Although the US government had begun stockpiling Tamiflu as early as 2003 within the context of its Strategic National Stockpile, it had initially only acquired relatively small quantities. As late as 2005 Roche would still have to remind the US Congress that US stockpiling efforts were lagging considerably behind those of other countries around the world. Roche warned Congress that "other nations are currently well ahead of the United States in Tamiflu stockpiling; and . . . the U.S. has to make commitments now to ensure a timely and adequate supply of Tamiflu" (US Congress 2005). The US government did begin to signal such a considerable change in its stockpiling ambitions later that year, as Secretary of Health and Human Services Michael Leavitt indicated his intention to build a much more sizable stockpile to Congress:

> I'd like to make an important point. Anti-virals are an important part of a comprehensive plan, but anti-virals are not the equivalent of preparation. There is no certainty of their effectiveness on any particular virus. There is no capacity to change the anti-viral if the virus adapts. There are distribution dilemmas. Nevertheless, it's a very important part of a comprehensive plan, and the plan does call for us to build a stockpile of 20 million courses. The vendors have represented to us that those could be delivered by the fourth quarter of 2006, and we could build our collective stockpiles to 81 million by the summer of 2007. Again, that's a date vendors are able to meet. (quoted in US Senate 2005)

That would allow for enough drugs to cover 25 percent of the US population (more than 75 million people), leaving another 6 million courses to contain any initial US outbreak (US Senate 2005).

The US stockpile was notable not only because of its large size (especially in absolute terms); it also stood out because the US government wanted the entire Tamiflu supply chain to be established within the territorial borders of the United States. The government was concerned that, in the event of a global pandemic, international distribution systems might encounter severe disruption. Given a global shortage of supply, moreover, other countries might also nationalize existing stock or production facilities. According to Secretary Leavitt, part of the rationale for the sizable US government order was thus to "enable manufacturers to make significant expansion in its U.S.-based manufacturing capacity—thereby positioning itself to meet future demands much more readily than currently is possible" and thus also helping the United States meet its longer-term pandemic preparedness and health security objectives (US Senate 2005: 11). Roche duly complied with the request, and the United States ended up building one of the world's largest stockpiles of Tamiflu.

It is more difficult to obtain reliable information about stockpiling in Europe. That is because Roche will not release information about government orders, insisting that it is up to those governments to disclose their orders if they so choose (Roche 2012: 9). However, it appears from several sources that 2005 marked the turning point for government stockpiling efforts in Europe as well. William Burns, head of Roche's pharmaceuticals division, pointed out in October 2005 that "following four ducks (that died) in Romania last weekend, Europe went mad. I don't think you'll find a single pack (of Tamiflu) in Paris. And this is not because we've had an influenza outbreak" (quoted in S. Turner 2005). The dead birds found at Europe's borders began to focus minds and would even begin to cause a run on Tamiflu in several countries. Roche's David Reddy observed at the time how "in one country we sold within a week the amount that we would normally sell in an entire year! We had to give priority to government orders as well as ensure treatment of people during the regular influenza season" (quoted in Samii and van Wassenhove 2008: 7).

Additional information about European stockpiling activities can be gleaned from a 2005 review of European pandemic plans conducted on the basis of information in the public domain at the time. It found that 20 countries in Europe had developed an antiviral-drug strategy (Mounier-Jack and Coker 2006: 1408). The study also found that 13 countries had publicly acknowledged stockpiling but that provision for individual countries varied greatly—ranging from 2% to 53% population coverage (Mounier-Jack and Coker 2006: 1410). A similar review of the situation undertaken only one year later (in 2006) pointed to a further increase in the stockpiling trend in Europe. Focusing on European national strategic plans for pandemic preparedness published before the end of September 2006, this study found that of the 29 plans it surveyed, "most plans stated an intention to stockpile antiviral drugs, with 14 noting that a stockpile had been secured" (Mounier-Jack et al. 2007). The study was supported by a grant from Hoffmann-La Roche, the manufacturer of Tamiflu.

Several public health experts interviewed for this book noted how such studies generated some unease in European policy-making circles. Indeed, the studies were perceived as exerting an unhelpful form of pressure on governments to explain how they had set their stockpiling levels—especially when some other governments appeared to have set higher targets. Several interview subjects also expressed the view that industry had been quite aggressive in pushing antivirals and that there was also peer pressure involved (e.g., Tegnell 2012). One senior European influenza policy maker working on influenza even pointed to the slightly awkward way in which these kinds of studies were carried out. After all, Roche would have known pretty accurately from its own order books which governments in Europe were stockpiling and at what levels, but because of the confidentiality clauses in the contracts, the company could not reveal this information. To get around that constraint, Roche essentially paid somebody to use the Internet to determine what levels could be reported based on public statements (European Influenza Expert 2012). "Personally," one policy maker recalls, "I was a bit unhappy about creating a culture of competitiveness in between the countries as to who's got the biggest useless stockpile because they couldn't deliver it" (European Influenza Expert 2012). Governments at the time would certainly have been looking over their shoulders to see what other countries were doing.

In retrospect, then, perhaps the most striking aspect about this competitive race to stockpile is that most European countries tried to go it alone rather than joining together. Given the many different European Union member countries that were simultaneously trying to obtain stockpiles, they could conceivably have taken a more coordinated EU-wide approach. In that way, the governments could also have presented a more united negotiating position vis-à-vis Roche. Speaking in 2007, the EU commissioner for public health at the time, Markos Kyprianou, indicated that he had made stockpiling one of his personal priorities. He certainly saw scope for a European stockpile that would not so much replace those of member states but could at least serve as an emergency stockpile for strategic use. The project never got off the ground, however, because of the absence of an appropriate EU competency in this area and a lack of support from some member states (Trakatellis 2007: 25). This stood in marked contrast to other regional groupings, most notably in Southeast Asia, where it was agreed to establish a regional stockpile (Trakatellis 2007: 25), with an antiviral stockpile of 500,000 courses to be held in Singapore (Ghosh and Soeriaatmadja 2006).

In either case, government stockpiling of Tamiflu would become a widespread international phenomenon over the coming years. By 2009 a total of 95 governments around the world had purchased or ordered pandemic Tamiflu stockpiles according to Roche. The company later also reported that it had supplied governments around the world with 350 million treatment courses (3.5 billion doses) of Tamiflu between 2004 and 2009 (Reddy 2010: ii35). Tamiflu was now effectively enjoying a second life as a medical countermeasure and first line of defense against the pandemic flu threat. In a complete reversal of its commercial fortunes, the pandemic threat meant that there was suddenly huge global demand for Tamiflu, and governments seeking to stockpile the antiviral for their populations now formed a significant chunk of that global demand.

Donald Rumsfeld and the Pentagon Stockpile

Many of those new Tamiflu stockpiles were aimed at the civilian population. Yet some governments also wanted to set up additional stockpiles for particular subgroups to ensure that core elements of the state would be properly protected and could continue to function during a pandemic. One particularly colorful chapter in the history of Tamiflu thus relates to the attempt by the US Department of Defense to create a Tamiflu stockpile specifically for the US military. The attempt generated a number of media headlines because of the close role that the secretary of defense at the time, Donald Rumsfeld, had previously played in Gilead Sciences—the company that invented the drug, owned its patent, and still received royalties on worldwide sales from Roche.

John Stanton, working at the time for the Washington, DC–based political news group Roll Call, researched the likely impact of the 2005 pandemic concerns on Donald Rumsfeld's financial fortunes at the time. Prior to being sworn in as secretary of defense, Rumsfeld had received a generous send-off from his colleagues at Gilead Sciences. John C. Martin, president and chief executive officer of Gilead, said at the time that "Don Rumsfeld's insight and contributions over the last twelve years have been invaluable as

Gilead has evolved from a promising biotech company into the worldwide biopharmaceutical corporation it is today" (Business Wire 2001). But what would happen with Rumsfeld's financial links to the company once he became secretary of defense? Upon taking up his new political office, Rumsfeld was not required to liquidate his extensive stock holdings in Gilead Sciences because the company was not a defense contractor (AFP 2005). Federal disclosure documents submitted by Rumsfeld at the time indicated the he had holdings in Gilead Sciences of approximately $5million to $25 million (Schwartz 2005a).

In characteristic style, Rumsfeld was deeply dissatisfied with the entire process of having to submit such financial disclosure documents. In a letter to the Office of Government Ethics, he complained at the time that the forms were "excessively complex and confusing" (AP 2002) and said of the forms that "they're so complex that no human being, college educated or not, can understand them" (quoted in *Washington Post* 2002). Rumsfeld was also unhappy about the fact that he had incurred more than $60,000 in accountant's fees just to fill out the forms (which he claimed he did not have time to complete himself) (AP 2002). The forms revealed assets worth between $53 million and $175 million at the time (*Washington Post* 2002) and indicated that Rumsfeld also had to sell between $20.5 million and $91.2 million in assets and investments as part of the process of becoming secretary of defense (AP 2002).

Following Rumsfeld's complaint, the director of the Office of Government Ethics at the time, Amy Comstock, dutifully responded. She acknowledged that the form was confusing and indicated plans to create simpler forms for the future. However, she also reminded Rumsfeld that public disclosure performs a "vital role" in preventing conflicts of interest from arising (*Washington Post* 2002). To this day, Rumsfeld continues to complain about the complexity of the tax code and that, despite employing accountants, he in not sure whether he is paying the correct amount of taxes (*Forbes* 2014). In either case, Comstock's warning about potential conflicts of interest would prove prescient when the issue later surfaced in relation to the decision by the Pentagon to create a Tamiflu stockpile.

It is likely that the value of Rumsfeld's Gilead shares appreciated significantly because of the rise of international pandemic concerns about H5N1. Rumsfeld reportedly sold some of those shares in 2004, generating $5 million in capital gains according to his financial disclosure report (Lean and Owen 2006). The following year, in 2005, amid rising pandemic fears, the value of Gilead stock prices increased further, from $35 to $47 per share, with *Fortune* magazine reporting that Rumsfeld would have made at least $1 million dollars on his Gilead stock (Schwartz 2005b). John Stanton has calculated that the rise in Gilead stock from the end of 2004 to the end of 2005 would have meant that the value of Rumsfeld's personal holding would have increased by between $2.8 million and $13.77 million—figures that do not include Gilead shares that Rumsfeld may have previously trans-ferred into a foundation and a trust that he controls or any investments in Gilead made by investment companies that Rumsfeld cofounded and main-tains a financial interest in (Stanton 2005).

Given his continuing financial interests in Gilead Sciences, Rumsfeld's role in the decision-making process around building a Tamiflu stockpile for the Department of Defense also attracted media scrutiny. The Pentagon placed an order for $58 million worth of Tamiflu to protect US troops around the world in July 2005 (Schwartz 2005a; AFP 2005)—a decision that could present a conflict of interest given Rumsfeld's role as secretary of defense. The issue was subsequently raised in a press conference on 1 November 2005. During the press conference Rumsfeld reportedly responded that—following consultation with the Senate Ethics Committee, Department of Justice at-torneys, and an attorney specializing in private securities—he had decided to maintain control of his stock but to not participate in any decision that might affect Gilead (Stanton 2005).

Rumsfeld said at the time: "I did consider every option and went to all of these people for advice, and finally made a decision that it would be a problem were I to sell it in the current situation" (quoted in AFP 2005). That was also the message put out by Gilead Sciences, a representative of which pointed out at the time: "Secretary Rumsfeld has no relationship with Gil-ead Sciences, Inc beyond his investments in the company. When he became Secretary of Defense in January 2001, divestiture of his investment in Gil-ead was not required by the Senate Armed Services Committee, the Office of Government Ethics, or the Department of Defense Standards of Conduct Office. Upon taking office, he recused himself from participating in any par-ticular matter when the matter would directly and predictably affect his financial interest in Gilead Science" (quoted in Lean and Owen 2006). Ac-cording to a spokesperson, this arrangement was also communicated to Department of Defense employees by Defense General Counsel William

Haynes in a letter on 27 October 2005. The letter reminded staff that Rumsfeld could not participate personally or substantially in any matter (including the prevention and treatment of flu) that could directly and predictably affect his financial interest in Gilead (AFP 2005).

Stanton also points out, however, that this letter was issued only *after* the Department of Defense had already decided to stockpile the medication (Stanton 2005). What is more, the memo stated that Rumsfeld could continue to deal with wider issues surrounding avian flu—including the issue of possible quarantines and the use of US troops: "The secretary may participate personally and substantially as these matters will not directly and predictably affect Gilead" (quoted in AFP 2005). As Stanton argues, "The Oct. 27 recusal also paints a much narrower picture of the types of decisions Rumsfeld will stay away from than the generic 'recusal' he has cited in public statements. According to the letter, Rumsfeld's recusal only applies to 'matters concerning avian flu dealing with the development and acquisition by the government of vaccines and/or treatments,' since those decisions 'may directly and predictably affect Gilead'" (Stanton 2005). Even after letter was sent, in other words, Rumsfeld would still be able to be involved in decisions, which—even if they were not so explicitly conflictual—could still conceivably have an indirectly beneficial impact on the company's fortunes (Stanton 2005). In either case, the creation of such specialist stockpiles for the armed forces shows that governments were not just interested in stockpiling Tamiflu to protect the civilian population; they were also becoming concerned about how the core institutions of the state would continue to function in the case of a pandemic.

Corporate Stockpiling: Developing the Business Continuity Market

Nor was such pharmaceutical stockpiling confined to governments. Many large corporations, too, wanted to create Tamiflu stockpiles as part of their business continuity plans to ensure economic damage is kept to a minimum during a pandemic. In the United States, government plans for pandemic flu actively assumed that the private sector would play a central role in pandemic preparedness planning. According to the then deputy secretary of health and human services Tevi Troy, "Stockpiling of antivirals is an essential act of preparedness for a potential flu pandemic, but it is one that is a shared responsibility that extends across all levels of government and all segments of society" (quoted in Business Wire 2008). He urged industry in particular to make a contribution to national efforts: "Planning efforts by business and private industry . . . comprise a fundamental part of our nation's efforts to ensure community resilience in a public health emergency. We encourage government, private industry and individuals to take action to prepare" (quoted in Business Wire 2008).

As the manufacturer of Tamiflu, Roche led the way by creating its own business continuity plan for pandemic flu. The plan aimed to ensure that during a pandemic Roche's business activities would not increase infection risk for employees or third parties, that employees had been issued Tamiflu prior to a pandemic materializing, and that company sites did not pose a danger for employees. Roche also wanted to be sure that it could continue manufacturing and distribution of lifesaving medicines in a pandemic and that the company could rapidly return to business. As part of the plan, all Roche employees and their close family contacts in the same household would receive Tamiflu, local laws and regulations permitting.

Beyond addressing its own business continuity needs, the Roche program also had a broader signaling function for other large corporations. Roche representatives thus made presentations about their own preparedness activities to wider business audiences, in which they would then ask the audience to also consider how well their businesses, in turn, would also cope in a pandemic—reminding them of their role in ensuring the welfare of their employees (R. Turner 2006). Roche proactively contacted other Fortune 500 companies about business continuity planning as part of this new marketing effort. As CEO and president of Hoffmann-La Roche, Inc., George Abercrombie recalled at the time: "It is the first time I have ever engaged a business in a dialogue over a prescription medicine" (Fox 2007). Yet there was clearly a market for such a program. Roche claims it received enquiries from more than 800 US-based companies and orders from more than 300 companies by June 2008 (Business Wire 2008). The high-level concern that many other businesses also had about the pandemic flu threat could also be seen very clearly in Davos in 2006, where the threat of a pandemic was now identified as a major global risk (WEF 2006).

In order to deal with such business continuity issues in the corporate sector, Roche also introduced a flexible "reserve" program in June 2008. In return for an annual charge, corporations could—as part of this new program—maintain access to their own corporate stockpile of Tamiflu for use during a pandemic: "The Roche Antiviral Protection Program (RAPP) holds one course of Tamiflu in its inventory for an annual reserve fee (which is low relative to the purchase price of the drug). The holder of a RAPP contract has the right to buy a single course at the regular price with delivery within 24–48 h. Thus, rather than immediately purchasing at the regular price to stockpile on its own, an organization can purchase the right to buy and thereby ensure supply" (Harrington and Hsu 2010: 438). While some companies preferred to predistribute Tamiflu directly to their employees, this scheme was designed to expand the market to those who were interested in having a Tamiflu capability but wanted different and more flexible planning options.

Yet this wider move to expand into corporate stockpiling would also touch upon a range of complex legal and regulatory sensitivities. In some cases, creating such corporate stockpiles required working with governments to alter legislation. One of the potential issues to emerge here was that this effectively constituted a way of marketing Tamiflu directly to businesses without going through doctors and other medical professionals. This even led to an employee allegation in May 2010 that Roche was putting sales staff under illegal pressure to sell Tamiflu to business continuity managers who were not doctors, a charge denied by Roche. The employee further alleged that he was asked to establish a special unit in 2006 for selling Tamiflu to companies and in the process discovered that there were no proper controls to ensure that sales staff only spoke to health-care professionals (Jack 2010). In either case, those corporate efforts show very clearly that stockpiling efforts were not confined to governments but spanned across many large companies as well.

Personal Stockpiling and Internet Sales

Many anxious individuals even tried to build up their own personal stockpiles of Tamiflu at home, especially as the pandemic flu threat received heightened media attention. In the age of the Internet, citizens who were concerned about the pandemic flu threat could easily seek out information about this antiviral on their own accord. Rather than relying on the government to protect them, they could simply try to secure their own supplies of the antiviral medicine (Ortiz et al. 2008). The extent to which citizens were trying to obtain information about Tamiflu, and perhaps even trying to acquire the drug over the Internet, can be gleaned by looking at Google Trends data.

Google Trends analyzes a sample of searches performed on the popular commercial search engine and then computes how many searches are being performed for a particular term relative to the number of searches done over time. These results are displayed in the search volume index. Although this only provides a rough approximation because of the use of data sampling methods and multiple approximations, it clearly shows the enormously increased Internet activity surrounding Tamiflu during recent pandemic scares. The search volume index for "Tamiflu" reveals two distinct and large spikes: one during the international fears of an imminent H5N1 pandemic in 2005 and a later one during the H1N1 pandemic that began to spread in April 2009. Those peaks coincide with periods of intense media reporting (Google Trends 2013). Although not conclusive, such data strongly suggest that many citizens wanted more information about and actively sought access to Tamiflu during those two pandemic scares.

There is also other evidence revealing the considerable lengths to which some citizens would go in trying to secure their own supplies of Tamiflu. During the H5N1 bird flu pandemic scare, for example, the popular Internet auction site eBay had to withdraw sales of Tamiflu through its website after prices reached more than £100 for a treatment course—more than three times its usual prescription price (Reuters 2005). Roche Canada had to cease distribution of Tamiflu to pharmacies in that country following concerns about citizens stockpiling the drug for personal use because of fears about H5N1, even though the government was also creating a national stockpile (Spurgeon 2005). During the subsequent H1N1 swine flu pandemic in April 2009, and despite UK government reassurances that the national stockpile was sufficiently large, online pharmacists again reported very dramatic increases in demand for Tamiflu as people tried to create personal stockpiles; in some cases demand was reportedly up by around 1,000 percent (Swaine and Smith 2009). Faced with the imminent threat of a pandemic, many citizens were actively seeking information about and demanding access to available pharmaceutical defenses.

The desperation of some people to secure their own personal Tamiflu supplies is further revealed by the way in which illegally operating groups even sought to profit from the sale of counterfeit Tamiflu. For example, four dozen shipments (51 packages) of counterfeit Tamiflu were seized by US federal customs officials at a post office in South San Francisco in November 2005 (Walsh 2005). The pills, marked "generic Tamiflu," had been ordered over the Internet and were shipped from China. Nor was this a one-off occurrence. The FDA would later also discover other sales of fraudulent Tamiflu. In June 2010 it had to issue a warning to consumers over a potentially harmful product called "Generic Tamiflu" that was being sold over the Internet by an online retailer claiming to be an online drug store. The product did not in fact contain oseltamivir but cloxacillin, an antibiotic substance (FDA 2010a). In the end, the emergence of pandemic fears about H5N1 had provoked a global stockpiling frenzy over Tamiflu spanning governments, corporations, and individuals alike, all now desperately clamoring to acquire the antiviral as the first line of defense.

Tamiflu's pivotal transition during this period of its life shows just how rapidly the introduction of security logics can alter the way a pharmaceutical product is perceived. Prior to the concerns about pandemic flu, the drug was largely viewed as a borderline drug—with a fairly limited role to play in the management of seasonal flu. With political fears now escalating about the pandemic flu threat, however, the economic calculations around the drug changed dramatically, and public demand for the product was radically transformed in many parts of the world. Tamiflu's early years of struggling for commercial viability now seemed like a distant memory, and the drug was fast becoming a lucrative source of income for Roche (and to a smaller extent also for Gilead Sciences). Tamiflu had become, in the words of Andrew Jack, the first "virtual" blockbuster medicine, "earning ten digit revenues to treat a virus that did not yet exist" (Jack 2009). Within a short period of time, the shift to a context of health security and pandemic preparedness had completely reversed the commercial outlook for Tamiflu.

This pivotal reversal in Tamiflu's fortunes also reveals two additional challenges that governments confront more generally when trying to build effective medical countermeasure capabilities. First, they have to accurately gauge and plan their demand for such medical countermeasures. Any new medical countermeasure would remain fairly useless if it is not available in sufficient quantities during a future emergency. To develop an effective medical countermeasure capability, governments thus need to have access to the right medical countermeasures in the right quantities at the right time. When it comes to many common diseases that are managed within the context of more routine health-care provision, this demand for pharmaceutical products remains fairly consistent, or the fluctuations in demand can at least be forecast with reasonable confidence. Demand for medical countermeasures, by contrast, can oscillate wildly and rapidly over time—in line with events unfolding on the ground, media coverage, political developments, and so forth. All of this means that demand for medical countermeasures is much more difficult to gauge properly, and governments will face difficult choices. In the face of their electorates, they must appear prepared during an emergency. At the same time, they must not be seen as wasting precious public resources on expensive medical countermeasures that might never be used and that will also eventually expire. Governments must therefore perform a difficult balancing act.

What is more, too much uncertainty about government demand for medical countermeasures might also further deter commercial developers of such products. From Roche's perspective, it appeared one day that nobody was interested in acquiring Tamiflu as a medical countermeasure, and the company was trying largely in vain to persuade governments to stockpile Tamiflu. The next day there was a new outbreak, and demand for the product suddenly mushroomed out of control as governments clamored to stockpile the drug. At that point, demand increased so rapidly around the world that Roche was unsure whether it would be able to adequately meet the spike in demand. From the commercial perspective, such high volatility around the demand for medical countermeasures only complicates matters further. Indeed, prospective commercial developers of medical countermeasures will likely struggle to forecast demand for medical countermeasures with the degree of certainty that would be required for their business models. As one industry analyst explains, "You have an uncertain regulatory path to approval, the government determining procurement volumes, and the government reserving the right to change its mind. That makes it all kind of scary" (quoted in Wizemann et al. 2010: 127–128). On both sides of the public-private equation, the unpredictability of demand for medical countermeasures thus generates a fifth challenge, *demand forecasting*. The most prominent way that many governments have tried to manage this challenge so far is by building new pharmaceutical stockpiles.

The fact that so many countries around the world did end up building sizable Tamiflu stockpiles also points to a possible strategy for improving the wider prospects for commercial medical countermeasure development in the future. If a new medical countermeasure could be simultaneously sold to many different governments around the world, then it might become possible for companies to achieve a higher volume of sales and thus improve their chances for achieving a sound commercial return on their investment. Roche's overall revenues achieved from Tamiflu stockpiling are difficult to calculate with accuracy, because most of the government contracts are confidential. But there can be little doubt that sales ran into billions. According to calculations by the Bureau of Investigative Journalism, for instance, worldwide orders for Tamiflu by 2010 exceeded $10 billion since 2004 (BIJ 2010b). Four years later, oseltamivir had reportedly generated cumulative sales exceeding $18 billion since the drug was commercially launched in 1999, around half of which was driven by government and commercial stockpiles (Abbasi 2014; Jack 2014). Even such ballpark figures should be substantial enough to form the basis of a viable business case for developing new medical countermeasures—provided enough countries decide to stockpile the product in sufficient volumes. Pooling of international resources could thus be one possible way forward in terms of building greater commercial demand for medical countermeasures in the future.

Yet we have also seen during this stage of Tamiflu's life that even stockpiling such medical countermeasure is not sufficient in and of itself. In fact, those expensive stockpiles will remain fairly useless if there is no way of rapidly, reliably, and securely distributing them to the public at large during a future emergency. Simply storing medical countermeasures in warehouses does not equate to a functioning and effective medical countermeasure capability. Governments also have to be able to get the medical countermeasures directly to people who need them, and they have to be able to do so very quickly in a context where normal distribution channels may cease to function properly. To do that, governments also need to put *logistical distribution* systems in place for medical countermeasures.

To be effective, such logistical distribution systems must meet a number of critical requirements. They have to be able to reach all the way down to the level of the individual citizen, with the "last mile" often being the hardest part of the chain to service. Governments must be able to activate distribution systems on fairly short notice, usually requiring that plans and processes be in place well in advance of an emergency. The logistical systems also have to meet the specific requirements of pharmaceutical products, such as maintaining a particular temperature range, humidity levels, and so forth. Finally, they have to work independently of normal pharmaceutical distribution chains, as those may become severely disrupted during an emergency.

Countries have already tried to develop a variety of models and logistical systems, some relying on the postal system, some signing advance contracts with logistics companies, some resorting to the armed forces, and some even planning to use school buses to distribute medical countermeasures in the event of an emergency. Irrespective of which option they take, *logistical mass distribution* emerges as a sixth key challenge surrounding medical countermeasures. Together with the issues of obtaining regulatory approval and accurately forecasting demand, it also completes the second set of challenges that comes into play *after* a new medical countermeasure has been developed. These additional acquisition challenges show very clearly how developing an effective medical countermeasures capability is not just a technical issue of designing new pharmaceutical products. It also entails carrying out a lot of additional planning work for governments to ensure that such products can be used effectively, such as making sure that sufficient volumes are available at the right time and that they can be quickly distributed in an emergency. Once a crisis or emergency arises and a medical countermeasure actually has to be distributed to the population, there is still a whole third set of *deployment* challenges that quickly comes into play.

III THE DEPLOYMENT CHALLENGES

6

In the Eye of the Storm

Global Access, Generics, and

Intellectual Property

The sudden surge in global demand for Tamiflu because of H5N1 soon gave rise to another problem. With so many governments, corporations, and individuals scrambling to stockpile Tamiflu, would Roche be able to quickly scale up pharmaceutical production and satisfy all of that rising demand? "What keeps me awake at night," the president and CEO of Roche in the United States confessed at the time, is that "we will be in the bullseye. People will want Tamiflu and we will not be able to make it fast enough" (Fox 2007). How the fortunes of Tamiflu had changed. Whereas Roche had previously been trying so hard to stimulate commercial demand for Tamiflu, it now faced the exact opposite problem of how to satisfy the seemingly overwhelming explosion in global demand. Access to Tamiflu was fast becoming a pressing international political concern.

The stakes in the access issue were high all around. If the company could not scale up production and a pandemic materialized, many people around the world could be left without access to an antiviral that might turn out to be lifesaving. Governments that had not managed to secure supplies in time would then appear unprepared in the eyes of their citizens and would have to explain to their electorates why they had not ensured proper access to the antiviral. From Roche's perspective it would mean that the company would be unable to fully realize the drug's newfound commercial potential—at the very moment that it was finally in high demand. More worrying still for Roche, if it could not meet the surge in demand, the resulting political pressure might well provoke concerted efforts to wrestle control over Tamiflu production away from the company.

That, in fact, is exactly what happened next. As Roche struggled to scale up Tamiflu production in line with rapidly rising global demand, the company soon came under intense pressure from three directions at once. Gilead Sciences, which had originally licensed the antiviral compound to Roche, now launched a legal challenge in an attempt to regain control of the drug's production. At the same time, governments in high-income countries threatened to invoke extraordinary legal procedures to sidestep the Tamiflu patent and to allow other pharmaceutical producers to produce the antiviral as well. Several governments in low-income countries similarly indicated that they wanted to do the same—by working more closely with a range of generic producers. On top of all those coalescing pressures, Roche now also faced a sensitive international diplomatic problem with how to ensure that even some of the poorest countries in the world would also have some access to Tamiflu in the event of a deadly pandemic.

The ensuing political battles over access to Tamiflu reveal the existence of a third group of challenges that can arise once an emergency transpires (or becomes immanent) and governments have to consider rolling out medical countermeasures to their populations in earnest. The first of these *deployment* challenges is how to rapidly scale up production of a medical countermeasure during a crisis, when there can be a massive spike in demand. The technical requirements of pharmaceutical production can be very complex in terms of the chemistry involved, the supply chains required, and the regulatory requirements that need to be satisfied. It may, therefore, not be possible to simply ramp up production on short notice during a crisis. At the same time, there are also commercial difficulties involved with maintaining a large surge production capacity in the absence of regular demand to underpin it. It would not make much commercial sense to have such spare production capacity sitting idly by without utilizing it on the off chance that a pandemic might materialize. How to best organize and make available such surge production capacity is thus another key challenge to arise around medical countermeasures more generally.

A second and closely related challenge that emerges at this stage is what governments should do about intellectual property and patents during such emergency situations. Here too the security context begins to complicate matters, because governments actually possess unique powers during a security crisis to sidestep or even override patents that have been previously granted to companies for their pharmaceutical products. Governments confronting such a crisis will have to make difficult political decisions about whether to uphold and respect, or alternatively to suspend, the intellectual property rights that companies have been granted for their pharmaceutical products. It is thus a peculiar feature of a medical countermeasure more generally that the very moment at which it is most likely to realize a commercial return—that is, during an emergency—is also the moment that governments possess the greatest political and legal leverage to override their patents on a drug. That too makes the whole area of medical countermeasures commercially much riskier. The question of how to deal with intellectual property and patents in order to maximize global access thus emerges as another major challenge in handling an emergency.

Scaling Up Production: The Race to Keep Up with Global Demand

With so many government orders for Tamiflu now flooding in, the first thing Roche had to figure out was how it could quickly scale up its production line for the antiviral so that everyone who wanted access to it could have it. The company would quickly have to take some pretty tricky and complex decisions. How far should Roche increase its production capacity for Tamiflu? When would it have to make those decisions, bearing in mind it would have to allow sufficient time for additional production lines to come on stream first? How much of the company's resources was it worth investing in this scaling-up process?

Even before the majority of new government orders flooded in, Roche decided to increase its production capacity for Tamiflu to 55 million courses over a two-year period. According to George Abercrombie, head of Roche in North America, "As early as 2003, before we had any firm governmental commitments, Roche recognized that responding to pandemic influenza would require enormous additional capacity. Since 2003, we have doubled our production capacity each year" (quoted in US Senate 2006). Roche also explored other ways of managing this projected demand. For instance, it gave governments the option of simply stockpiling the active pharmaceutical ingredient (as a powder) rather than having to purchase Tamiflu in finished capsule form (Samii and van Wassenhove 2008: 1–2). For either option, however, Roche would still have to navigate a number of commercial and technical risks in scaling up Tamiflu's production.

Given the time and costs involved in ramping up production, there was a difficult guessing game to be played here in terms of exactly how much supply would be required over the coming years. Pharmaceutical production facilities like those for Tamiflu have to be built to high specification and often have to comply with the complex regulatory requirements of multiple countries simultaneously (Cole 2013: 25). Yet no one could know for sure when, or even if, a new flu pandemic would actually materialize, where it would spread, or how severe it might be. Even if such a pandemic did occur, moreover, no one could be certain whether the pandemic influenza virus strain would be susceptible to Tamiflu or whether antiviral resistance would rapidly arise. Forecasting demand was thus shrouded in immense uncertainty.

Nor was that demand simply driven by events on the ground. Media coverage also played a pivotal role, and—like government demand—it too was highly volatile. Roche employees felt at the time that media coverage seemed to oscillate rather unhelpfully between fear and apathy. There were thus significant difficulties for Roche in managing media coverage of Tamiflu and in the need to balance "sensationalism" with "maintaining the focus and interest when the media is quiet" (R. Turner 2006). Overall, it remained very challenging to properly align pharmaceutical production cycles with the shifting ebb and flow in media attention and events unfolding on the ground. All of this made demand forecasting even more difficult moving forward.

Roche also had to juggle several technical constraints associated with scaling up the Tamiflu production process. Roche representatives pointed out that the Tamiflu production process consists of at least 10 steps. Some of those steps are technically very challenging and require specialized equipment. Parts of the production process were also potentially dangerous because of the use of azide chemistry (chemistry similar to that used to rapidly inflate the airbags found in cars). The latter had to be carried out under controlled conditions. As they involve a potentially explosive reaction (van Koeveringe 2006: 10–11). Speaking before Congress, Dr. Dominick Iacuzio, medical director for Tamiflu at Hoffmann-La Roche, summed up the challenge as follows:

It is imperative that Tamiflu be stockpiled in advance of a pandemic since inherent complexities in production severely limit our capability, our ability, to rapidly meet large-scale, unanticipated demand. The manufacturing process for Tamiflu takes 8 to 12 months from raw materials to finished product. The process involves many inputs and steps, including a unique starting material and a potentially explosive production step that can be carried out only in specialized and very costly facilities. Historically, Roche has not produced the levels of Tamiflu required for global stockpiling. However, since 2003 we have increased total Tamiflu production capacity nearly eight-fold. (quoted in US Congress 2005)

To better communicate these many challenges to the wider world, Roche even offered media representatives tours of their production facilities. Roche's David Reddy recalls: "By the time the media left our production facilities, they understood, with a certain degree of clarity, the complexity involved in the manufacture of Tamiflu. They better appreciated why the average production cycle time is close to one year and that more of the product cannot be made by a simple turn of the switch" (quoted in Samii and van Wassenhove 2008: 4).

Limited availability of key raw materials for making Tamiflu was another constraint Roche had to manage during this period. The production of Tamiflu relied on star anise—a key but also scarce ingredient. David Lapre, head of Roche Global Supply Chain Management at Basel, Switzerland, explained the problem in the following terms: "As one can imagine, with bird flu and Tamiflu so prominent in the news, the price of star anise—the main raw material for Tamiflu—went up exponentially to the point where our suppliers started delaying deliveries and pushing us to revise our supply contracts" (quoted in Samii and van Wassenhove 2008: 2). Although this problem was eventually resolved through the development of a synthetic version, it showed how a surge in global demand can quickly also lead to shortages in key raw materials and drive up prices, creating new bottlenecks in the pharmaceutical production process (Cole 2013).

Overall, then, Roche had to simultaneously juggle a number of different factors in trying to rapidly scale up Tamiflu production: varying and uncertain levels of government demand, difficulties in managing media coverage of the pandemic flu threat, a technically complex and highly regulated production process, and access to scarce key raw materials. It was certainly not an easy juggling act, and by the end of 2005 there was already a backlog of one year to fill government orders (Samii and van Wassenhove 2008: 3).

Just as Roche was weighing all of these considerations toward the end of 2005, moreover, another significant event occurred—an event that would prove decisive in convincing Roche that real change was needed in the international scale of Tamiflu production.

In August 2005, in the immediate aftermath of Hurricane Katrina, senior managers at Roche's pharmaceutical division were unexpectedly called in to a videoconference. The reason for the urgent meeting was that the US government had just asked the CEO of Roche in the United States about the company's ability to supply 200 million treatment courses in the United States, which would amount to two billion capsules (Samii and van Wassenhove 2008: 1). It was a highly credible government enquiry for a potentially enormous order of Tamiflu. Yet in a context where the production capability was 55 million treatment courses per year at the time, an enquiry of such magnitude would require Roche to undertake a major rethink of its production targets. As Lapre recalls, "After discussions with the US government in 2005, we realized that our planning had been on the wrong scale and had not taken into account concerns regarding restrictions on material flow across borders. Just one country demanded five times our annual capacity and an end-to-end supply chain within its territory" (quoted in Samii and van Wassenhove 2008: 2). Following further meetings with US officials, Roche revised its annual production target upward to 400 million treatment courses by the end of 2006. That represented a significant 15-fold increase over 2004 production capacity (Samii and van Wassenhove 2008: 2).

Moving to such a scale of production meant that Roche would have to bring additional production partners on board. That would generate further questions still—especially about who those partners would be, who should carry the costs of scaling up production, and how that additional production capacity (once created) would be sustained and utilized after initial orders were filled. After considering a long list of potential companies, Roche was able to identify a group of 18 partner companies (spread across 10 countries) that could become part of the expanded network of global production for Tamiflu (Samii and van Wassenhove 2008: 3). Due to those efforts, the international production network for Tamiflu had grown to encompass more than 12 production facilities in the supply chain by 2006, with materials being sourced from over 50 outside suppliers (van Koeveringe 2006: 12). The costs for this expansion in production capacity, from capital investments and regulatory filings to technical transfer activities and qualification/registration work, were covered by Roche (Samii and van Wassenhove 2008: 3).

All of these experiences with the scaling up of Tamiflu production reveal a much wider challenge surrounding medical countermeasures in general. Because demand for them will oscillate immensely in response to events on the ground (or indeed media reporting), the question of how to rapidly increase their production during a crisis becomes another major challenge. There are a number of complicated factors that have to be taken into account, and often it may not be possible to simply scale up production in a way that would rapidly satisfy an explosion of international demand. In the case of Tamiflu, global demand continued to outpace supply despite all of Roche's efforts. As a result, Roche would soon find itself in a position of having to fight rear-guard actions on three different fronts, as other actors now desperately moved in and tried to wrestle control over its production away from the company. The initially technical question of how to scale up production was fast turning into a political issue about whether the patents on Tamiflu should be sidestepped and whether other actors should be allowed to produce the antiviral as well.

The Gilead-Roche Dispute: Legal Pressures to Revoke the Tamiflu License

One source of new pressure came from Gilead Sciences, the company that initially discovered the new molecule on which Tamiflu is based and then licensed it to Roche. As international demand for the drug soared and Roche struggled to keep up with demand, Gilead Sciences mounted a legal challenge aimed at terminating the existing licensing agreement with Roche. There were multiple grounds for their legal challenge. The company alleged that Roche had not marketed Tamiflu adequately, that there had been problems with the manufacturing processes leading to shortages in product supply, and that there had been incorrect calculation (and payment) of royalties owed to Gilead (Gilead Sciences 2016). Gilead also alleged that Roche had not adequately demonstrated its commitment to the product and had not allocated the necessary resources for its commercialization— including a failure to launch the product in a number of markets where the product had been approved (Gilead Sciences 2016). Overall, the company essentially believed that Roche was not making its "best efforts" to market the drug (Pollack and Wright 2005).

Penny Ward, who had worked on Tamiflu for Roche, recalls that the company had initially seen Tamiflu as one of the key drugs that could take Roche from a company predominantly selling to hospitals to one that could also sell directly to the general market. Once it transpired that Tamiflu was not going to become such a blockbuster drug for seasonal flu, the product moved to the back burner. That was no doubt a commercial disappointment for Gilead, which had seen it as a billion-dollar product (Ward 2015).

So how could these conflicting commercial expectations of the two companies be reconciled? The original licensing contract between Gilead Sciences and Roche included a mechanism for canceling the agreement in the event of a "material breach" of its terms. Amid growing concerns about the pandemic flu threat and soaring global demand for the drug, Gilead Sciences thus delivered a notice of termination to Roche for material breach of the 1996 agreement on 23 June 2005. If the claim was successful, the rights for Tamiflu could have ultimately reverted back to Gilead—and just at the time when international demand for Tamiflu was rampant. The timing for Roche could not have been worse.

Not surprisingly, perhaps, Roche denied the charge. It countered that there had simply been little interest in the drug from consumers or governments until the recent fears of a flu pandemic (Pollack and Wright 2005). Franz Humer, chief executive of Roche at the time, argued that "it became a drug which was difficult to commercialize. . . . We sat there with a drug in which we had invested a significant amount of development and where we had sales that were less than exciting" (quoted in Pollack and Wright 2005). With the growing pandemic threat, however, all eyes were now firmly fixed on Tamiflu once more, and it was imperative to get the dispute resolved rapidly. Too much was at stake for this issue to linger unresolved.

Fortunately, the initial agreement between Gilead Sciences and Roche also envisioned the option of using an arbitration process in order to deal with any possible disputes that might arise further down the line. The companies agreed to proceed with arbitration and on 16 November 2005 announced that they had reached an amicable settlement. According to John F. Milligan, Gilead's chief financial officer, "Both Roche and Gilead recognized the urgent need to resolve our dispute and remove any distraction that might in any way impede Roche's ability to address an important global health need" (quoted in Pollack and Wright 2005).

The details of the settlement included an amendment to the original agreement, according to which Roche would reimburse Gilead $62.5 million in retroactive cost of goods adjustments. Gilead would also retain the $18.2 million that Roche had paid under protest concerning royalties owed from 2001 to 2003 (Yeh 2007: 5). Moving forward, the overall royalty levels based on net sales of Tamiflu would remain unchanged: (1) 14 percent of the first $200 million in worldwide net sales in a given calendar year; (2) 18 percent of the next $200 million in worldwide net sales during the same calendar year; and (3) 22 percent of worldwide net sales in excess of $400 million during the same calendar year (SEC 2005). Both companies would thus continue to benefit commercially from international Tamiflu sales.

In addition to these financial arrangements, the two companies also agreed to create a new joint committee to oversee the coordination of global manufacturing as well as a joint committee to oversee the commercialization of Tamiflu for seasonal sales in the most important markets, such as the United States (Rollerhagen and Braxton 2016: 8). The dispute was settled by the end of 2005; Roche's David Lapre would later sum up the agreement in the following terms: "After sharing the details of our expansion plan, we ended with a compromise. They became actively involved in the effort. We met with them on a regular basis and gave them the opportunity to provide input on our decisions" (Samii and van Wassenhove 2008: 3). Roche had managed to resolve the dispute with Gilead Sciences, but moving forward the company would also have to share some control over Tamiflu production plans with Gilead Sciences. And Gilead Sciences was not the only one putting Roche under more pressure.

Political Pressures in the United States

Politicians too were beginning to pile more pressure on Roche. Governments would have overall responsibility for managing the societal effects of a pandemic, and their citizens would understandably be looking to them for protection in that eventuality. With pandemic fears reaching fever pitch, many governments now wanted to bulk-purchase large quantities of Tamiflu. They also wanted to secure those stocks as soon as possible, at the best possible price. When they discovered that Roche had only limited supplies available, governments began to think more creatively about how it might be possible to increase the international supply of Tamiflu in other ways. In particular, they now wanted Roche to allow other pharmaceutical companies to produce Tamiflu.

However, as the commercial producer of Tamiflu, Roche was not very keen on this course of action at all. In fact, Roche explicitly—and repeatedly—refused to allow this. "Roche," spokesman Terry Hurley stated as late as October 2005, "fully intends to remain the sole manufacturer of Tamiflu" (quoted in Russell 2005). The company's public justification for not licensing a generic version of Tamiflu was because of the complex, lengthy, and potentially dangerous nature of the manufacturing process. The limited global Tamiflu supply thus ended up pitting the interests of governments and populations directly against those of the commercial manufacturer. With pandemic anxieties continuing to escalate around the world, Roche would soon find itself fighting a rearguard battle to defend its line of argument.

Governments actually have quite significant leverage to pressure a company like Roche into letting other producers manufacture an antiviral. Especially when it comes to security crises and national emergencies (like a pandemic), many governments possess extraordinary powers. In such circumstances, they can authorize a third party to supply an equivalent drug, even without first requiring the explicit consent of the patent holder (Hamied 2003). Governments could simply decide to sidestep Roche if they felt they had to. Threatening to invoke such special procedures of "compulsory" licensing could thus serve as a powerful "stick" for governments to threaten Roche with in their quest to increase the international supply chain (or even just to reduce the price) for Tamiflu. If Roche did not play ball, governments had other options.

Some of these power battles between Roche and governments over Tamiflu production played out quite publicly. In the United States, for example, prominent members of Congress began to openly propose that public health provisions permitting the federal government to wrestle control of the drug away from Roche should be invoked. Congressman Dennis Kucinich complained vociferously about Roche: "They're getting rich as the world gets sick. . . . The company is able to control the supply and the price [of Tamiflu], and it's very dangerous for the health of this country to let them make all the decisions" (quoted in Schmit 2005). In his view, these were clearly extraordinary times, given the pandemic threat, and the supply of Tamiflu should therefore not just rest with one company. He was not alone in feeling this way.

Senator Charles E. Schumer was another vocal congressman piling public pressure on Roche. Schumer proposed that the company should voluntarily license production to other companies as a way of rapidly increasing production: "Roche must engage in an active campaign to license Tamiflu production to 5 U.S. drug companies in the next 30 days. Roche is putting their own interests ahead of world health. They should not be slow-walking this process when we have a potential pandemic that could occur at any time" (*Wall Street Journal* 2005). Schumer also argued that "if we increase the number of manufacturers producing Tamiflu, we can protect many more Americans should a pandemic hit" and "knowing we have enough Tamiflu, just in case, would go a long way towards calming the public about potential shortages and hopefully dissuade people from buying, stockpiling or even taking a drug they currently don't need" (*Wall Street Journal* 2005). Like Kucinich, Schumer felt that because of the pandemic flu threat now confronting the United States, business as usual would not be acceptable. Something would have to give.

Yet a third congressman, Bernie Sanders, also joined in the growing chorus of political voices publicly calling for expanding the number of pharmaceutical companies producing Tamiflu. Whereas Schumer was calling for Roche to voluntarily enter into licenses with other companies, Sanders's call went even further by also directly threatening to sidestep the company altogether: "When you have a national crisis, you do not have to give enormously profitable pharmaceutical companies the price they want. That is why we're here, to protect the American people, and if they want profits rather than serving the people, I think the law is very clear, that we have a right to go outside of that company [to break their patent]" (quoted in Hoyt 2012: 149). With such calls by influential Congressmen growing in the United States, Roche would now also have to battle on a second front. In addition to managing the legal challenge from Gilead Sciences, Roche had to respond to the growing chorus of politicians calling for the government to override the Tamiflu patent in one of the world's most profitable pharmaceutical markets—the United States.

All the while, other groups were beginning to chip away at Roche's public justification for maintaining such tight control over Tamiflu production. One high-profile consumer group disputing Roche's official line, for example, was the Consumer Project on Technology (CPT). The organization was founded by Ralph Nader in 1995 and has since been renamed Knowledge

Ecology International. In November 2005 CPT issued a statement actively disputing the argument put forward by Roche about the complexity involved in the manufacturing process for Tamiflu. It alleged, "Roche has clearly exaggerated and misled government officials about the difficulties in manufacturing generic Tamiflu. . . . The Roche prices are also unaffordable for consumers in developing countries. If Roche does not act now, governments should issue the appropriate compulsory licenses in order to assure the competitive generics sector can legally sell generic copies of the drug. Further delays by governments are not helpful, and increasingly hard to defend" (Love 2005b). The group similarly tried to persuade lawmakers in the United States and Europe to invoke procedures that envision the overriding of patents in times of national emergencies, even without the explicit consent of Roche.

Roche could not easily ignore such calls, as the US federal government is indeed authorized, through the "Takings Clause" of the Fifth Amendment of the US Constitution, to take private property for public use. The use of intellectual property is explicitly included in this provision and is further codified in 28 USC 1498(a)—albeit subject to a reasonable compensation being paid to the patent holder. According to section 1498(a), "Whenever an invention described in and covered by a patent of the United States is used or manufactured by or for the United States without license of the owner thereof or lawful right to use or manufacture the same, the owner's remedy shall be by action against the United States in the US Court of Federal Claims for the recovery of his reasonable and entire compensation for such use and manufacture" (quoted in Yeh 2007: 11). If the federal government decided to take this route, neither Roche nor Gilead Sciences would be able to prevent generic manufacturers from producing and selling generic Tamiflu to the US government. The only recourse for the companies would be to turn to the US Federal Claims Court in order to eventually recover some compensation as envisioned in the law further down the line (Yeh 2007: 11).

Roche was clearly not in favor of taking this route. Most pharmaceutical companies are highly protective of their patents. They make products that are costly to develop but in many cases also easy to copy (at least by those with the relevant knowledge of how to do so). Pharmaceutical companies thus depend heavily on patent protection for sustaining their business models. That is also why they would want to resist a situation where governments routinely issue compulsory licenses in health emergencies.

From the commercial perspective, doing so could further undermine industry efforts and incentives to develop new antivirals and vaccines for managing future public health crises (Bradsher 2005). The government might score a quick political victory on the day, but in the longer term such a move for the development of future medical countermeasures could be very negative. Moving forward, pharmaceutical companies might well conclude that developing new medical countermeasures is too risky commercially because during any future crisis governments would simply invoke these extraordinary powers. Not surprisingly, Roche wanted to forestall this eventuality at all costs.

Was there any way that Roche could resist these growing calls? Would the company have any leverage to counter the growing chorus of prominent politicians? Beyond the industry's wider political influence, Roche did actually possess some leverage—mostly in the form of the considerable technical and manufacturing expertise it had acquired about how to make Tamiflu. Although others might be able to manufacture the drug, nobody at the time had a greater understanding of the intricacies of Tamiflu production or of all the detailed aspects surrounding it. We have also seen that the US government had made some special requests of Roche—such as increasing its production capacity located geographically on US soil. If the US government went down the route directly opposed by Roche, it would run the risk of jeopardizing any active cooperation it might receive from Roche in this area. Indeed, some observers asserted, "Breaking the patent through a compulsory license would actively discourage Roche from either producing the drug or lending its expertise, which would be directly counterproductive" (Van Gelder 2005).

Such countervailing pressures from the manufacturer side meant there was ultimately a very difficult political call to make for the US Department of Health and Human Services secretary at the time, Michael Leavitt. Should the government invoke the powers of the state to allow others to produce Tamiflu against Roche's will? Weighing in on one side of the argument was the lurking pandemic threat that the government wished to protect the population against. On the other side, the government would not want to send a signal that would discourage the development of new medical countermeasures in the longer run. In the end, Leavitt broadly accepted the reasoning of the pharmaceutical companies and was reassured that Roche was working with other partners to increase supply of the drug. Despite the vocal threats coming from Congress, the US government ultimately did not pursue the compulsory license route, and Roche was able to maintain control over Tamiflu production in the United States.

Nevertheless, the protracted political battles over the compulsory licensing of Tamiflu point to another commercial risk for companies involved in the development of medical countermeasures more generally. In a crisis situation, many governments will be very tempted (and indeed come under intense popular pressure) to invoke their emergency powers to secure access to a drug or to at least negotiate prices significantly downward. Their priority will understandably be to protect the population, and political pressure on governments to "do something" in a crisis can be immense. Pharmaceutical companies can also be in quite a vulnerable position in terms of their public relations in such situations—especially when they do not enjoy a positive reputation and are perceived to be putting profits before lives during a crisis. Yet from the perspective of a company considering to develop a new medical countermeasure, such an emergency may also be the only time it can actually achieve a major return on its product. So if a patent is not respected under those circumstances, a company may well wonder how medical countermeasures are ever supposed to achieve a commercial return on its investment.

All of these developments reveal the essentially double-faced nature of health security threats. While the anxieties around pandemic dramatically increased commercial demand and revenues for Tamiflu, those anxieties also became so strong that governments then began to question whether production of the drug could actually be left solely in the hands of a single company like Roche. There was a real risk that the company might thus lose control over Tamiflu's production at the very moment that its product was finally in high demand. Like the legal pressure from Gilead Sciences, the threat of compulsory licensing to increase access to the drug thus emerged as another battle line between governments and pharmaceutical companies. And that was just the situation in high-income countries such as the United States.

Low-Income Countries: TRIPS, Generic Antiflu, and Indian Companies

On top of all these coalescing pressures, governments in low- and middle-income countries too were now demanding access to Tamiflu in order to protect their populations against H5N1—even if they often lacked the necessary financial resources to acquire sizable Tamiflu stockpiles. Their largely unsuccessful efforts to acquire Tamiflu echoed earlier struggles around unequal international access to life-prolonging antiviral medicines for people living with HIV/AIDS. During the AIDS pandemic, there had been huge and heart-wrenching discrepancies in the global access to such medicines. Now it seemed that many low- and middle-income countries might also have to ride out a flu pandemic—again without access to the kinds of pharmaceutical protection available to many high-income countries. Politically, it threatened to be déjà vu all over again.

What leverage did those governments have to ensure that their populations would not be left out again and that they too would receive access to Tamiflu? The formative experiences with access to HIV/AIDS medicines suggested a different mechanism that they might use to override the patent on Tamiflu—via the agreement on Trade-Related Aspects of Intellectual Property Rights (TRIPS). TRIPS is an international agreement that sets out minimum standards for the international protection of patents (as well as copyrights, trademarks, and so forth). The TRIPS agreement formed a core component of the international treaties creating the World Trade Organization (WTO) in 1995, as compliance with TRIPS is a precondition for WTO membership. Yet the TRIPS agreement also contains provisions for countries to issue compulsory licenses in some circumstances (Löfgren and Williams 2013). The existence of a "national emergency," in particular, could allow governments to act quickly—and without first having to negotiate with the patent holder for obtaining a possible voluntary license.

Against the backdrop of the AIDS pandemic and other pressing global health challenges, this mechanism was further clarified by the WTO in 2001 and 2003. In 2001 the "Declaration on the TRIPS Agreement and Public Health," also known simply as the "Doha Declaration," explicitly affirmed that the agreement should be implemented in a way that supports the protection of public health and access to medicines for all. Crucially, the declaration gives the right of determining what constitutes such a national emergency to member states. Each member state thus has "the right to determine what constitutes a national emergency or other circumstances of extreme urgency, it being understood that public health crises, including those relating to HIV/AIDS, tuberculosis, malaria and other epidemics, can represent a national emergency or other circumstances of extreme urgency" (WTO 2003).

During the negotiations, the US government had actually wanted to restrict the scope of this provision. It specifically opposed including the wording of "other epidemics" in the text. After some debate, the issue was eventually put to a vote. The United States lost the vote by a landslide—148 to 1, in fact—so the wording was included (Hamied 2003). The inclusion of this additional provision meant that, irrespective of what the US government may decide to do domestically, there was now also a credible and established international mechanism that could be invoked to allow the generic production of Tamiflu. If a country possessed a domestic manufacturing base and determined that a pandemic threat constituted a national emergency, it could, in accordance with the detailed procedures stipulated in article 31 of TRIPS, make a case for issuing a compulsory license. This international picture was thus another battle line that emerged between governments and Roche. Even though Roche had largely retained control of production in the United States, things could turn out very differently in many low- and middle-income countries.

Even after clarification of this procedure through the Doha Declaration, however, at least one important obstacle still remained with invoking these TRIPS exceptions. There are many low-income countries that do not possess a domestic pharmaceutical manufacturing base of their own. How would those countries get access to generic drugs? Would these countries simply be denied access, or would they perhaps be allowed to import Tamiflu from a generic producer located in a different country? In order to address this problem, the WTO also permitted member states—under strict conditions—to import generic drugs produced under compulsory license in other countries (WTO 2003). Even if a country could not make its own medicines, in other words, it could still be entitled to import generic medicines from other countries. This additional provision paved the way for a geographically much wider application of the TRIPS emergency provisions.

Even though all of these issues were initially negotiated against the backdrop of HIV/AIDS, they now quickly resurfaced in the case of Tamiflu because of the pandemic flu threat. People began to explore in earnest whether the "national emergency" provisions could also apply to Tamiflu (Yeh 2007). Roche's position of remaining the sole producer and supplier of Tamiflu thus invited vocal public criticism from prominent international leaders at the time. United Nations Secretary-General Kofi Annan, for instance, argued that intellectual property laws should not be a barrier to developing countries acquiring antiviral medications in emergency situations (Bradsher 2005). Access to Tamiflu for low- and middle-income countries was fast becoming a pressing international political issue. In 2006 several Asian countries were reportedly already contemplating invoking article 31 of TRIPS and—for those without a domestic manufacturing base—the Doha agreement paragraph 6 relating to importing under compulsory license (SEARO 2006: 11). By this point, the battle over controlling Tamiflu production was clearly no longer just confined to high-income countries; it was also spreading to low-income countries concerned about how their populations would be protected in the event of a pandemic.

But who could actually produce such a generic version of Tamiflu that might be aimed at low- and middle-income countries? All of these discussions would remain fairly hypothetical if a credible and competent producer of generic Tamiflu could not be found quickly. Here all eyes quickly turned to India. India was just starting to become fully integrated into the TRIPS system around that time. By virtue of the peculiarity of the Indian patent laws, patents in India only covered manufacturing processes and not the products themselves. Historically, this had allowed Indian pharmaceutical companies to produce equivalent generic drugs through different manufacturing processes and then sell them at lower prices without violating patent laws in India. That is also why India has often been described in recent years as the "pharmacy for the poor."

With concerns about pandemic flu now on the rise, some Indian pharmaceutical companies began to argue that Roche did not have a valid patent for Tamiflu in India and that they could therefore produce generic versions of the drug for the Indian market (but not for export). Cipla was one of the most prominent companies making this argument. The Indian pharmaceutical company had risen to international fame by producing inexpensive generic AIDS medicines. The much lower cost of their generic AIDS medicines suddenly made the rolling out of antiretroviral treatments to people living with HIV in many low-income countries a viable option. Now Cipla also wanted to enter the market with a generic version of Tamiflu, with the intention of also selling it to other Asian countries (Feddersen 2007: 12). "Right or wrong, we're going to commercialize and make oseltamivir," said Yusuf Hamied, Cipla's charismatic chairman, in October 2005 (quoted in McNeill 2005). Hamied also pledged to sell a generic version of Tamiflu "at a humanitarian price" in low-income countries rather than aiming at the European and American markets (McNeill 2005).

During an interview in Mumbai, Hamied explained in greater detail how his discussions with Indian health authorities made him realize just how exposed India would be in the event of a pandemic. He concluded that generic production of Tamiflu was a serious challenge for the country and instructed his research and development staff to obtain all the information they could on oseltamivir. Hamied also possessed crucial contacts in China from his earlier work on HIV/AIDS drugs. Those contacts could help to supply him with star anise—the critical ingredient that was native to China but not India. Within three months, Cipla had successfully produced a few kilograms of oseltamivir, and the company subsequently received permission from the Indian regulators to market it under the brand name Antiflu in India (Hamied 2014).

The timing in all of this was deeply significant. The integration of India into the WTO meant that new Indian patent laws would recognize patents filed in India by Western companies after 1 January 1995. The Tamiflu patent in India had been filed with a "priority date" of 26 February 1995, technically falling into this period. Hamied thought, however, that the Indian government would be unlikely to fight over a difference of two months, especially if the lives of millions of Indians were at stake (McNeill 2005). So Cipla decided to press ahead with making a generic version of Tamiflu.

All the while further doubts were also emerging about the accuracy of Roche's explanation about how difficult and dangerous the production process is. In early November 2005, the *Wall Street Journal* reported that Cipla and Taiwan's National Health Research Institutes had just finished the work of reproducing small quantities of Tamiflu (Zamiska and Dean 2005). The Taiwanese claimed that once they had secured all the publicly available documents about the drug, it took them only 18 working days to complete the task. Others also challenged the argument about the danger of the production process and the potentially explosive step. According to the *Wall Street Journal*, "That step—which involves a chemical reaction with sodium azide, whose explosive potential has made it the common choice in automobile air bags—turns out to be relatively routine, according to some pharmaceutical executives and scientists familiar with the chemistry. Although it is still dangerous, the process is well within the abilities of university chemistry labs, let alone the world's top generic-drug makers, these scientists say" (Zamiska and Dean 2005). David Reddy, speaking on behalf of Roche at the time, did not challenge this. In fact, he subsequently acknowledged that Roche's earlier estimates might have been too cautious. However, he did counter that there was still a big difference between laboratory reproduction of small quantities of a drug and larger-scale processes for mass manufacturing it. Moreover, both Cipla and the Taiwanese scientists also acknowledged that even if the production process itself was not that challenging, the key obstacle that remained to producing large quantities of generic oseltamivir would be to secure significant supplies of shikimic acid— the critical ingredient mostly extracted from Chinese star anise at the time (Zamiska and Dean 2005).

In either case, Roche's inability to scale up production sufficiently quickly had now put it on a confrontational course with at least three different sets of actors. From one direction, Roche was under legal pressure to share control of Tamiflu production with its corporate partner, Gilead Sciences. From another direction, Roche was subjected to credible political threats to sidestep patents coming from high-income countries like the United States. And now it was also confronting a third threat of generic production emanating from companies in low- and middle-income countries desperate to ensure that their populations would also have access to Tamiflu. Roche was indeed in the eye of a perfect international political storm. The issue of access had quickly morphed from a largely *technical* question about scaling up production, into a much wider international *political* question of whether patents and intellectual property should be respected during an emergency situation.

Breaking the Deadlock: Sublicenses, International Stockpiles, and the Tamiflu Reserves Program

Who would win all those political battles in the end? Would Roche be able to retain control over the international production of Tamiflu, as it had so firmly set out to do from the beginning? Roche essentially used three different strategies for navigating through this political storm. First, the company decided to enter into voluntary sublicensing agreements with third parties as a way of increasing international Tamiflu production. Under the combined pressure from world leaders, politicians, and generic manufacturers, and unable to service this spike in demand by itself, Roche finally opened discussions with other countries on possible sublicensing agreements in October 2005. Taking this route meant that the company would have to cede some control over Tamiflu production, as it would now also have to bring other producers on board. Overall, however, the company felt that this route would still be preferable—especially when compared to the alternative of entertaining compulsory licenses that several governments were now threatening.

Indeed, there would still be a number of commercial advantages for Roche in entering into such voluntary licenses compared to having governments issue compulsory licenses. Voluntary licenses meant, for instance, that Roche would still receive licensing fees from sales of Tamiflu. Those fees would likely be higher than the compensation they would eventually be able to get through court settlements on compulsory licenses (where that legal option even existed). Estimates at the time indicated that under a compulsory license agreement Roche would likely have been entitled to royalties of around 3–5 percent. Even then, however, it would still lose the ability to control the sale price of the drug, and the existence of a generic version could eventually translate into smaller royalty payments (Yeh 2007: 15–16). Further advantages associated with the voluntary sublicensing route are that Roche could still retain some control over things like the price of Tamiflu; the volume of generic drugs being produced; who the drug is sold to (restricting it to government stockpiles, for example); the reexporting of supplies; and the duration of licenses (Yeh 2007: 16). If Roche could not retain complete control of Tamiflu production, then voluntary sublicenses were effectively the next best option for the company.

Yet Roche still insisted that it would only enter into such sublicensing agreements where third parties had a realistic chance of supplying substantial volumes of the drug for emergency pandemic use, in line with stringent safety, regulatory, and quality conditions. After entertaining bids from a number of different companies, Roche eventually came to a sublicensing agreement with Hetero, based in Hyderabad, India. The terms of the license would allow Hetero to sell the drug in India and to export it to almost 100 countries across Asia, Africa, and Latin America. Another agreement was reached with China, where sublicenses were granted to Shanghai Pharmaceuticals and the HEC Group to produce a generic version of Tamiflu for China (Reddy 2010: ii38). Finally, Roche also gave the technical know-how to a company in South Africa—Aspen Pharmacare—to support supply of oseltamivir for African countries (Samii and van Wassenhove 2008: 3; Reddy 2010: ii38).

Faced with simultaneous pressure from a variety of different directions, then, Roche had little choice in the end but to back down from its aspiration to remain the sole manufacturer of oseltamivir. International political pressure for access to Tamiflu had simply proved too intense. Yet by taking the route of voluntary sublicensing agreements, the company had at least managed—from its perspective—to fight off the much less desirable threat of compulsory licensing. Entering into voluntary sublicensing agreements thus formed one critical component for navigating the political storm around access to Tamiflu in the midst of which Roche suddenly found itself.

Creating a new international Tamiflu stockpile under the auspices of the World Health Organization formed a second strategy used by Roche. As fears of a pandemic escalated, it became clear that, new sublicensing arrangements notwithstanding, many low-income countries would still find it very difficult to secure access to the drug. That represented a source of considerable anxiety for those countries. In many cases those governments were just as keen to access Tamiflu supplies as their counterparts in high-income countries, but they were simply unable to do so, because their countries lacked either the requisite resources or a domestic pharmaceutical manufacturing base or both. Their likely plight meant that Roche was now also coming under greater ethical or normative pressure not to put profits ahead of lives—especially for some of the poorest populations living around the world.

Such global justice considerations again echoed earlier—and for the industry quite bruising—confrontations with civil society organizations and low-income countries around international access to life-prolonging HIV/AIDS medicines. In the case of HIV/AIDS there had been strong grassroots mobilization and campaigning for equitable international access to medicines. The pharmaceutical industry was widely seen at the time as having lost the public relations battle—not least when they were perceived to have sued the South African government to protect their financial interests over the plight of those dying from AIDS-related illnesses. With pandemic fears escalating, Roche would have to be mindful of the possibility that there could be a damaging repeat of this kind of public backlash in the case of Tamiflu.

In order to help countries that did not possess their own stockpiles, Roche began to work with the World Health Organization to create an international stockpile of Tamiflu. In 2004 Roche donated 125,000 treatments of Tamiflu to be used by WHO in affected countries in Asia and Eastern Europe (Roche 2012: 9). Roche also shared its order book with the head of the Influenza Unit at the World Health Organization in March 2005. The order book revealed that governments in Asia had placed very few orders for Tamiflu, even though many expected a pandemic to originate in Southeast Asia. This, David Reddy explains, meant that "an eventual outbreak would just rage and spread. As few governments at that time had indicated to the WHO their willingness to share their stockpiles with others, we needed to find a viable alternative solution" (quoted in Samii and van Wassenhove 2008: 5). All of this would pose a problem not just for countries directly affected by an outbreak but potentially for *all* countries—especially if it meant that an outbreak could not be contained before going on to cause a much wider pandemic. There was thus mutual interest among many countries in creating an international stockpile of Tamiflu that could be deployed on short notice to those countries directly affected by an outbreak but unable to source their own pharmaceutical supplies.

Perhaps such a stockpile would be able to stop an initial outbreak at the source, saving many lives in the long run. Even if it could not completely contain an outbreak, however, such an international stockpile might still be useful in terms of at least slowing down the early phase of a pandemic. That could still give governments and health systems more time to prepare for what was coming. Such scenarios thus became the subject of more extensive modeling. A 2004 study modeled on assumptions similar to the 1957–1958 pandemic, for example, concluded that "targeted antiviral prophylaxis has potential as an effective measure for containing influenza until adequate quantities of vaccines are available" (Longini et al. 2004: 623). Another influential modeling study, published in *Nature* in September 2005, similarly argued that "elimination of a nascent pandemic may be feasible using a combination of geographically targeted prophylaxis and social distancing measures, if the basic reproduction number of the new virus is below 1.8. We predict that a stockpile of 3 million courses of antiviral drugs should be sufficient for elimination. Policy effectiveness depends critically on how quickly clinical cases are diagnosed and the speed with which antiviral drugs can be distributed" (Ferguson et al. 2005: 209). Bolstered by such modeling,

WHO negotiated with Roche the further donation of a "fire-blanket stockpile" of three million treatment courses in August 2005. The stockpile would be colocated in the United States (Joppa, Maryland) and Switzerland (Basel), with 1.5 million treatment courses in each location that could be shipped at short notice (Roche 2012: 9; WHO 2011b: 9). This stockpile was expanded in January 2006, when Roche donated a further two million treatment courses to be held as stockpiles in particular regions (Samii and van Wassenhove 2008: 5). These were donated to WHO for use in developing countries most likely to be affected by human infections with H5N1 that could not economically afford to purchase the drugs (Roche 2012: 9). Such donations to international stockpiles thus formed a second strategy used by Roche to manage the difficult issue of global access and the political storms it was creating.

Roche subsequently also deployed a third strategy for dealing with access issues for low-income countries. In response to later concerns about pandemic H1N1, Roche announced the launch of its Tamiflu Reserves Program in July 2009. The program was explicitly geared toward developing counties (India was excluded from this program on the basis that it has its own generic manufacturing capacity). Through the program, Roche offered those countries to produce and store pandemic stockpiles of Tamiflu at a reduced price, with the cost also being spread over multiple years. In the event that a pandemic is announced, Roche would then ship out the supplies upon request by these governments. Roche also promised not to raise prices during a pandemic unless there is an increase in the underlying cost of raw materials needed for making the drug, the manufacturing process, transportation, taxes, and so forth (Roche 2012: 10). Overall, then, Roche had sought to address the needs of low-income countries through a trio of measures—the introduction of new sublicenses for Tamiflu production, the creation of an international Tamiflu stockpile through WHO, and the launch of its Tamiflu Reserves Program.

These international battles over Tamiflu production reveal just how critical the issue of access to medical countermeasures can become during an emergency. People will understandably be desperate to protect themselves against a potentially lethal threat. Governments will come under intense political pressure to ensure that their citizens have access to any available medical countermeasures and will want to be reassured by companies that they can secure sufficient supplies to protect their populations. Yet companies may find themselves struggling to provide such assurances because of the significant challenges involved in rapidly scaling up production of a pharmaceutical product on short notice.

The resulting tension over international access to medical countermeasures generates two wider challenges around medical countermeasures during an emergency. The first is a largely technical challenge around how to ensure that there is sufficient production capacity for a medical countermeasure. We have seen from the Tamiflu experience that there are a number of reasons why scaling up production on short notice is not always possible during a crisis. At the same time, it also does not appear very realistic to expect commercially operating pharmaceutical companies to maintain a large volume of spare production capacity simply on the off chance that there might be a pandemic or outbreak at some point in the future. "Over-production," Roche warns in this respect, "is not sustainable from a business perspective and production output will be modified to meet real demand" (Roche 2012: 6). In the absence of a continuous stream of orders, in other words, a company will likely need to deploy production capability in other and commercially more rewarding ways rather than electing to have it idly on hand.

That is also exactly what soon happened in the case of Tamiflu. Once the immediate fear of an H5N1 pandemic subsided, so too did government interest. Roche then began to struggle to maintain an adequate supply network for Tamiflu. As two spokespeople for Roche explain,

> This supply network was in place by the end of 2006, but by the end of 2007, it was becoming increasingly challenging to sustain. We were trying to generate the data needed to extend the shelf life of the product purchased by governments, and this was reducing the orders made with our partners. Some started to reassign their capacity, which meant the network capacity started to deplete. At this stage, we started working with our government partners to agree how we could establish a more sustainable approach. Today, surge capacity is only one part of pandemic preparedness. We are able to produce 130 million treatments within six months and 200 million within one year. However, to do this requires us to hold inventory equivalent to more than 100 million treatments across the production supply chain. (Rollerhagen and Braxton 2016: 3)

Once the backlog of government orders is filled and network utilization drops, Roche would thus have to scale back the production line once again, making it much more difficult to scale things up again the next time around.

By the end of 2007 it thus appeared that not very many lessons had been learned about how companies and governments might better cooperate in the area of medical countermeasures. If anything, things seemed to be heading back to square one. "If the pandemic does not come," Roche's Lapre argued, "some will criticize the efforts and monies spent on stockpiles. Much worse, if it does come and develops along the lines of a more extreme scenario, stockpiles could be quickly depleted. What if the production network has degraded to a point where it cannot respond?" (quoted in Samii and van Wassenhove 2008: 8). Tensions around the scaling up of mass production, or sustaining spare capacity that can be utilized during an emergency, are thus a seventh major challenge that can arise around medical countermeasures more generally—especially during an international emergency.

If sufficient quantities of a medical countermeasure are not available during such a crisis, then another challenge can also quickly arise for governments as to whether they should continue to respect the intellectual property and patents around medical countermeasures. We have seen that governments have the option of invoking their extraordinary powers during an emergency—powers that they do not possess under normal political circumstances. In a crisis, governments could deploy those special powers to wrest control over the production of a patented pharmaceutical away from a pharmaceutical company like Roche. This may seem like a simple and straightforward decision. Yet governments again have to strike a difficult balance between the immediate need to protect their populations against an impending threat and not sending a longer-term signal to the pharmaceutical industry that patents will simply be routinely sidestepped during crises. The latter route could have the effect of deterring the future development of other new medical countermeasures.

From the perspective of the pharmaceutical companies, the fact that governments even have this option of sidestepping intellectual property rights during an emergency only increases the commercial risks around medical countermeasures further, as they may suddenly see the patents on their products being overridden. Indeed, it is a peculiar feature of a medical countermeasure that the very moment at which it is most likely to realize a commercial return—that is, during an emergency—is also precisely the moment when governments and other actors possess the most political and legal leverage to sidestep a patent or to negotiate prices significantly downward. How to handle such intellectual property and patent issues during emergencies thus forms an eighth major challenge arising more generally in the quest to secure populations pharmaceutically. Those challenges were eventually diffused through voluntary sublicensing agreements and an array of other international initiatives in the case of Tamiflu.

These challenges, moreover, show how the quest to secure populations pharmaceutically cannot be confined to the initial development of new medical countermeasures alone or even to their subsequent acquisition by governments. There is still a third set of deployment challenges that arises once an emergency actually occurs. To address these additional challenges, BARDA has—as part of the medical countermeasures enterprise in the United States—already invested in the creation of three new Centers for Innovation in Advanced Development and Manufacturing in the United States. Those centers are designed to easily switch production between different product lines in order to quickly scale up production of medical countermeasures during an emergency. These new centers have been activated on several occasions and in response to a number of recent outbreaks, such as avian influenza, Ebola, and the Zika virus (Fassbender 2016). They mark some of the most significant attempts made by the US government to date to address this complex but equally critical piece of the medical countermeasure puzzle.

7

"Ode to Tamiflu"

Side Effects, Teenage "Suicides," and

Corporate Liabilities

International efforts to stockpile Tamiflu for pandemic preparedness purposes soon became mired in yet another controversy. Speculation suddenly surfaced in the media that Tamiflu might also have rarer but potentially more harmful side effects. New medicines are usually approved on the basis of clinical trials that only enroll a comparatively small cohort of people compared to the size of the overall population. Often trial participants are also selected specifically for the purposes of carrying out those clinical trials. That means they may not fully reflect the diversity of people eventually taking the medicine and might not include people suffering from all the same coexisting medical conditions that are present in the general population. As more people utilize the new drug under "real-world" conditions, continued monitoring is therefore necessary to ensure that the new medicine is not causing unintended harms.

Tamiflu was no exception in this regard. During this postmarketing phase of its life, concerns arose in public that the antiviral might also have rarer but much more serious side effects—especially in Japan, where the antiviral was being widely prescribed for seasonal flu. The mere suggestion that Tamiflu could have potentially more harmful side effects immediately provoked a cascade of further issues. For the public, it generated questions as to whether people should continue to take the antiviral—even though it had been officially approved by the regulators. For doctors, it meant they had to decide whether to continue prescribing Tamiflu to their patients. For governments, it raised concerns about whether their regulatory agencies had done their job properly and—if the existence of such harms was confirmed—could also cast significant doubt on the wisdom of all those stockpiling decisions they had since taken. For the pharmaceutical companies, in turn, such speculation could generate extensive financial or other legal liabilities, as well as undermining future sales of Tamiflu. Both Roche and the regulators would therefore have little choice but to respond to the public speculation. This chapter explores how those concerns about more harmful side effects initially arose in the Japanese media and how government regulators and Roche subsequently tried to manage the public alarm caused by the reports.

Collectively, these postmarketing experiences with Tamiflu point to another major challenge that can also arise around medical countermeasures more generally when they are rolled out to the population: how to deal with the sensitive issue of harmful side effects and their associated liability implications. This is an issue potentially affecting all new medicines, but it is particularly salient in the case of medical countermeasures. We have already seen that it can be much more difficult to run the clinical trials needed to properly gauge the full safety profile of medical countermeasures in advance of their use because of the exceptional danger that many of those pathogens pose to human life. Medical countermeasures used during a crisis also face the prospect of being rolled out to a very large number of people in just a short period of time. If a new medicine produces rare but harmful side effects inside the human body, this may only begin to manifest itself at that point in time. Some governments are therefore already beginning to adapt their legal frameworks governing the deployment and use of medical countermeasures during emergencies in order to address this vexing issue of harmful side effects.

Tamiflu and the Possibility of Neuropsychiatric Side Effects

Medical students are often taught that every medicine they prescribe will have one effect that it is intended to have but also at least one other effect that it is *not* intended to have. The possible side effects of medicines are particularly critical to consider when governments take decisions to mass-administer a new medical countermeasure to their population. The experience with Tamiflu in the United Kingdom is a good example. In England, the government widely distributed Tamiflu to the general population via its National Pandemic Flu Service during the H1N1 pandemic of 2009–2010. Citizens could use the Internet (or contact a call center) and then go through a simple symptom-based algorithm to determine whether they would qualify for the antiviral. Those who did were issued a unique reference number and were then asked to collect their Tamiflu packs from a local collection point. It was the quintessential example of a rapid and mass administration of a drug in order to manage a public health emergency.

One of the many people taking Tamiflu in the United Kingdom at the time was a thirteen-year-old boy named Harry Houseago. Harry lived in Tulse Hill (an area of south London) and was a pupil at Alleyn's School in Dulwich. One day Harry found himself stuck at home because his school had closed temporarily in May 2009 because of swine flu fears. Lying in bed and idly playing his guitar, Harry composed a song called "Ode to Tamiflu." When he subsequently posted a performance of the song on the Internet, it rapidly began to attract media attention:

ODE TO TAMIFLU
I fall asleep and wake up feeling queasy
And ev'rything's reeling,
It's not very pretty,
I'll have to go . . . to the loo again.
I remember they gave us pills
Saying: "This is so you don't get ill."
But now I know
This is worse than any cold.
Oh Tamiflu, it's down to you
That I'm feeling very nauseous,
And now I've got a pain in my head
So I think I'd better stay in bed.

Harry later clarified that the song was not prompted by symptoms he experienced personally. Rather, he had been moved to write the lyrics after reading the extensive warning label accompanying the medication, which listed numerous potential side effects (Houseago 2009). That is also why Harry's song mostly revolves around the more common and well-known "milder" side effects of Tamiflu, such as nausea and headaches.

Generally speaking, the basis for assessing the side effects of medicines consists of a small number of clinical trials, often as few as just two or three. Depending on the trial, it may also only run for a short period of time. Although there are also examples of larger trials, many clinical trials range between 1,000 and 3,000 participants (Light 2010: 7). This means that once a new drug is approved, it is likely to be prescribed to many more people than are able to participate in the initial clinical trials. Side effects occurring with a lower frequency than that may therefore not be properly captured in clinical trials (Avorn 2005: 71). If, for example, a medicine is associated with a serious side effect that occurs on average once in every 10,000 cases, this would not necessarily be captured by a standard-sized clinical trial (Elashoff 2012). Even at that rate, however, it could still become a pertinent issue in the mass administration of a medical countermeasure to a large proportion of the general population.

Another significant issue here is that the persons enrolled in clinical trials may not fully reflect the diversity of patients to whom the drug is later prescribed. Scholars studying the broader processes around clinical trials have identified a number of different strategies that pharmaceutical companies might use to minimize the appearance of side effects at clinical trial stage. Such strategies could entail excluding patients with more complex risk profiles, running shorter (or smaller) trials, selective reporting of toxic side effects, ruling out patients with other health problems even if there is a good chance that such patients would later be prescribed the drug, and so forth (Light 2010: 15–16). Commercially operating pharmaceutical companies would want their new medicines to look as effective and safe as possible at the clinical trial stage. Postmarketing surveillance under "real-world" conditions—also known as pharmacovigilance—is therefore necessary to confirm, revise, or deny the safety profile of the drug determined in the initial clinical trials.

In the case of Tamiflu all eyes regarding the existence of such possible side effects would be on Japan because of the high use of Tamiflu in that country. Although initial uptake of Tamiflu for seasonal flu was much lower than expected in most major pharmaceutical markets, Japan marked a notable exception. The country's widespread use of Tamiflu for seasonal flu rapidly propelled Japan to the status of the world's largest consumer of Tamiflu—especially prior to the rise of government stockpiling for pandemic preparedness. More than 75 percent of all Tamiflu prescriptions worldwide issued between the influenza seasons of 1999–2000 and 2006–2007 were dispensed in Japan, translating into a total of 36.4 million prescriptions according to Roche (Toovey et al. 2008: 1100).

There are several likely reasons for the higher level of Tamiflu consumption in Japan. One is the high density of the Japanese population, with people living in close proximity to one another in narrow streets and intermingling in crowded subways. That makes infectious diseases an ongoing concern in Japanese society. It is not at all unusual, for instance, to see people wearing protective face masks as a routine precaution on public transportation networks, even if there is no immanent concern about an infectious disease outbreak. The views of medical authorities and the health-care systems in Japan are also likely factors. Academic experts in Japan strongly recommended the use of Tamiflu for seasonal flu. Many Japanese patients also benefit from easy access to medical facilities, including rapid influenza testing. Being able to obtain timely laboratory confirmation of influenza infection can strengthen the clinical case for using antivirals. That is because the diagnosis of influenza can then be made rapidly enough to initiate Tamiflu within the recommended 48-hour window after onset of symptoms. Finally, there is also a preexisting culture of managing influenza medically in Japan, with doctors traditionally prescribing several kinds of medicines even for the common cold. All these factors probably contributed to turning Japan into the world's largest market for Tamiflu.

Yet such a comparatively high level of Tamiflu consumption also made Japan the likely place for rarer and potentially more harmful side effects to surface if they existed. It was therefore particularly concerning when Japanese doctors first raised the prospect of Tamiflu possibly having such side effects—especially in children and adolescents. In June 2004, the Japanese health ministry notified doctors about neuropsychiatric adverse events possibly associated with Tamiflu—issuing instructions that doctors should be alerted to these risks. A scientific meeting held in November 2005 was then told of reports about two teenage Japanese boys who died a year apart (in February 2004 and February 2005) in apparent suicides after taking the drug (Cohen 2014). The cases also attracted significant media attention in Japan. In total, the Japanese Pharmaceuticals and Medical Devices Agency reported at the time that it had received reports of 64 cases of psychological disorders, delusional states, or other abnormal behavior (Laurance 2005). If a causal link between some of those events and Tamiflu were substantiated, it could prove a very difficult situation for Roche as the commercial producer of the antiviral, for all the governments now in the process of stockpiling the antiviral for pandemic preparedness purposes, and indeed for the regulators that had initially approved the use of the antiviral in children.

Rokuro Hama and the Early Cases in Japan

One person who is more familiar than most when it comes to many of those Japanese cases is Rokuro Hama. Hama is chairman of a small non-profit organization called the Japan Institute of Pharmacovigilance, based in Japan's second largest city of Osaka. Hama possesses detailed knowledge about these cases because he published articles about them and provided expert opinions on three deaths with suspected links to the use of Tamiflu in Japan. With the help of a translator, I managed to visit him at the modest offices of the Japan Institute of Pharmacovigilance. Soft-spoken and welcoming, Hama shared his views about many of those issues at length and alerted me to some of his publications on the subject.

One of those deaths happened during a nap that was taken by a young boy aged 2 years and 9 months who had tested positive for influenza and had taken Tamiflu dry syrup on 5 February 2005 (Hama 2005; Laurence 2005). A second death involved an older, 14-year-old boy, who had similarly tested positive for influenza. After taking Tamiflu on 4 February 2005, the boy reportedly watched television with his sister for about one and a half hours. Around half an hour after he had gone to bed, his mother decided to check in on him but could no longer find him in his room. The boy was later found outside of the building lying on the ground, believed to have fallen out of his room on the ninth floor of the condominium. He sustained fatal injuries from the fall (Hama 2005, 2008). Andrew Jack, who covered the story for the *Financial Times* at the time, conveys the human dimension of such events in a way that medical case reports and statistics cannot. Reporting on his visit to the boy's mother, Jack writes:

> In the Japanese industrial town of Chiryu I go to visit . . . Ryuko, and she kneels in front of the shrine in the corner of the living room in her small modern apartment, placing the bouquet of white flowers I have given her next to a candle beneath a photograph of her son, Kohei. Memorabilia of Kohei's 14-year life are also there: a baseball and bat, a hat, some toys. On the table is a photo from the local newspaper, showing an assembly at his school. Ryuko explains: "Each

person's name on the register was called out, and when it came to Kohei's turn, all 194 children said 'yes.'" (Jack 2006)

Yet a third death had occurred the previous year and involved a 17-year-old high school boy. He too had tested positive for influenza and took Tamiflu via capsule on 5 February 2004. Around two hours after taking the medication, while his other family members were away from the home, the boy suddenly ran across the snow outside, jumped over a concrete fence, crossed a railway and jumped over the guardrail of a highway. He was hit by an oncoming truck and died (Hama 2005). All of these cases involved young patients—ranging from 2 to 17 years in age—who all had a history of taking Tamiflu shortly before their deaths. Their experiences thus raised concern about whether Tamiflu could potentially have some much more serious side effects that medical authorities were not aware of.

In considering the possibility of a causal relationship between Tamiflu use and these deaths, Hama points to a number of possible factors: the rapid time within which these episodes emerged after taking the medication; that the emergence of such cases coincided with the commencement of the marketing of Tamiflu for children in Japan in 2002–2003; and that similar mechanisms had also been observed in some animal toxicity studies (Hama 2008: 19). Masato Tashiro, head of influenza at Japan's National Institute of Infectious Diseases at the time, told reporters that the institute knew very little about this issue, yet he expressed concern that Tamiflu might be entering the brain by crossing the blood-brain barrier—a critical layer of tissue that usually prevents many chemicals from crossing from the bloodstream into the brain (MacKenzie 2007). Roche had itself warned that the drug should not be given to infants younger than 1 year because animal experiments showed that in animals too young to have a fully formed barrier the drug depressed brain activity and caused death (MacKenzie 2007).

A frequent counterargument made by the pharmaceutical industry (as well as several regulators) is that influenza illness can itself cause delirious and abnormal behavior induced by high fevers often associated with the illness. That makes it much more difficult to disentangle the effects of influenza itself from those possibly caused by Tamiflu. Hama, however, is not persuaded by this argument. He points out that some of the patients showed signs that their body temperatures were already decreasing, casting doubt in his mind on whether these could be explained by reference to fever delirium and so forth (Hama 2005).

In either case, Hama's reporting of these initial cases eventually led to the identification of five further cases. That increased the total number to seven suspected "sudden onset" cases that occurred shortly after taking the first or second dose of Tamiflu. A further "delayed" case had also emerged, occurring only after the full course of Tamiflu had been taken and continuing for some two weeks thereafter. Of the seven sudden onset cases, two were accidental deaths attributed (in all likelihood) to nonsuicidal abnormal behavior, while another three deaths occurred suddenly during sleep and another two cases were life threatening but not fatal (Hama 2008). All of this would understandably begin to cause considerable unease, as well as disconcerting media headlines, in Japan (and beyond). Governments, and indeed Roche, would have little choice but to respond to the growing public speculation and anxiety.

Government Agencies Respond with Additional Warnings

People principally look to their governments to ensure that medicines are safe. As public attention turned toward these alarming cases, the Japanese Ministry of Health, Labour and Welfare (MHLW) thus began to look more systematically into the issue. The ministry found that between 2001 (when marketing of oseltamivir began in Japan) and the end of May 2007, a total of 1,377 adverse reactions had been reported. Of these, 567 were considered serious neuropsychiatric cases, with 211 showing signs of abnormal behavior. Among the 71 deaths reported by MHLW, accidental deaths resulting from abnormal behavior was noted in 8 individuals (Hama 2008: 14). Looking into all of those cases more systematically would prove difficult, however, because Japan did not have an information system to track the nationwide drug utilization at the time. Even though claims are centrally collected, they were in paper form and therefore not amenable to computer analysis (Okamoto 2010).

Outside of Japan other regulatory agencies similarly felt compelled to investigate the matter further. In the United States, the FDA began looking into the possibility of neuropsychiatric side effects in 2005. The agency was puzzled by the fact that the vast majority of these reports emanated from Japan. As Japanese dosing recommendations were similar to those found in the United States and Europe, one would normally have expected to see a fairly even distribution of such cases occurring across all countries where the drug was being used. Even though Japan was by far the largest consumer of Tamiflu, one would still have expected to get reports from other countries if there was a causal relationship between Tamiflu use and such side effects.

The FDA explored several possible hypotheses. Perhaps Japanese patients metabolized the drug differently. Perhaps they had higher levels of the drug in their bodies. But the FDA could not find evidence of either. What is more, the FDA also acknowledged that there was evidence of neuropsychiatric events occurring with patients infected with influenza but who did *not* have treatment with Tamiflu:

> Beginning in the mid-1990s, there have been many reports in the pediatric scientific literature describing a syndrome of influenza-associated encephalitis (inflammation of the brain) or encephalopathy. These reports originated primarily from Japan where pediatricians described a pattern of rapid onset of fever, accompanied by convulsions and altered level of consciousness, progressing to coma within a few days of the onset of flu symptoms. This syndrome frequently resulted in death or significant neurologic sequelae. These reports prompted nationwide surveillance of influenza-associated encephalopathy in Japan. This syndrome was described and the surveillance in Japan was in progress before Tamiflu was approved for the treatment of influenza. (FDA 2005)

On the basis of its 2005 deliberations, the FDA determined that "we cannot conclude that there is a causal relationship between Tamiflu and the reported pediatric deaths" (FDA 2005).

That said, the FDA remained sufficiently concerned about the cases to demand that Roche amend the product label for the drug in 2006 to also include the possible side effects of delirium, hallucinations, and other related behavior (FDA 2006). What is more, a separate analysis of the FDA's Adverse Event Reporting System database (2005–2010) carried out years later by the Southern Network on Adverse Reactions would find that in children aged 19 years and younger "the incidence of oseltamivir-related npAEs [neuropsychiatric adverse events] in the United States is approximately equivalent to the frequency reported in Japan once controlling for the lower rate of oseltamivir prescription in the US" (Cohen 2014; Lu et al. 2014). That finding casts doubt on the view that this is primarily an issue associated with Japan, and the FDA has since further updated the Tamiflu label a number of times—as has the European Medicines Agency (Cohen 2014).

The Japanese authorities, who were on the front line of this issue, decided to issue their own alerts. Toward the end of February 2007 they warned doctors not to prescribe oseltamivir to adolescents aged 10–19 years. A Japanese study conducted during the 2005–2006 winter season had initially appeared to clear the drug. The study followed 2,846 children during the winter of 2005–2006. The researchers concluded that there was no significant difference in the frequency of abnormal behavior between those children who took Tamiflu and those who did not (Yokota et al. 2007; see also Fuyono 2007: 358). The study was led by Shunpei Yokota, a pediatrician at Yokohama City University's graduate school of medicine. However, there were lingering concerns about some shortcomings associated with the study—concerns that Yokota himself acknowledged (Fuyono 2007: 358). So the matter ultimately remained unresolved.

To try to settle the question more conclusively, Yokota and his team launched a second study. This was a much larger one of around 10,000 persons aged between 10 and 18 during the following winter of 2006–2007 (Fuyono 2007: 358). Yet this second study soon became enveloped in public controversy. It transpired that two members of the study group (including Yokota himself) had been paid in the past by the Japanese pharmaceutical company Chugai for pediatric research and teaching. Yokota had reportedly been paid 10 million yen between 2001 and 2006 (around $85,000 at the time it was reported) and Tsuneo Morishima, 2 million yen in 2005 (Fuyono 2007: 359). Why was that a problem? It was a problem because Chugai was not just any pharmaceutical company. Chugai was the Japanese subsidiary of Roche—and thus also the main distributor of Tamiflu—in Japan. The financial connection with the company thus raised concerns about the independence of the study and possible conflicts of interests.

After details of the payments emerged, Shunpei Yokota was replaced by Yoshio Hirota—a professor at Osaka City University. An interim analysis reported no association between neuropsychiatric symptoms overall with oseltamivir (Hirota 2008). However, the results were quickly challenged by other analysts—including Rokuro Hama—and before this study could present its final report, the Japanese authorities decided to limit the use of the drug (Cohen 2014). Following media reports of two more deaths, of a 14-year-old boy and a 14-year-old girl in 2007, who jumped to their deaths after taking oseltamivir, the Japanese authorities decided that inserts warning against giving the drug to those aged between 10 and 19 years would need to be included in the packs (Fuyono 2007: 358; Cohen 2014). Politically, the Japanese government had little choice in the end but to respond to the public concern, which it did by commissioning further scientific studies, asking its regulatory agencies to look into the problem more closely, and ultimately issuing additional warnings.

Roche-Sponsored Studies: Managing the Commercial Fallout

How would Roche, in turn, respond to these sensitive issues? As the commercial manufacturer of Tamiflu, the company too would now be in the public spotlight. Roche also had to be mindful of the fact that pubic speculation about potentially more serious side effects could have financial implications for the company. The mere possibility that a product might have more serious side effects can be commercially significant and quite damaging for companies. Yet in this case there was also the added potential for such concerns about side effects to undermine confidence in the government stockpiling of Tamiflu. If such a link existed and was established, it could throw a major wrench into ongoing stockpiling and pandemic preparedness plans. Roche too would therefore have little choice but to respond to the public speculation.

Roche's principal counterargument was that these events might not be caused by Tamiflu but more likely by influenza itself. In making that argument Roche had considered its own preclinical and clinical trial data on Tamiflu. The company also looked at its postmarketing spontaneous events reporting. Roche even considered wider epidemiological data drawn from health claims and medical database records in the United States and the United Kingdom. The company's analysis concluded that "the evidence strongly supports that the [NPAEs, neuropsychiatric adverse events] events are more likely to be caused by the disease itself than by oseltamivir, which is consistent with UK GPRD [General Practice Research Database] medical records analysis showing that the risk of NPAEs in influenza patients is significantly higher than in the general population" (Toovey et al. 2008: 1112). The study also pointed to literature describing children with influenza in Taiwan and Japan reportedly also experiencing such NPAEs without, or prior to, treatment with oseltamivir (Toovey et al. 2008: 1107). Roche later published additional studies looking at an association between the use of oseltamivir and neuropsychiatric events using information from a large US medical claims database but that were not able to find one (Smith and Sacks 2009).

According to Penny Ward, who worked for Roche on Tamiflu, there is also a wider data challenge that arises with issues like this. When dealing with a problem occurring in 1 in 10,000 cases (or an even less frequent), she argues, one would need hundreds of thousands of participants on both sides of the equation to run a proper randomized trial. In her view, it is therefore not possible for anyone—including Roche—to say categorically that there are not some people who are susceptible to neuropsychiatric difficulties because there is just no feasible way of demonstrating that conclusively, hence the solution of including this warning on the product labeling (Ward 2015). It would be a question that quickly runs up against the limits of what is knowable within the confines of current techniques for assessing such effects.

Others argue that the Roche-sponsored studies were not sensitive enough to capture these kinds of effects and that only a very careful prospective and period-defining study could detect this difference (Hama 2014). A 2014 review by the Cochrane Collaboration also raises a number of other possible reasons why the Roche studies may not have detected an association (Jefferson, Jones, Doshi, and Del Mar et al. 2014). The authors of the review further point to other, prospective studies from Japan which, in their view, indicate that such prospective and intentional collection with a large scale of participants may be necessary in treatment-randomized control trials (Jefferson, Jones, Doshi, and Del Mar et al. 2014). Yet even scholars at the forefront of investigating these issues acknowledge that "opinion on causal association between oseltamivir use and serious adverse events including sudden death and abnormal behaviors remains controversial" (Hama and Bennett 2017: 149).

It is beyond the scope of this book to evaluate or adjudicate between different claims about the safety profile of oseltamivir. What does matter very much for the purposes of this study, however, is the fact that this whole issue of harmful side effects quickly erupted as another major source of tension and controversy in the case of Tamiflu, just as governments were in the process of building their pandemic stockpiles. As the authors of the Cochrane Review argue, even findings of rare events would matter in this case because of "the distribution of oseltamivir to large numbers of asymptomatic individuals following pandemic plans" (Jefferson, Jones, Doshi, and Del Mar et al. 2014). The mere suggestion of such an association with more harmful side effects can thus become a particularly significant and sensitive issue for medical countermeasures. It also meant that Roche, as the manufacturer of the drug, would have little choice but to respond. The company did so mostly by carrying out its own studies and responding to additional data requests from regulators.

Yet if all this controversy posed new challenges for regulators and companies alike, the most serious impact was undoubtedly felt by the families who had suffered these devastating losses. At the end of the day, children had died and families were bereaved. Those families would want to know if the drug had played a role in the deaths of their loved ones. Beyond their immediate sense of personal loss, moreover, some relatives would also want to explore whether they would be financially compensated for these losses. Japan does have a compensation system for dealing with such issues, which is operated through funds provided by pharmaceutical companies. Yet according to Hama none of the Japanese families have received any compensation because the companies involved "have never accepted the causality of Tamiflu and neuropsychiatric symptoms, sudden death and death from abnormal behaviors" (Hama 2014). Similar compensation claims have since also surfaced outside of Japan. In the United States, for instance, law firms specializing in injury claims are now actively seeking clients whose children have taken Tamiflu and subsequently experienced side effects (Parker Waichman LLP 2015).

The emergence of such claims in multiple countries shows how the issue of a medicine's potentially harmful side effects is ultimately also tied to wider questions around the financial and legal liabilities for the harm they may cause. Beyond the particular experiences with Tamiflu, such liability questions can become particularly significant in relation to medical countermeasures more generally. That is because new medical countermeasures might be mass-administered to a large proportion of the population in a short period of time during a crisis, much as was done with Tamiflu during the 2009–2010 H1N1 pandemic. What would happen if more harmful side effects then suddenly began to manifest themselves? Who would then be liable for them—the governments, the companies, or even those involved in administering them? Who would ultimately have to pay? Could there even be criminal charges?

Harmful Side Effects and the Liabilities
for Medical Countermeasures

The potential for harmful side effects has to be considered in relation to all medicines of course. Yet the issue becomes particularly salient in the case of medical countermeasures. That is because the principal means through which a company (and regulators) would come to a comprehensive view about the safety profile of a drug is through clinical trials. Yet we have already seen that running such clinical trials can be much more difficult for many of the health security threats against which governments would like to see new medical countermeasures developed. The diseases they address may not occur naturally, may occur only in very small numbers, or may be very dangerous, potentially even lethal. In such circumstances, it is more difficult (if not impossible) to design and carry out large-scale clinical trials that can yield meaningful information about safety and efficacy in the way that would be routinely done for many more common diseases. When it comes to medical countermeasures, in short, there may be much greater uncertainty about the presence of such harmful side effects.

From the commercial perspective, this heightened uncertainty only adds to the financial risks associated with taking on the development of new medical countermeasures. If it is not possible to carry out proper clinical trials prior to a health security threat materializing, how can companies effectively manage the risk of costly lawsuits that might subsequently emerge? As the Tamiflu experience shows, there is a very real prospect that those taking medical countermeasures and who believe they suffered harm as a result will seek financial compensation for the harm incurred. It could be an enormous financial and legal risk for any company to take on, especially if the product is later distributed very widely to the general population.

Nor is it just the pharmaceutical companies that face risks here. The administration of medical countermeasures also involves many other groups as well, such as government agencies, public health authorities, medical professionals, health-care workers, and so forth. All of those groups could potentially face the risk of lawsuits if they are directly involved in the administration of a product that ends up causing serious harm to people. Unless there is a clear legal framework for dealing with the liabilities for injuries resulting from the use of medical countermeasures, pharmaceutical companies and the many other actors relied upon for their administration may be deterred from becoming involved with them. Some governments have therefore already begun to adapt their legal frameworks specifically governing the administration of medical countermeasures.

The PREP Act: New Legal Protections for Pharmaceutical Companies

The United States has been particularly proactive in this area and has already introduced three key changes. First, the US government passed new legislation to manage the issue of potential lawsuits. The Public Readiness and Emergency Preparedness Act (PREP Act) of 2005 introduced the possibility of granting pharmaceutical companies new legal protections from such lawsuits in the case of a public health emergency. A related goal was to address the liability concerns of a wide range of other actors, such as health-care providers, public health professionals, public-private partnerships, and others involved in the distribution and deployment of such medical countermeasures (Binzer 2008: 2). The PREP Act thus specifically provides the US secretary of the Department of Health and Human Services with the power to issue a declaration providing immunity from tort liability.

Tort is an area of law where a person who suffers an injury might initiate a lawsuit to receive compensation from those responsible for causing the damage or injury. The PREP Act's provisions are intended to cover claims related to the administration of medical countermeasures in an emergency and to protect "entities and individuals involved in the development, manufacture, testing, distribution, administration, and use of such countermeasures" (IOM 2010: 6). The legal protections would thus extend to a wide array of stakeholders involved in the administration of medical countermeasures including pharmaceutical companies. These legal protections are triggered when a formal declaration is issued under the provisions of the PREP Act (Binzer 2008: 2).

The types of loss covered by the PREP Act are wide ranging. They include death; physical, mental, or emotional injury, illness, disability, or condition; and loss or damage to property (IOM 2010: 22). However, the protection from tort liability is also limited, in the sense that the act does not provide protections for death or serious injury arising from any *willful* misconduct (IOM 2010: 22). If a product is used under a declaration, citizens could still sue in the United States if they could demonstrate willful misconduct by the company—such as fabricating data, knowingly withholding information, and so forth. Crucially, there is no judicial review of declarations—mostly in order to protect the secretary's decision to issue such declarations and to prevent delay from lawsuits (Binzer 2008). Yet it is also important to bear in mind that all of these protections only pertain to US law, leaving unresolved a set of wider issues around potential lawsuits occurring in other countries (Binzer 2008: 2).

This new mechanism for extending tort liability protection to producers of novel medical countermeasures has already been invoked on a number of occasions. Over the years it has been used for acute radiation syndrome, anthrax, botulism, pandemic influenza, and smallpox. Tamiflu, moreover, is one of the medical countermeasures that was explicitly covered by such declarations in the past (IOM 2010: 24). According to a senior Roche executive speaking at the time, these provisions were crucial for stockpiling the antiviral for pandemic preparedness purposes: "We believe the protections contemplated under the recently enacted Public Readiness and Emergency Preparedness Act of 2005 framework should address our significant concerns regarding the liability implications of the provision of Tamiflu for the pandemic stockpile. . . . Thus, in addition to other contractual protections, we will be asking the Secretary of HHS to include Tamiflu in any declaration triggering liability protections for pandemic countermeasure products" (quoted in US Senate 2006). The unprecedented patient population, higher dosing duration and levels, and greatly reduced physician supervision were key factors for the company to consider (US Senate 2006).

The extension of special legal protections for the manufacturers of new medical countermeasures (as well a wider set of health-care providers) thus marks the first key legal adjustment that the US government has already undertaken in order to secure the greater cooperation of pharmaceutical companies in the manufacture and stockpiling of medical countermeasures like Tamiflu. They have essentially used the powers of the state to grant them immunity from prosecution for the potential harms caused by such products. In Europe, by contrast, such a centralized procedure for dealing with liability issues associated with medical countermeasures does not yet exist, and such issues would mostly still be a matter of national legislation in member countries (EMA Officer 2013). That said, lawsuits for claiming compensation are not the only legal issues that need to be addressed in relation to the use of medical countermeasures during emergencies. Other legal complexities that could arise during an emergency also need to be addressed.

Emergency Use Authorization: New Pathways for Using Unapproved Drugs

A second type of legal difficulty that could easily transpire during an actual emergency is that a government may wish to roll out a new medical countermeasure that has not yet been granted official regulatory approval because it is still deemed to be the best (or perhaps only) medicine available at the time. Doing so would be illegal, however, because the medical countermeasure has not yet been officially approved. Such legal uncertainty could thus potentially preclude a government from using a medical countermeasure in this kind of scenario.

A third, closely related, legal ambiguity could arise even if a government just wants to deploy an approved medical countermeasure for purposes that are different from those for which it was originally approved by the regulators—because it thinks it may also help to deal with a new threat that has just materialized. Doing so would again be illegal because the drug has not been approved explicitly for those purposes. Yet the US government encountered precisely this scenario when it wanted to use Tamiflu during the 2009 H1N1 pandemic. Strictly speaking, Tamiflu did not have regulatory approval for the use against *pandemic* flu in the United States—only for *seasonal* flu. That raised a difficult question as to whether it could legally be given to the population, increasing the risks of legal action if side effects were to then emerge unexpectedly.

In order to deal with the legal issues around those two closely related scenarios, the US government also introduced another new legal instrument. This new procedure would make it lawful for the government to deploy medicines under certain emergency conditions—even if they have not yet been approved. It would also allow the government to legally use medicines for purposes and indications that are different from those for which they were initially approved. The new mechanism is called an emergency use authorization (EUA) and was established in 2004 as part of the Project BioShield Act. Formally, an EUA is "an authorization issued by the Food and Drug Administration (FDA) for the use of an unapproved medical product or an unapproved use of an approved medical product during a declared emergency involving a heightened risk of attack on the public or U.S. military forces, or a significant potential to affect national security" (IOM 2010: 5).

The new procedure gives government planners much more flexibility in responding pharmaceutically to health emergencies. Susan Sherman of the Office of General Counsel of the Department of Health and Human Services argues that "from a legal perspective, there are a lot of situations where EUA helps get past all those requirements. . . . You can change the labeling. You can change the information. You can change the dosage. You can give it to populations for which wasn't approved" (IOM 2010: 26). In the case of Tamiflu, for instance, the declaration enabled the antiviral to be used to treat and prevent influenza in children under the age of 1, to use it at later times after the onset of symptoms, to be distributed without all the FDA-required prescription labels, and to use some medicines beyond their expiration date (FDA 2010b).

Procedurally, the determination of such an emergency can be made by either health or security authorities—specifically the Department of Health and Human Services, the Department of Homeland Security, or the Department of Defense. The declared emergency can be a military, domestic, or public health emergency, but it should be one that affects, or has a significant potential to affect, national security. The agents covered by the procedure include chemical, biological, radiological, or nuclear agents (IOM 2010: 27). However, such an EUA cannot be made lightly. Before making any EUA determination, the HHS secretary must first be satisfied of several conditions: the agent the countermeasure is addressing can cause serious of life-threatening disease; the product may be reasonably believed to effective in either detecting, treating, or preventing the disease; the known and potential benefits outweigh its known and potential risks; no adequate alternative is approved and available; and any other criteria prescribed in the regulation are met (Gottron 2014: 4). Nor is the role of the FDA as the government regulator completely sidestepped during this procedure, as it is still up to the FDA to review the EUA request, which can then be issued by the FDA commissioner via a formal letter of authorization.

More recently, this EUA mechanism has been further adapted through the Pandemic and All-Hazards Preparedness Reauthorization Act of 2013. The act built on the earlier procedure but significantly broadened its scope in at least two directions. First, it allowed the HHS secretary to declare an EUA following the determination that significant *potential* for a public health emergency exists (Gottron 2014: 13). It would no longer be necessary, in other words, to wait until an outbreak had already happened before issuing an EUA; one could now be activated much earlier in anticipation that such an emergency may be imminent—perhaps because an outbreak had occurred elsewhere in the world and there was a reasonable possibility it could spread to the United States. Second, the secretary could now also issue an EUA for all countermeasures acquired through Project BioShield, regardless of whether a separately declared emergency or potential emergency exists (Gottron 2014: 13). In either case, the procedure essentially would make it legal to use medicines in ways for which they were *not* initially approved, or even to use unapproved ones, in order to deal with an emergency.

Like the PREP Act declarations, this new procedure too has already proved useful to the US government on several occasions. The procedure was first used for a medication designed to deal with inhalation anthrax in 2005, when it was requested by the Department of Defense (Nicholson et al. 2016: 22). It was subsequently also invoked to cover antibiotic emergency kits (in 2008), and Tamiflu (as well as Relenza) during the influenza A (H1N1) pandemic of 2009 (IOM 2010: 25). Such EUAs have since also been issued for H7N9 influenza, MERS, Enterovirus D68, Ebola virus, and Zika virus in recent years (FDA 2014: 31). The introduction and use of these new legal instruments thus put the US government very much at the forefront of efforts to address some of the legal and liability issues associated with medical countermeasures.

Other governments around the world have also been looking to introduce similar procedures. The European Commission has spent much of the past decade developing its own health security framework—focusing on prevention, preparedness, and responses to threats (European Commission 2011). A new agreement on strengthening EU health security reached in 2013 "provides for the possibility that the Commission recognizes a situation of public health emergency for the purposes of conditional marketing authorizations for medicinal products" and that "this would allow accelerated marketing of medicinal products or vaccines in an emergency situation" (EU 2013). Subject to specific obligations, a conditional marketing authorization could be granted on the basis of less information during an emergency (Cavaleri 2016; EMA Officer 2013). In Asia, moreover, Japan introduced an "expedited review for antiterrorism measures" as early as 2001. That measure would temporarily allow medical countermeasures for bioterrorist threats to be approved (Shimazawa and Ikeda 2015: 131). In addition to the United States, several governments around the world are thus similarly adapting their legal frameworks governing medical countermeasures and are suspending a number of legal requirements that would normally apply under more routine circumstances in order to enable governments to better manage an emergency situation pharmaceutically.

The challenges surrounding medical countermeasures, then, do not end with their initial development or even their subsequent acquisition by governments. There are also additional deployment challenges that arise once they are actually administered to the population during an emergency—including issues around their potential to cause more harmful side effects. Because many of the pathogens that medical countermeasures are designed for are so rare and dangerous, it can be much more difficult for companies to conduct proper large-scale human clinical trials. This can ultimately lead to greater uncertainty about the existence, extent, and seriousness of potentially harmful side effects.

Yet there is still the very real prospect that such a product could then be suddenly administered to a very large number of people over a short period of time. In such a scenario, even a harmful side effect that may only occur in only one in a thousand people will still cause a significant number of cases if, say, 100,000 people are given the medical countermeasure (Cole 2013: 14). In the worst-case scenario, evidence of a new medical countermeasure's rarer but potentially more harmful side effects may thus only manifests itself once it is actually administered on a larger scale during an emergency. If that were to happen, people would suffer, companies and public health authorities could face potentially enormous liabilities, and public trust could become quickly undermined.

That is why managing the legal and liability issues associated with harmful side effects emerges as another major—and ninth—challenge that can arise around medical countermeasures more generally. Again, it is a challenge that puts governments in a particularly difficult position. On the one hand, citizens will expect governments to use their regulatory powers to ensure that any medical countermeasure they are asked to take is safe (and indeed effective). At the same time, governments wishing to encourage the commercial development of new medical countermeasures will also need be sensitive to the needs of pharmaceutical companies that develop and produce them. They will need to bear in mind that pharmaceutical companies could be deterred by the prospect of extensive legal and financial culpabilities that may result from the sudden emergence of such harmful side effects during a crisis. Governments, in other words, have to strike a balance between acknowledging the concerns of pharmaceutical companies and not doing so at the expense of the safety and well-being of their populations.

It is possible for governments to try to address this problem. Indeed, we have seen that they can do this by introducing greater legal flexibilities and new legal instruments for medical countermeasures. That route, however, also introduces new tensions of its own. As governments become more closely invested in the development of new medical countermeasures, they also run the risk of undermining public confidence in the impartiality of their advice. Perhaps nothing exemplifies this tension more clearly the case of Kohei, one of the boys who died in Japan whom we encountered at the beginning of this chapter. Asked about how she viewed the issue of Tamiflu in Japan, Kohei's mother observed: "In Japan they have bought pandemic stockpiles of Tamiflu. Because of their policy, they probably don't want to say that it's related" (quoted in Jack 2006). Her response is revealing in that it shows how her trust in the government had been profoundly shaken by the fact that the government had also invested so heavily in stockpiling Tamiflu for pandemic preparedness purposes.

8

Data Backlash

Roche and Cochrane Square Up

over Clinical Trial Data

Between 2009 and 2010 the twenty-first century experienced its first influenza pandemic. A new H1N1 influenza virus was discovered in North America, from which it rapidly spread to other continents. By this point many governments had already developed extensive pandemic prepared-ness plans because of the earlier H5N1 bird flu threat. In many cases, those older plans could simply be dusted off and then quickly activated for H1N1. Tamiflu once again moved into the public spotlight as the first line of de-fense against pandemic flu. A number of governments now also made their newly acquired Tamiflu stockpiles available to their populations for the first time. Those decisions would usher in the next significant stage—and con-troversy—in the life of Tamiflu.

With so many more people now taking the antiviral, several groups sud-denly came forward demanding access to *all* the clinical trial data for Tamiflu. Doctors wanted to reassure themselves about the drug's benefits before prescribing it to patients during the pandemic. That was especially important given the lingering concern about Tamiflu's potential side effects prompted by the reports emanating mostly from Japan. Some journalists and research organizations also wished to scrutinize the data because of the considerable costs incurred to the public purse in creating the Tamiflu stock-piles, and because of the significant revenues that Roche was suddenly achieving from the drug. Access to the full clinical trial data for Tamiflu thus became the key battleground for issues surrounding its effectiveness, safety, and value for the money. There was just one problem: none of those groups could actually access all that clinical trial data for the simple reason that much of it was not in the public domain.

Historically pharmaceutical companies have not routinely made all of their clinical trial data publicly available. Nor were they legally required to do so. Pharmaceutical companies like Roche were thus accustomed to carrying out the clinical trials for their products. Once completed, they would then confidentially share some of the data with the regulatory agencies during their applications for marketing approval. At their discretion, pharmaceutical companies could also permit selected studies to be published in scholarly journals—particularly where the studies pointed to a clinical benefit of their product. That is precisely how things initially unfolded with Tamiflu. Roche carried out the clinical trials and then shared information with the relevant regulatory agencies as required and permitted some studies to be published in academic journals. Yet all of this also meant that a significant proportion of the clinical trial data on Tamiflu was never made public.

Widespread use of Tamiflu during the H1N1 pandemic began to put considerable public pressure on those conventional arrangements around the handling of clinical trial data. One of the groups—a particularly influential research network called the Cochrane Collaboration—now wrote directly to Roche demanding access to *all* the detailed data. When Roche refused, it provoked a protracted public battle with the Cochrane Collaboration that would last for several years. Frustrated by their continued inability to access all the clinical trial data, those campaigning for greater public access to clinical trial data even turned Tamiflu into the new poster child for their wider campaign. Tamiflu quickly become the focus of much broader and politically charged questions like, Who should generate clinical trial data? Who should have access to it? How should the data be analyzed? Those bruising public confrontations point to a tenth, and final, challenge that is becoming increasingly salient in the quest to secure populations pharmaceutically: access to clinical trial data.

The Case for Tamiflu as a Pandemic Preparedness Drug

With the arrival of a new flu pandemic in 2009, governments were preparing themselves for increased levels of illness in the population and for heightened pressure on their health systems. Many governments therefore wanted to know whether Tamiflu could also help to prevent—or at least reduce—influenza-related complications leading to hospitalizations. If it could, that might help not only with saving lives but also with reducing the intense pressure on stretched health-care facilities expected during a pandemic. The question of whether Tamiflu would—beyond reducing the duration of symptoms by around one day in otherwise healthy adults—also deliver such "harder" public health outcomes thus became critical for the purposes of managing the looming H1N1 pandemic.

Roche clearly believed that the drug could have such an effect and stated so publicly on many occasions. Indeed, it put this message out via a variety of different media and communication channels. For example, in one of its factsheets on Tamiflu published in 2005 (around the time that governments were considering the creation of stockpiles for H5N1) Roche claimed: "When administered according to its approved dosage (75mg twice daily for 5 days), Tamiflu delivers a 38 per cent reduction in the severity of symptoms, a 67 per cent reduction in secondary complications such as bronchitis, pneumonia and sinusitis in otherwise healthy individuals and a 37 per cent reduction in the duration of influenza illness. These data were derived from seasonal outbreaks of influenza" (Roche 2005: 1). This statement is doubly significant. First, it represents an unequivocal statement by the manufacturer of Tamiflu that it believes the drug to be able to reduce influenza-related complications. Second, the statement also makes clear that the data underpinning this claim stem from trials carried out with *seasonal* influenza, not with *pandemic* flu. We have already seen in an earlier chapter that such data could not be generated for pandemic flu because nobody could really know in advance exactly what a new pandemic virus would look like.

Beyond this fact sheet, similar claims about Tamiflu's ability to reduce complications could also be found in other company communications. Some of Roche's websites, for instance, made very similar claims (Jefferson et al. 2010: 79–80). Roche employees, too, would emphasize this message in public presentations. David Reddy, for example, invoked a modeling study that estimated how Tamiflu stockpiles might reduce and delay hospitalizations during a pandemic (Tierney and Reddy 2005). Penny Ward, working for Roche at the time, made a very similar observation in a special supplement in the *Journal of Antimicrobial Chemotherapy*: "If the goal is reduction in complications, hospitalizations and deaths and the consequent utilization of resources, then treatment seems a viable option" (Ward et al. 2005: i18). Such claims would prove integral to launching Tamiflu's second life as a medical countermeasure for pandemic flu.

Yet where did the data underpinning those claims actually come from, and were those studies carried out by Roche or by independent groups? Looking back at the recent history of pandemic preparedness planning, it is clear that one study in particular proved pivotal to making such claims. That was a pooled analysis of 10 clinical trials involving a total of 3,564 patients and published by Laurent Kaiser et al. in the *Archives of Internal Medicine* in 2003. The aim of the Roche-funded study was to assess the effect of oseltamivir on the incidence of lower respiratory tract complications (LRTCs) leading to antibiotic treatment and hospitalizations following influenza illness. According to the now infamous study, "Our analysis found that early treatment of influenza illness with the neuraminidase inhibitor oseltamivir significantly reduced influenza-related LRTCs, associated antibiotic use, and the risk of hospitalization" (Kaiser et al. 2003). The study, in short, seemed to confirm that Tamiflu could also deliver those crucial public health outcomes as well.

The Kaiser study was published in 2003, before many governments decided to stockpile the antiviral. Yet it would later prove highly influential in repositioning Tamiflu as a medical countermeasure for pandemic flu. Others have already documented how several key organizations and health agencies later referred to the Kaiser study as evidence for the claim of the medicine's utility for pandemic preparedness planning. The CDC, for example, cited it for several years to support the claim that Tamiflu reduces the risk of complications and pneumonia, and the study was also referenced in the US Pandemic Influenza Plan (Jefferson et al. 2010: 78). In the United Kingdom, the Kaiser study was also cited by the UK Department of Health in its decision to stockpile the drug (DOH 2009; cited in Cohen 2009). It was further cited by Professor Fred Hayden, who was also a named author on the paper and who advised the UK Department of Health and the World Health Organization (Cohen 2009: 1342). The Kaiser study thus became very influential in the context of worldwide pandemic preparedness efforts—and in ways that were not properly anticipated by the authors at the time they published it. Kaiser himself later revealed in a television documentary about Tamiflu that "I had never foreseen that my study would have been so extensively cited, even mis-cited and for sure cited out of context, to justify the use of Tamiflu and to buy millions of doses of this drug during the 2009 pandemic in England" (Tinari et al. 2011: 15).

There were at least two perceived problems with the Kaiser study. First, it was based on data that had been generated by Roche and analyzed through studies funded by Roche. Because running clinical trials is a complicated and costly enterprise, responsibility for carrying out or contracting them has historically mostly fallen to the companies making the drug. Yet this close connection between the manufacturer and the studies can also raise questions around potential conflicts of interests and about whether such studies have the proper levels of independent scrutiny.

This problem was compounded by a second one. Many of the trials forming the basis for the Kaiser study were not publicly accessible. Pharmaceutical companies would usually submit clinical trial data to the regulators in confidence, as would be required for the purposes of obtaining regulatory approval. Yet such data would *not* be made publicly available as a matter of course. Nor were pharmaceutical companies legally required to do so. Like many other companies, Roche could thus exert a considerable degree of control over the public disclosure of the full clinical trial data on Tamiflu. However, with all eyes now on Tamiflu as the first line of defense for pandemic flu, the clinical trial data on Tamiflu would begin to come under much more intense public scrutiny. In fact, the authors of the now notorious Kaiser study could hardly have predicted what would happen next.

Digging Deeper: Hayashi's Email Query to Cochrane

It all started with a fairly unassuming query left on a public website by a Japanese pediatrician from Osaka named Keiji Hayashi. Hayashi was prescribing oseltamivir to children with influenza presenting in his clinic at the time, just like many other Japanese pediatricians. Yet he was becoming concerned about Tamiflu's possible side effects (Tinari et al. 2011). He was also aware of the of the possibility of the rare but potentially severe side effects documented by Rokuro Hama, who was also based in Osaka (Cohen 2009: 1342). Sitting with his wife in the reception room of his pediatric practice, Hayashi recounted the fascinating story of what happened next (Hayashi 2014).

Hayashi explained how the arrival of pandemic flu in 2009 generated a difficult clinical dilemma for him. On the one hand, he remained concerned about Tamiflu's potential side effects, which made him think twice before prescribing the antiviral to his patients, especially children. On the other hand, if the Kaiser study was correct, there could be potentially lifesaving benefits for those who became infected with the new pandemic H1N1 flu virus. In that case he would probably not want to withhold treatment. If, in other words, the claim about complications was accurate, then the benefits would have to be balanced against the risk of side effects in his clinical decisions about whether to prescribe Tamiflu (H. Epstein 2011). So, with patients in his busy practice to attend to, Hayashi was keen to find out for himself if the justification for the claims about Tamiflu was sound (Hayashi 2014). Does Tamiflu actually work to reduce complications in the way that was being widely claimed?

Where would be the best place to find unbiased and reliable information on Tamiflu's effectiveness? Hayashi initially turned to the highly regarded Cochrane Collaboration—an independent nonprofit and nongovernmental research organization made up of tens of thousands of volunteers around the world who review the evidence for medicines. Reviews carried out by the Cochrane Collaboration enjoy the international reputation of representing the "gold standard" in medicine because they summarize all the available data on a medicine and are periodically reviewed as more data become available (Goldacre 2014). When Hayashi consulted the latest Cochrane reviews of Tamiflu (oseltamivir) from 2006, he saw that they had endorsed the claims about the reduction of complications described in the 2003 Kaiser study. To see backing for this claim from the trusted Cochrane Collaboration would normally have been highly reassuring.

Yet Hayashi also spotted a potential problem with the Cochrane group's finding. Like so many other official government documents, the Cochrane review too appeared to have relied on the Kaiser study to evidence the claim. The Kaiser study, in turn, was a pooled analysis of ten other clinical trials of oseltamivir. To be absolutely sure, Hayashi also wanted to personally review these ten clinical trials himself so he could double-check that their analyses had been performed soundly. So he set about to locate the original data for the ten clinical trials forming the basis of the Kaiser analysis.

That quest yielded a remarkable discovery. A quick look at the references for the ten trials forming the basis of the Kaiser analysis revealed that most of those studies had never been fully published. Of the ten studies, only two were published in full, another seven were published only as abstract proceedings of conferences, and one was not published at all (Sheridan 2016: 47). The two that were published, moreover, did not appear to provide evidence of these effects. It was therefore impossible for Hayashi to obtain the information that he needed in order to make his prescribing decision. As he explains in a documentary:

> His [Kaiser's] literature reviewed ten data. I found that two had been published. When I looked at the two data, I found that Tamiflu lacked superiority in preventing complications such as bronchitis. So actually the eight remaining data, that are not published, are the ones that prove Tamiflu's effectiveness in preventing complications. And another thing is when looking at the authors' affiliation; four aside from Kaiser were from Roche. And another was a consultant who is paid by Roche. So I thought the literature was basically written by Roche. (Tinari et al. 2011: 4)

Hayashi could not get to the bottom of the matter because eight of the ten clinical trials used in the Kaiser study were not publicly accessible. How, then, could he decide with confidence whether or not to prescribe Tamiflu to his patients concerned about the H1N1 pandemic? Nor, for that matter, was it clear how the Cochrane reviewers could have obtained direct access to this trial data in order to support the claims in their independent analysis.

Fortunately for Hayashi, the Cochrane website gives readers the option of posting comments online. So on 14 July 2009, Hayashi's next move was simply to leave a comment on the Cochrane Collaboration website. His comment pointed to the fact that the Cochrane conclusion too appeared to depend on the Kaiser study and not its own independent analysis of the underlying data: "We strongly suppose that the reviewer's conclusion about the complications was mainly determined by these 8 RCTs [randomized control trials], we should appraise the 8 trials rigidly. Without this process it is difficult to conclude that Oseltamivir can prevent lower respiratory tract complications" (Hayashi 2009). Hayashi would not have realized it at the time, but his comment on the Cochrane website would soon go on to trigger a cascade of further events that eventually ended up helping to transform the way in which clinical trial data are published today.

Under the rules of the Cochrane Collaboration, the authors of the Tamiflu review were obliged to reply to Hayashi's comment within six months. The relevant Cochrane review had been carried out by Thomas Jefferson along with a number of coauthors. Looking at the comment, Jefferson—by his own admission—realized fairly quickly that he had made a mistake in relying on the Kaiser study. So he set out to get the original data directly from the scholars who authored the Kaiser study. He first emailed Professor Frederick Hayden, who was the corresponding author for the Kaiser study. Hayden replied that he could no longer locate the data for a number of reasons and that Cochrane would need to go to Roche instead. Jefferson received a similar response when he next contacted Professor Laurent Kaiser, the study's lead author (Cohen 2009: 1343). This meant Jefferson would have little choice now but to approach Roche directly and get the data from the company.

When Jefferson wrote to Roche requesting the data, the company insisted that he first sign a confidentiality agreement preventing him from sharing the data openly. According to the proposed confidentiality agreement, Jefferson would not even be permitted to publicly disclose the existence of the confidentiality agreement (Doshi 2009). That request posed a dilemma for Jefferson. After all, the whole ethos of the Cochrane Collaboration is to make its data sources and methods public so that others can also understand how the conclusions are arrived at and even contest them if they think errors have been made. As Jefferson felt that the Roche requirements for this confidentiality agreement were contrary to the Cochrane ethos, he was not willing to sign the agreement (Jefferson et al. 2010: 77). When he queried this stipulation with Roche, he did not receive a reply (Cohen 2009). David Reddy, head of Roche's pandemic task force at the time, later explained that there was a legal issue at stake for the company, because the data included patients' initials and birthdates, which legally could only be seen by regulatory agencies, doctors, and Roche's study managers, but not by others unless they promised confidentiality (MacKenzie 2009).

When asked, in the context of researching this book, why the company did not immediately release all the data to Cochrane, spokespeople for Roche also pointed out that it would not have been standard practice to do so. Such a request, they argued, would have been unprecedented at the time: "Our strategy for dealing with Cochrane was one of caution. It was an unprecedented request, and while we had shared information with regulatory authorities, we were not set up to provide the requested clinical documents to a non-statutory body. Our primary concerns were to make sure we could protect the confidentiality of patients and to ensure any scientific assessment was completed using valid methodology. As mentioned before, we had and maintain serious reservations about the approach suggested and then employed by Cochrane" (Rollerhagen and Braxton 2016: 6). Roche therefore proceeded very cautiously in response to the Cochrane request.

However, Roche did then get in touch with Cochrane again in October 2009 in response to a follow-up email by Jefferson—this time to inform Cochrane that it had since given the data to a different group for further analysis. This, the company now claimed, prevented it from also providing the data to Cochrane (Cohen 2009; Goldacre 2012: 84). Ben Goldacre, who described the story in his book *Bad Pharma*, counters that such a response from Roche "was a non-sequitur: there is no reason why many groups should not all work on the same question. In fact, since replication is the cornerstone of good science, this would be actively desirable" (Goldacre 2012: 84). Perhaps that also helps to explain why, only shortly thereafter, Roche did then send Cochrane seven documents—each around a dozen pages long—containing excerpts of the clinical study reports for the 10 trials that formed the basis for the Kaiser study (Cohen 2009; Goldacre 2012: 84). It looked like the Cochrane group was finally making some progress in the matter.

Again, however, disappointment soon followed. Upon closer inspection of the documents sent by Roche, the Cochrane researchers quickly realized they did not include all the detailed information that they felt they needed in order to properly analyze the issue of complications (Goldacre 2014), and they struggled to reconstruct the unpublished data sets on the basis of the information they had just received (Cohen 2009). They were also stumbling across other startling discrepancies and inconsistencies. One striking finding, for instance, was that different regulatory agencies—who would have seen clinical trial data as part of the process of regulatory approval—had come to very different conclusions on the issue of Tamiflu's effect on complications. The relevant European regulator EMEA (subsequently renamed EMA) indicated in its 2009 review of product characteristics that oseltamivir did reduce the risk of complications (Cohen 2009: 1344). Yet a 2008 review of the information contained on the product label approved by the FDA in the United States read: "Serious bacterial infections may begin with influenza-like symptoms or may coexist with or occur as complications during the course of influenza. *TAMIFLU* has not been shown to prevent such complications" (quoted in Cohen 2009: 1344).

That last finding was again doubly significant. First, it showed that different regulators had come to differing conclusions on the issue of complications after looking at the clinical trial data. Second, it meant that one of the internationally most highly respected regulators had explicitly found that there was *not* sufficient evidence to make such a claim about complications. When asked further by the *BMJ* and *Channel 4 News* about this discrepancy, an FDA spokesperson explained: "The clinical trials in a variety of different populations (healthy adults and children, nursing home patients, adults and children with underlying cardiac/respiratory conditions) failed to demonstrate any significant difference in rates of hospitalization, complications, or mortality in patients receiving either Tamiflu or placebo, probably because these are relatively rare events. The clinical trials, although relatively large, were not powered to detect these clinical endpoints" (quoted in Cohen 2009: 1344). All of this leads to the question of how different regulators looking at the clinical trial data could come to such differing conclusions. It would be very difficult to know for certain without being able to access all the detailed clinical trial data for Tamiflu.

What is more, the Cochrane Collaboration now also faced a dilemma of its own. The group had since been commissioned by UK and Australian government agencies to update its review of oseltamivir (Cohen 2009: 1343). Unable to secure access to the full clinical trial data underpinning the Kaiser study, and with their internal deadline for their update looming, what position should the Cochrane team now take on the crucial issue of Tamiflu's effect on complications? The group decided on methodological grounds that it would have to exclude the Kaiser data in its next evaluation of Tamiflu—to be published in December 2009—because it could not independently verify the data. It was a highly significant decision leading to an important change from the previous Cochrane review. The updated 2009 Cochrane guidance concluded that it was impossible to say whether or not oseltamivir reduces complications (Jefferson et al. 2010).

Not surprisingly the group's decision caused quite a political stir at the time. After all, such claims had underpinned the costly public investments made by governments in creating extensive Tamiflu stockpiles for pandemic preparedness purposes. At the same time, their contentious decision also appears to have spurred Roche into finally committing to make the full clinical study reports of the clinical trials available. Why was access to those full clinical study reports so critical for the Cochrane researchers? When later recounting the story from their perspective, some of those involved in the effort explained: "Clinical study reports contain the same information as journal papers . . . but have far more detail: the study protocol, analysis plan, numerous tables, listings, and figures, among others. They are far larger (hundreds or thousands of pages), and represent the most complete synthesis of the planning, execution, and results of a clinical trial. . . . When regulators decide whether to register a new drug in a manufacturer's application, they review the trial's clinical study report" (Doshi, Jefferson, and Del Mar 2012). Following the crucial change in Cochrane's position on the issue of complications, Roche now pledged to release the "corresponding full study reports" for the 10 trials "within the coming days to physicians and scientists undertaking legitimate analyses" (J. Smith 2009)—though the company would not actually do so for another several years (Goldacre 2012: 86). Some of the stated reasons Roche cited for not releasing all the detailed information sooner included ongoing concerns about patient confidentiality, questioning the independence of some of the Cochrane researchers, and complaining that journalists were being copied onto email correspondence with the company (Goldacre 2014).

Even after the critical change in the Cochrane assessment, Roche continued to assert considerable control over who would have access to the full clinical trial data for Tamiflu. None of this was illegal. Yet with all eyes now on Tamiflu because of the H1N1 pandemic, the whole question of who should be able to access all of the clinical trial data was fast becoming a hot political issue and the new battleground for verifying all the claims about its effectiveness, safety, and utility against pandemic flu. The issue even began to attract high-level attention from several professional societies, public health organizations, medical journals, the media, and investigative journalists.

Tamiflu as a Poster Child for the Data Access Campaign

All of this public attention on Tamiflu suddenly also made it very attractive to campaigners advocating for greater transparency around clinical trial data more generally. They now seized upon the Cochrane Collaboration's frustrating experience with Tamiflu as a particularly vivid illustration of all the problems surrounding existing arrangements for accessing clinical trial data. Those arrangements meant that researchers could not independently review all the clinical trial data for the simple reason that they could not get access to it. Regulators could see the data but in the past would not share all such data with third parties. Those wanting to review the data would have no choice but to rely only on those studies openly published in the scientific literature.

What exactly is the problem with relying on such published data alone? There are at least two different issues at stake. First, researchers have no way of knowing how many clinical trials have been conducted in total and therefore what proportion of the existing data they are looking at. Second, pharmaceutical companies can also be quite selective in terms of which studies they permit to be published. Studies with negative or inconclusive findings may never be published—either because companies would not have a commercial interest in publishing them or because many journals tend to be less interested in publishing them than ones with positive findings. Both of those problems generate a risk of publication bias, whereby only the most favorable studies are published, leading to a potentially skewed picture of a drug's overall efficacy and safety in the published literature.

This problem of publication bias is certainly not new, but campaigners now sensed a valuable tactical opportunity to use the ongoing experiences with Tamiflu as a way of reinvigorating their wider campaign. Tamiflu, Ben Goldacre explains in an interview for this book, "is a poster child [for the campaign] because of the amount of money that was spent on it. It means you can go on TV and say here is an example Tamiflu, and this is no small thing because of the amount of money spent and it is very rigorously documented" (Goldacre 2015). In fact, those campaigning on this issue could publicly portray the Tamiflu situation in seemingly incredible and almost comical terms. As Fiona Godlee, editor in chief of *BMJ* (formerly the *British Medical Journal*), put it in a documentary, "In this case almost all of the data is in the hands of the manufacturer of the drug. So the data were generated by employees of the company, they were evaluated by employees of the company, they were authored by employees and people paid by the company—academics paid by the company. So we have no independent evaluation of this drug and because the data aren't available we have to say, we cannot judge the effectiveness of this drug" (Tinari et al. 2011: 5). Under Godlee's leadership, *BMJ* would remain at the forefront of international efforts to highlight this problem over public access to clinical trial data for many years to come.

Yet given Roche's steadfast refusal to make all of the Tamiflu data public, what tangible leverage did the campaigners actually have to materially improve the situation? How could they go up against such a powerful and well-resourced pharmaceutical company as Roche? The campaign first tried to mobilize public opinion in order to create greater pressure on the company. *BMJ* thus teamed up with investigative journalists to expose the way in which key influenza scientists with industry links had also been involved in developing WHO guidance on neuraminidase inhibitors (Cohen and Carter 2010). Their joint investigation found that "key scientists advising the World Health Organization on planning for an influenza pandemic had done paid work for pharmaceutical firms that stood to gain from the guidance they were preparing. These conflicts of interest have never been publicly disclosed by WHO, and WHO has dismissed inquiries into its handling of the A/H1N1 pandemic as "conspiracy theories" (Cohen and Carter 2010). Many of those links were described in a startling exposé published in *BMJ*— casting doubt on the integrity of the guidance and the decision making, as well as strengthening the case for greater independent scrutiny of the underlying clinical trial data.

The public reach of the story was considerable. Many international newspapers, newswires, and radio and television outlets covered it. The report into the potential conflicts of interest at WHO was mentioned more than 1,000 times by media organizations around the world (BIJ 2010a). Yet all this public pressure notwithstanding, Roche was still not budging. The company continued to refuse to release all of the detailed data that the Cochrane Collaboration wanted access to. So the Cochrane Collaboration next turned to a second strategy.

Targeting the Regulators

If Roche was not going to release all the data voluntarily, perhaps there was someone else with access to the data who could be persuaded to share it instead. Regulators, in particular, would have to have seen at least some of the data in the course of deliberating the regulatory approval of Tamiflu. Perhaps they could be convinced—or even pressured—to release it. Members of the Nordic Cochrane Centre had earlier deployed such a strategy in the area of antiobesity drugs, where there had been a very similar issue over access to unpublished trial data. In that case, researchers wrote to the European regulator (EMA) in June 2007 requesting the data from them. The EMA responded at the time that it would not release the data—citing intellectual property and the commercial interests of pharmaceutical companies as relevant factors to consider (Goldacre 2012: 71). Initially this alterative strategy of turning to the regulator therefore looked like another dead end.

Before giving up, however, there was at least one other angle the Cochrane Collaboration could try. If it could not persuade the regulators to hand over the data voluntarily, perhaps there was someone else who had the power to compel the regulator to do so. Thus, they next approached the little-known office of the European Ombudsman. This organization is charged with independently and impartially investigating instances of maladministration in the institutions of the European Union. It can launch investigations either on its own accord or in response to formal complaints. Openness and public access to documents is one of its primary areas of activity, covering around a third of its inquiries per year (European Ombudsman 2011).

The researchers from the Nordic Cochrane Centre now decided to make two complaints to the ombudsman over the EMA's refusal to hand over information on the diet drugs: first, that the agency had provided an insufficient justification for its decision to withhold information, and second, that the claim about commercial interests could not be justified in that the data requested only related to safety and efficacy of the drugs (Goldacre 2012: 73). The EMA did not respond for four months, maintained its position over the coming year, and—two years into the standoff—then raised additional concerns about patient confidentiality that might be breached by such releases (Goldacre 2012: 73–74).

After going through some of this information itself, however, the European Ombudsman came to the view that the EMA had indeed failed in its duty to give an adequate explanation and made a preliminary finding of maladministration (Goldacre 2012: 74; Gøtzsche and Jørgensen 2011). The ombudsman instructed the EMA to either release the data or provide a better explanation for not doing so (European Ombudsman 2010; Goldacre 2012: 74). Eventually, the EMA agreed to allow the claimants access to the data (European Ombudsman 2010). The Ombudsman's full report was published at the end of November 2010, a good three years after the initial complaint (Goldacre 2012: 78). The researchers finally received the data they had requested about the antiobesity drugs from the EMA in February 2011

(Gøtzsche and Jørgensen 2011). However, another crucial outcome of the whole episode was that it also led to a fundamental change in the data release policy at the EMA (Jefferson, Jones, Doshi, and Del Mar et al. 2014: 496).

Sensing, perhaps, that the political winds were beginning to change in relation to clinical trial data access, and also confronted with the significant change in the Cochrane assessment, Roche finally sent the Cochrane Collaboration some 3,195 pages of study reports from the Tamiflu treatment trials on 31 December 2009—only a few weeks after the 2009 Cochrane update had been published (Doshi, Jones, and Jefferson 2012; Jefferson, Jones, Doshi, and Del Mar et al. 2014: 494). This may initially sound like quite a large volume of information. Upon closer inspection, however, it turned out that the documents only included the first "module" of each clinical study report, although the tables of contents indicated that these reports contained four to five modules each (Doshi, Jones, and Jefferson 2012). When they wrote to Roche again requesting the *full* study reports, Roche replied that it believed that the group now had all of the information it needed to do its job (Jefferson, Jones, Doshi, and Del Mar et al. 2014: 494).

So the Cochrane Collaboration next turned to the regulator and filed a Freedom of Information request with the EMA for additional information on these studies—especially as the EMA had in the meantime introduced its new data release policy (Jefferson, Jones, Doshi, and Del Mar et al. 2014: 496). The EMA then sent the Cochrane Collaboration another 25,453 pages of material covering module 2—but still mostly missing modules 3–5 (Doshi, Jones, and Jefferson 2012). Yet those last three modules were especially crucial to the Cochrane researchers, because they detailed the trial protocols and amendments. The Cochrane researchers were therefore adamant about wanting access to the *entire* clinical study reports to carry out their independent review properly. In the meantime, however, they would use this additional data just obtained from the EMA (along with some other data) to publish a further update of their review in January 2012 (Jefferson, Jones, Doshi, and Spencer et al. 2014).

How, then, could the Cochrane group obtain access to those remaining modules? EMA had already confirmed that it did not hold these additional modules (Doshi, Jones, and Jefferson 2012). So, following a similar strategy to the one that the Nordic Cochrane Centre had earlier adopted in relation to the diet drugs, Thomas Jefferson next submitted a formal complaint specifically about oseltamivir to the European Ombudsman on 15 October 2012. He alleged that the European regulator made its 2002 authorization decision regarding Tamiflu on the basis of incomplete information (Jefferson 2012). The complaint asked the ombudsman to request that "EMA correct their error by summoning the missing data from Roche and either reanalysing it or make it widely available to the scientific community" (Jefferson 2012). The group had since also submitted a separate freedom of information request to the FDA in January 2011, who they believed also held the relevant data (Doshi, Jones, and Jefferson 2012). Getting full access to *all* the clinical trial data on Tamiflu was proving to be a slow and arduous process—with neither Roche nor the regulators initially appearing to be particularly accommodating in opening access to the full clinical trial data (see Goldacre 2012).

In a further escalation of public pressure, *BMJ* then also decided to openly publish the Cochrane Collaboration's extensive correspondence relating to its ongoing efforts to obtain the full data for Tamiflu on a dedicated and high-profile website: http://www.bmj.com/Tamiflu. That correspondence also formed the basis for a wider *BMJ* open data campaign and helped to stimulate the prominent AllTrials campaign (Jefferson, Jones, Doshi, and Del Mar et al. 2014: 497). Under such mounting public pressure, the major breakthrough finally occurred in April 2013, when Roche emailed the Cochrane Collaboration that it could get access to the clinical study reports for all 74 Roche-sponsored trials on Tamiflu over the next couple of months—running to more than 100,000 pages (Jefferson, Jones, Doshi, and Del Mar et al. 2014: 497; PMLive 2013).

Roche indicated that these data would now be released in a staggered process in which the documents would first be assessed for issues of patient confidentiality and commercial interest (Cohen 2013). According to the company, "Due to their age, some of the documents requested were not in a fully electronic format (hard copy documents had been scanned) and as such we had to identify a process and redact the documents semi-manually. In total, clinical study reports for 74 studies were shared, amounting to more than 138,900 pages of documents. Collating, sorting and redacting this volume of material was a huge undertaking, especially when such care needed to be taken to ensure patient privacy was maintained" (Rollerhagen and Braxton 2016: 6). With all the data being finally released, Cochrane could now begin the painstaking processes of independently reviewing all of the original Tamiflu data—especially the claims about its impact on complications that had proved so critical for pandemic preparedness and international stockpiling efforts.

Most people would probably have given up trying to get access to all the clinical trial data for Tamiflu much sooner—especially given the great resistance the group encountered along the way. However, the Cochrane team's dogged determination and unconventional tactics had finally begun to pay off. After a protracted battle with Roche, the Cochrane Collaboration had managed to break new ground with this significant development. Indeed, its Tamiflu report would mark the first time in its history that a Cochrane review would be based on "all relevant full clinical study reports of a family of drugs, integrated by regulatory comments" (Jefferson, Jones, Doshi, and Spencer et al. 2014). It was a major breakthrough the Cochrane Collaboration had fought fiercely and long to achieve, and Tamiflu stood at the center of all of these fascinating developments.

Updating the Cochrane Review

What conclusion did the Cochrane team come to after having the chance to analyze all of the additional data? After the many years of battling on, had they actually discovered anything markedly new or different from what the company had initially claimed? The updated Cochrane review (Jefferson, Jones, Doshi, and Spencer et al. 2014)—which runs to well over 500 pages—found that oseltamivir reduces time to first alleviation of symptoms in adults by 16.8 hours, representing a reduction from 7 to 6.3 days. That was broadly in accordance with the findings of several other studies that had already been published. However, the authors also concluded that "treatment trials with oseltamivir or zanamivir do not settle the question of whether the complications of influenza (such as pneumonia) are reduced, because of a lack of diagnostic definitions" (Jefferson, Jones, Doshi, and Del Mar et al. 2014). The study, in other words, did not find sufficiently compelling evidence to support Roche's earlier and very public claims about Tamiflu's ability to reduce complications that had also formed part of the rationale for government stockpiling.

Among many other findings, the Cochrane review also reminded readers that any benefits of the antiviral would still have to be balanced with its harms: the "trade-off between benefits and harms should be borne in mind when making decisions to use oseltamivir for treatment, prophylaxis, or stockpiling" (Jefferson, Jones, Doshi, and Spencer et al. 2014). In characteristic style, Ben Goldacre helps to visualize some of these "trade-offs" in much more accessible—if also quite graphic—terms: "Since percentages are hard to randomize, we can make those numbers more tangible by taking the figures from the Cochrane review, and applying them. For example, if a million people take Tamiflu in a pandemic, 45,000 will experience vomiting, 31,000 will experience headache and 11,000 will have psychiatric side-effects. Remember, though, that those figures all assume we are only giving Tamiflu to a million people: if things kick off, we have stockpiled enough for 80% of the population. That's quite a lot of vomit" (Goldacre 2014). The updated review, in short, was not a great outcome for Roche and would do little to rebuild public trust in the public battering that Tamiflu's reputation had already taken. Not surprisingly, Roche quickly contested the findings of the 2014 Cochrane study. "We disagree with the overall conclusions," the company pointed out in a statement and warned that this could also "potentially have serious public health implications" (Gallagher 2014). Roche has since also written an extensive and detailed response to the Cochrane review (posted on the Cochrane website) running to some 69 pages (Clinch et al. 2014).

Broadly speaking, there are at least three key areas of contestation between Roche and Cochrane. One of Roche's chief concerns is that the Cochrane report fails to take into account the totality of data available for Tamiflu—namely, that it only considered 20 out of 77 clinical trials available to them in the end and that it excluded real-world data from observational (nonrandomized) trials (Rollerhagen and Braxton 2016: 6). One key area of ongoing debate between the researchers and the company thus revolves around the question of which kinds of data should be included in forming a view on this issue. Should all of the clinical trials be included or only a proportion of them? Moreover, should analysts solely consider randomized controlled trials or also other forms of evidence, such as that coming from nonrandomized studies that observe patients in their clinical settings?

A second major area of ongoing debate is the extent to which data from *seasonal* flu can be applied to making decisions about *pandemic* flu. Roche argues that "clinical data reviewed by Cochrane specifically looks at the effectiveness and safety of Tamiflu in *seasonal* influenza, and excludes data relating to the use of the medicine in a pandemic setting. To this end, it is insufficient to infer conclusions on the use of Tamiflu in pandemic influenza"

(Rollerhagen and Braxton 2016: 6). The clinical trials, in other words, were designed with the intention of obtaining regulatory approval for *seasonal* flu and not really to answer wider questions about their public health use (ECDC 2016: 18). Irrespective of the findings of the Cochrane review, there would therefore be limits to how well the findings based on seasonal flu data could also be applied to a future flu pandemic—as the Janus-faced nature of flu begins to rear its head once more.

Yet a third area of contestation revolves around the question of whether these studies were ever designed to be sufficiently powerful to answer this question of complications. "The included trials in the latest [2014] systematic review," three influenza experts argue, "were not appropriately designed or powered to assess the effect of neuraminidase inhibitors on life-threatening complications, and absence of a reliable signal on the reduction of complications from such underpowered RCTs does not imply absence of effect" (Nguyen-Van-Tam et al. 2014). Peter Openshaw, director of the Centre for Respiratory Infection at Imperial College, London, even expressed concern that because of the media headlines generated by the 2014 Cochrane review "we risk losing one of the few weapons we have, because of overly negative publicity" (quoted in Butler 2014).

On the one hand, then, the political campaign around making the Tamiflu data public has been remarkably successful. The combination of mobilizing public opinion, targeting the regulators, and using the little-known office of the European Ombudsman seems to have eventually forced Roche's hand and produced the desired outcome for the Cochrane Collaboration. On the other hand, the major breakthrough has arguably also come at a price. Some members of the scientific and public health communities are concerned that the lines between science and campaigning may have become blurred in the course of the protracted Tamiflu skirmishes. Kevin McConway, a professor of applied statistics at Open University in the United Kingdom, thus argues that the Cochrane review was an impressive piece of work but that "it is a potential limitation of this study that the work has been carried out alongside campaigning on access to trial data" (quoted in Gallagher 2014). In his view "The writers of the review have a clear position in this controversy, and, although I personally do generally agree with their position, I feel it does at times lead to some confusion between reporting the results of the review of these particular drugs and commenting on the general position on access to and use of unpublished data" (quoted in Galla-gher 2014).

Even though the campaign on Tamiflu was ultimately successful in terms of getting the data released, then, some remain uncomfortable about the perceived blending of science and campaigning that occurred along the way. It is also worth noting that, the generally very high reputation of Co-chrane reviews notwithstanding, in the case of Tamiflu its findings have not been accepted uncritically. Both the CDC and the Infectious Diseases Soci-ety of America, for instance, issued statements explicitly clarifying that they would not be changing their recommendations in light of the latest Co-chrane report.

All of that said, there is also one final twist to this whole chapter in the life of Tamiflu. It is not very widely known that Thomas Jefferson, who led the Cochrane review of Tamiflu, had himself worked for Hoffman-LaRoche as an ad hoc consultant in the past. Anyone who takes the time to read the small print on his publications can easily discover this for themselves, as Jefferson has openly declared this relationship within the context of conflict-of-interest disclosures required by many scientific journals. An ar-ticle from 2011, for example, notes that Thomas Jefferson "has been an ad hoc consultant for Hoffman-La Roche" (Cochrane Neuraminidase Inhibitors Review Team 2011: 1303). His employment at the company was also con-firmed by Roche: "Thomas Jefferson was a consultant for Roche; he worked on data sets related to Tamiflu. He contributed to a number of abstracts ex-ploring the efficacy of Tamiflu and its impact on reducing complications" (Rollerhagen and Braxton 2016: 7). It turns out that the researcher leading the Cochrane review of Tamiflu was himself a former consultant for Roche who had worked on Tamiflu for the company.

The Roche Response: Managing the Cochrane Fallout

By this stage in the ongoing data "wars" over Tamiflu it looked as though events were beginning to overtake Roche and that the company was going to have to surrender a significant degree of control over access to the full clinical trial data for Tamiflu. Given its concerns about the Cochrane ap-proach, what options did the company have to pursue its own interests? Even though the company could not control what Cochrane ultimately did with the Tamiflu data, Roche could still use its considerable financial muscle to populate the public space with a number of additional studies that would—it hoped at least—show Tamiflu in a more favorable light. Roche was certainly not going to roll over without putting up a fight.

First, Roche approached other leading scientists and invited them to re-analyze the clinical trial data underpinning the original Kaiser study. In 2010 Roche thus made the Tamiflu data available to Marc Lipsitch at Harvard University. This new Harvard analysis would end up broadly confirming an effect of Tamiflu on complications, albeit a slightly more modest one than the Kaiser study had initially reported (Hernán and Lipsitch 2011: 277). Yet if Roche had hoped that this new study would resolve the brewing controversy, it was mistaken. The Cochrane Collaboration quickly countered by raising a number of concerns about the Harvard study. It questioned whether it was even possible to meta-analyze complications in this manner—especially as the trials did not use standardized definitions of secondary complications. The Cochrane group was also concerned that the study appeared, in its view, to engage in selective reporting, or "cherry-picking," by focusing only on some indicators of complications but not others. Finally, the group also expressed concerns whether sufficient cross-checks had been performed on the data and reiterated the need to secure access to the full clinical study reports (Jones 2011). Instead of resolving the issue of complications, the battle over access and control to the data only heated up further.

Roche next funded a separate, larger study of the impact of Tamiflu on complications. To do so, the company even helped to set up a whole new consortium called the Multiparty Group for Advice on Science (MUGAS) which would help enhance "public health security by addressing unsolved scientific issues that hamper public health guidance" (MUGAS 2014b). The core idea was that the new MUGAS consortium could provide greater clarity in areas where there are confusing, ambiguous, or mixed messages: "When confusion threatens to hamper public health policies, the MUGAS Foundation offers a solution to settle the scientific debate" (MUGAS 2014a). Tamiflu's role in reducing complications was the first controversy ever to be considered by the new MUGAS consortium. In fact, it remained the only project the initiative has taken on at the time of writing.

In the case of Tamiflu, the MUGAS study wished to analyze the impact of oseltamivir in the treatment of seasonal influenza, looking at symptom alleviation, complications, and safety. Rather than just carrying out yet another study with the data for the original Kaiser study, however, this would now be a bigger study including *all* published *and* unpublished Roche-sponsored randomized placebo-controlled, double-blind trials of 75 mg oseltamivir administered twice a day in adults (Dobson et al. 2015). The new study would also be based on individual patient data rather than on aggregated study results—which is often seen to be preferable for meta-analyses (Kelly and Cowling 2015: 1701). Like the Harvard study before it, the results of the MUGAS study seemed to broadly confirm the earlier findings of the initial Kaiser study (Dobson et al. 2015: 1729).

And just like the earlier Harvard study before it, the new MUGAS study too would not settle the controversy. That is because the entire initiative was perceived to suffer from at least one major drawback. The MUGAS study was funded through an unrestricted grant from Roche. The grant clearly stipulated that Roche would not be involved in the analysis in any way, barring providing the necessary data dictionaries and data sets (Dobson et al. 2015: 1732). Roche provided access to the individual patient data via secure web access and provided data clarifications, but it was not involved in the design, conduct, or reporting of the meta-analysis (Dobson et al. 2015: 1730). The results were also not shared with Roche until the analysis had been completed (Dobson et al. 2015: 1732). Still, the MUGAS initiative tends to divide opinion. For some people, including members of the Cochrane Collaboration, the fact that the funding still comes from the industry ultimately taints the findings and undermines its overall credibility (Couzin-Frankel 2015; Silverman 2015). Those backing the MUGAS initiative counter that these questions are ultimately very important for public health and that it would be extremely complicated to try to secure public funding for such studies.

In either case, the arrival of the H1N1 swine flu pandemic in 2009 would also present Roche with a third opportunity for generating more information about this vexing issue—this time by considering a different type of data altogether. The two studies discussed above had been carried out with randomized, placebo-controlled trials for *seasonal* flu. Generally speaking, randomized controlled trials are viewed as the least biased type of evidence for assessing pharmaceutical products. That is also why the Cochrane Collaboration only uses such trials for conducting its meta-analyses. Yet public health organizations often also consider other types of "weaker" data, such as observational data, especially where such trial data do not exist. With the arrival of the H1N1 pandemic, it would now be possible to also look at such observational data from the use of Tamiflu during the H1N1 pandemic.

Professor Jonathan Nguyen-Van-Tam, who also worked for Roche in the past but now works at the University of Nottingham, led a team carrying out a meta-analysis of patient data to look at the effects of neuraminidase inhibitors on deaths for hospitalized patients with confirmed or suspected H1N1 infection. The Post-Pandemic Review of Anti-Influenza Drug Effectiveness (PRIDE) study was again made possible by an unrestricted educational grant from Roche. The headline results suggested that neuraminidase inhibitors were associated with statistically significant reductions in mortality risk (Muthuri et al. 2014). As Nguyen-Van-Tam put it at the time, "I continue to believe neuraminidase inhibitors are a useful drug for patients with severe flu who are hospitalised. Cochrane only accepted randomised control trials. If we had that sort of data we would give it primacy, but we don't live in that world. We needed to use observational data" (quoted in Jack 2014).

Like the previous two studies, however, this one too would not put an end to the controversy. Within 48 hours of the study being published in *Lancet Respiratory Medicine*, the *BMJ* published an article claiming that the new study "was based on flawed analysis" (Nguyen-Van-Tam 2014). Nguyen-Van-Tam expressed both concern and surprise that the PRIDE consortium, which had undertaken the study, received no forewarning about the *BMJ* piece. The group was also not offered the customary right of reply (Nguyen-Van-Tam 2014). Yet such heated exchanges reveal just how contested and tense the whole debate about Tamiflu had become over the years. Indeed, a different study of the effect of oseltamivir on mortality in 2009A/H1N1 influenza patients has since also found insufficient evidence to support the view that oseltamivir reduces the risk of mortality for such patients (Heneghan et al. 2016).

It cannot be the aim of this book to determine who is right or wrong in these debates about the role Tamiflu in reducing complications and mortality. Some of those involved in the extensive Cochrane review themselves acknowledge how "even among institutions that aim to provide the least biased, objective assessments of a drug's effects, determining 'the truth' can be extremely difficult" (Doshi, Jefferson, and Del Mar 2012). Yet there are a number of reasons why all of these protracted controversies and disputes around Tamiflu are also highly significant for the whole area of medical countermeasures more generally.

First, they reveal just how intense the interest in the full clinical trial data (and also other data) became once Tamiflu entered into the political limelight as the first line of defense against pandemic H1N1 flu. It was precisely at the moment when there was the very real prospect of Tamiflu being administered to large parts of the population that the whole question of complications suddenly erupted as a major source of tension, debate, and controversy, putting the clinical trial data for Tamiflu under unprecedented scrutiny. Too much was at stake now to simply leave the analysis of all those data to the companies or the regulators alone. For any medical countermeasure that is going to be widely distributed to the population during a future emergency, there is likely to be intense public pressure to make *all* the data publicly available for further scrutiny.

Second, they suggest that in the face of such pressure, even powerful pharmaceutical companies (and regulatory agencies) will struggle to preserve traditional arrangements for accessing detailed clinical trial data. As a large pharmaceutical company, Roche tried to use its considerable power and influence to manage the persistent requests to hand the data over to the Cochrane Collaboration. Roche did this mostly by using its financial muscle to fund a number of additional studies on the issue. Those financial resources stood in stark contrast to the workings of the Cochrane Collaboration, which is a much looser network of people carrying out their work on what is, by comparison, a shoestring budget. According to Jefferson, the members carrying out the Cochrane review mostly "talk through Skype or via e-mail because we are penniless! We receive funds from the English government to perform this review, but they are pretty meagre" (Tinari et al. 2011: 8). The power differentials at play between different stakeholders in the Tamiflu data wars could not be starker.

Yet Roche still ended up releasing the information in the face of mounting public pressure. The European Medicines Agency too has since introduced a whole new policy on open access to clinical trial data for all new medicines approved for human use in the European Union. It has now become the first regulatory agency in the world to commit to making all clinical study reports submitted by pharmaceutical companies as part of their marketing applications openly available to researchers in the future (EMA 2016). All of this suggest that companies and regulators will ultimately struggle to preserve traditional arrangements in this area—especially when it comes to high-profile medical countermeasures used in an emergency.

Finally, the various responses and debates prompted by those additional studies also show that none of Roche's three strategies have ultimately succeeded in putting the Tamiflu controversy to bed once and for all. Despite the underlying power differentials and the multiple new studies produced, groups like the Cochrane Collaboration can still have a significant impact on the public debate and can be quite effective in terms of getting their voices heard—through use of the media, through online networking, through public campaigning, and so forth. Overall, this has led to an increase in the plurality of actors now commenting on these kinds of issues and to a diversification of perspectives on some of the key questions involved.

As a result, there are now several contrasting views circulating about which data sets should be included in analyses about the potential role of Tamiflu in pandemic preparedness. There are also diverging views among stakeholders about how exactly such analyses should be performed and who should pay for them (Boseley 2015). Different organizations even place different emphasis upon what types of data should ultimately count, on how to weigh different categories of evidence, and on what lessons can also be extrapolated from seasonal flu data for pandemic preparedness purposes (Hurt and Kelly 2016). Nor does it appear likely that much more meaningful clinical trial evidence will emerge over the next 5 to 10 years to clarify this issue, because of the difficulties associated with running such trials (Hurt and Kelly 2016). All of that also makes it much more challenging to create certainty and clarity for the publics who may eventually be asked to use—and ultimately also pay for—medical countermeasures like Tamiflu.

In the end, then, the protracted battle between the Cochrane researchers and Roche over access to Tamiflu's full clinical trial data also points to the tenth challenge that can arise around medical countermeasures more generally: access to data. During an actual emergency, detailed clinical trial data are likely to become the battleground for answering key questions about a medical countermeasure, such as "Does it work?" and "Is it safe?" The pressure for full public disclosure of all those data will probably be intense during such an emergency, when a medical countermeasure faces the very real prospect of suddenly being mass-distributed to the population in a short period of time.

In the case of Tamiflu, securing access to the data was thus deemed to be particularly important precisely because of the prospect of it being rolled out on a population-wide basis. "While the evidence base for all approved drugs should be sound," the Cochrane Collaboration argued in this regard, "the evidence base for public health drugs must be of the highest quality, publicly available and open to independent scrutiny" (Jefferson et al. 2010: 79). Medical and public health groups will be keen to have access to *all* the data in an emergency so that they can review it independently, while patients will also want to have independent reassurances that the product is safe and effective before taking it.

Yet there are also wider political reasons why calls for independent scrutiny of clinical trial data are likely to intensify for medical countermeasures, such as the considerable public expenditure involved in their procurement and stockpiling. Governments do not want to be seen by their electorates as squandering vast amounts of scarce public resources on treatments that cannot be shown to be effective or as unnecessarily propping up the profits of the pharmaceutical industry. Such financial considerations also formed a significant motivation for governments in commissioning the Cochrane Collaboration to update its review of Tamiflu. "The Cochrane Review update," Ben Goldacre explains, "was specifically triggered by the British and Australian governments writing to Cochrane and saying: we are considering spending a lot of money on stockpiling this, could you please update your review. So, the Cochrane review was actively solicited by governments because they were stockpiling" (Goldacre 2015). There are thus both public health and political considerations generating stronger demand for access to *all* the data for medical countermeasures.

More generally, then, recent experiences with Tamiflu also suggest that traditional arrangements for accessing clinical trial data—whereby access is principally controlled by pharmaceutical companies and restricted to regulators—may not be politically viable in relation to medical countermeasures during future emergencies. Too much is at stake, and other groups will also want to see all the data because of the potential safety issues and costs involved. Yet control of such data is also something that has historically been very important to the pharmaceutical industry, and which it has fought very hard and long to retain. At the end of the day, those pharmaceutical companies do not just produce "bare" molecules but what Andrew Barry calls "informed materials"—that is, molecules embedded in a thick "informational" and data-laden environment (Barry 2005). Companies view the data produced along the commercial development pathway as being absolutely integral to the pharmaceutical products that they end up selling. The fact that there will likely be greater political pressure to make all such data publicly available during an emergency can thus complicate matters further—especially from the perspective of pharmaceutical companies considering the development of new medical countermeasures. Determining which groups can access the full clinical trial data—and how—is therefore a tenth challenge to arise more generally around medical countermeasures. This tension also completes the final group of deployment challenges that can arise once an emergency has transpired and a new medical countermeasure is actually distributed to the population.

9

"To Boldly Go . . ."

Pharmaceutical Enterprises and Global Health Security

Tamiflu is approaching the end of its patent at the time of writing, and the sun is slowly beginning to set on the life of this prominent antiviral. What lessons does its checkered history yield for the wider quest to develop new pharmaceutical defenses in the twenty-first century? Three lessons stand out above all. First, the experiences with Tamiflu reveal just how complicated the process of securing populations pharmaceutically is in practice. Retracing the many unexpected twists and turns in the life of Tamiflu unearths a complex array of policy tensions and competing stakeholder interests present at every stage of a medical countermeasure's life. Securing populations pharmaceutically thus entails a lot more than just designing a few new pharmaceutical products. Governments also need to put into place the many wider systems necessary for ensuring that they can use such products effectively during future emergencies.

Second, the Tamiflu story shows that the introduction of security logics into commercial processes of pharmaceutical production generates a lot of added tensions. The extraordinary security context within which medical countermeasures would be deployed gives rise to new problems at pretty much every stage in the life course of a medial countermeasure—from its initial development, via its acquisition by governments, all the way through to its eventual use during an emergency. The many challenges surrounding the development of new medical countermeasures thus also differ in crucial respects from the ones associated with more routine pharmaceutical products. If developing safe and effective new medicines is complicated at the best of times, it is even more so when it comes to medical countermeasures intended to address an array of much more unpredictable biological threats.

Finally, the Tamiflu story also reveals that there is no "magic bullet" that will suddenly stimulate companies to develop such new pharmaceutical defenses. There are just too many steps, costs, risks, and uncertainties involved in the process. Governments are only likely to improve outcomes by designing much broader policy initiatives that concurrently address the many overlapping financial, legal, regulatory, developmental, production, and distribution challenges that arise over the life course of a medical countermeasure. That is why some governments are already taking the seemingly quite drastic step of designing new and specialized pharmaceutical regimes for the explicit purpose of developing such new medical countermeasures.

This chapter reviews some of the broader lessons about medial countermeasures that governments and companies are taking away from their formative experiences with Tamiflu over the past decade. It then goes on to map the extensive new medical countermeasure enterprise that has begun to take shape in the United States in response to those challenges. Finally, it moves on to the bigger question of whether that US enterprise could also form the basis for a geographically much wider initiative to strengthen global health security in the twenty-first century. What, in other words, would it actually take for governments to arrive at a point at which in the future they could make lifesaving medical countermeasures rapidly available to the world in response to deadly outbreaks occurring around the world?

Governments Take Stock: To Stockpile . . . or Not to Stockpile?

With the dust beginning to settle on Tamiflu, what lessons do the major stakeholders take away from their experience with the antiviral over the past decade? Many governments, for one, are now stuck with all those sizable and costly Tamiflu stocks they acquired from Roche as part of their pandemic preparedness planning. The major problem they face is that those stocks will eventually expire. When governments first began stockpiling Tamiflu, no one knew for certain how long the antiviral's shelf life would be. Pharmaceutical products are not really designed to be stockpiled for long periods of time. The shelf life for Tamiflu capsules was initially set at five years. With governments starting to stockpile in 2004, decisions about replenishing would have had to be made as early as 2009 (Reddy 2010: ii38).

As longer-term stability data for Tamiflu subsequently became available, however, Tamiflu's shelf life was extended from five to seven years in the United States and Europe (Reddy 2010: ii38). That bought governments valuable time to figure out the best way forward. Yet sooner or later governments will have to make some difficult decisions.

Are governments still likely to replenish those stockpiles following all the controversies that have engulfed Tamiflu over the intervening years? We have seen that some of the initial rationales for government stockpiling have since become subject to more extensive debate—especially around the issue of complications. New concerns about the possibility of rare but potentially more harmful side effects have also surfaced since many of those initial stockpiling decisions were taken. Overall, the wider debate about the wisdom of stockpiling Tamiflu has thus become much more contested with the passing of time. One of the coauthors of the 2014 Cochrane Review, Carl Heneghan, even argues that, after all the clinical trial data are reviewed, there is "no credible way these drugs could prevent a pandemic" and that stockpiles were "money thrown down the drain" (quoted in Butler 2014). All of this means that government decisions about stockpiling will become more difficult moving forward.

Yet governments will likely also consider a range of other factors when making their final decisions about stockpiling. Governments may conclude that in the event of a pandemic even a small or modest effect would still be beneficial when aggregated to the level of the population. "Even small individual effects," Jonathan Nguyen-Van-Tam argues with regard to neuraminidase inhibitors, "can have a large impact when applied across whole populations" (Van-Tam 2010: ii3). Irrespective of the issue of other outcomes—such as complications, hospitalizations, and mortality—a modest reduction in symptom duration could be seen to be significant in a pandemic context. If Tamiflu could also achieve such a reduction during a pandemic (which nobody can know for certain in advance), governments might conclude that this would have desirable effects at the aggregate population level and tip the balance in favor of stockpiling. Of course, officials would then still need to weigh any such potential benefits against the possible harms.

Beyond that, antivirals also remain one of the few measures that governments would have available at their disposal during the *early* phases of a pandemic, when a virus-specific vaccine would not yet be widely available.

One influenza scientist, Wendy Barclay, argues that "they should replenish the stockpile. What else can you do if a pandemic strikes? We won't have a vaccine for the first six months. . . . If it works a little bit in seasonal flu, the chances are they'll work quite a lot better in a pandemic situation and get more people back to school and work' (quoted in Gallagher 2014). Even today, Tamiflu is still one of the few pharmaceutical interventions that governments could utilize while they wait for a strain-specific pandemic influenza vaccine to eventually become available. This point was also echoed by the UK's chief medical officer, Dame Sally Davis, who explained before Parliament that "we have to protect our public in that first six to 12 months. The only known protection is the antivirals, and we knew that if we waited for a pandemic, everyone would be panicking and demanding them" (PAC 2013). That remains the case today, much as it was when the stockpiles were created.

During the onset of a new pandemic, governments will likely also be under considerable political pressure simply "to do something" (Jack 2009). Some have therefore come close to portraying such antiviral stockpiles as being akin to an expedient mass placebo—but one that could nevertheless help with stemming social anxiety and panic during a pandemic. Pandemics, a famous saying goes, always arrive as twins. There is the "biological," or "epidemiological," pandemic, but it is usually accompanied by an equally debilitating social pandemic of fear and panic (Strong 1990). Even if the drug turns out not to be that effective clinically during a future flu pandemic, governments also need to manage the social fear and anxiety that such events provoke. In her capacity as editor in chief of *BMJ*, Fiona Godlee made a very similar point when addressing a UK parliamentary committee about the Tamiflu stockpile: "I think it was politically expedient. There was an outbreak of potentially serious influenza. . . . The UK was confronted with a situation in which it wanted something. There isn't anything else for pandemic flu. To cut a long answer short, I would say it was bread and circuses to keep the populace happy, and I think it was misleading and wrong, especially as the alternative, paracetamol, is well understood, and Tamiflu has adverse effects, apart from its cost" (PAC 2013). Even she acknowledged, though, that this was ultimately a difficult call for politicians (and medical officers) to make—as they were facing a serious problem (PAC 2013).

Finally, governments will probably also contemplate the political risks involved with deciding *not* to stockpile. What would happen if a deadly influenza pandemic subsequently materializes and it then transpired that the government had decided *against* stockpiling—meaning that citizens were now unable to access potentially lifesaving antivirals? "Pandemic planners," some influenza experts argue, "must consider all evidence and weigh this against the risks of inaction and the likely public outcry if potentially life-saving drugs are not available in the face of unpredictable, but potentially severe, future influenza outbreaks" (Van-Tam et al. 2014). In the event of a pandemic, the decision *not* to stockpile could conceivably have career-limiting effects for any officials involved and could be electorally extremely damaging for any government as a whole. After all, people will likely look to their government in the first instance to protect them during a pandemic.

Perhaps such thinking also helps to explain why some experts were not at all surprised that so many governments decided to stockpile Tamiflu in the end. When asked about those stockpiles during an interview, one expert even immediately turned the question around and asked: "Who would have dared *not* to stockpile a medicine that clearly has efficacy against influenza? It would have been very courageous not to stockpile" (Kurki 2015). Given that in some countries the protection of the individual is even considered the paramount duty of government, such a decision would have been very difficult to justify politically. Confronted with this choice, many politicians and public health planners would prefer to err on the side of caution. As Patrick Mathys of the Swiss Federal Agency for Health (*Bundesamt fuer Gesundheit*) put it with exemplary candor, "Perhaps some will later say we were exceedingly cautious and went too far. But I can live very well with this accusation" (quoted in Vetterli 2009; my translation).

The entire question of whether or not to stockpile Tamiflu thus continues to pose a profound political dilemma for government officials. If they replenish the stockpiles and there is no pandemic, they are open to accusations of wasting scarce public resources. If they do not stockpile, a pandemic arrives, and the antiviral proves effective against the virus, they could then be open to accusations of negligence. Angus Nicoll and Marc Sprenger explain this wider predicament with reference to their experiences with pandemic preparedness efforts in Europe: "In all this unpredictability it seems one certainty was that when a pandemic happened the policy makers would be criticized. If it was a bad pandemic they would be criticized for not doing enough. If it was not so bad (and European Centre for Disease Prevention and Control and others have argued that the 2009 was about the best pandemic Europe could have hoped for) they would be criticized for over-preparation, wastefulness and *shroud-waving*" (Nicoll and Sprenger 2011: 191). Decisions about whether or not to stockpile remain shrouded in an irreducible degree of scientific uncertainty, and political factors will also have to be taken into consideration in the end. That was also the conclusion that a high-profile parliamentary inquiry in the United Kingdom arrived at: "the case for stockpiling antiviral medicines at the current levels is based on judgement rather than evidence of their effectiveness during an influenza pandemic" (PAC 2013).

In either case, government decisions about future stockpiling have undoubtedly become more complex since those early days and on the back of all of the public controversies that have engulfed Tamiflu over the intervening years. During this time, citizens have also been confronted with at least two major pandemic flu scares. The first threat—H5N1 (or bird flu) in 2003–2006—did not become a pandemic. The second one—H1N1 (or swine flu) in 2009–2010—did become a pandemic according to the World Health Organization but did not match the more apocalyptic scenarios that many had feared. Yet many members of the public were still asked by their governments to take the antiviral drug and have also seen substantial public funds used to create and maintain large Tamiflu stockpiles—from which pharmaceutical companies profited considerably. Overall, these experiences are likely to have weakened public confidence in such stockpiles, a problem that even the industry acknowledges. Richard Bergstrom of the European Federation of Pharmaceutical Industries and Associations thus argues:

> We also need to reflect on why is it that in the eyes of the public this was so strange that you would buy products for tens of millions of euros or hundreds of millions of euros and stockpile it in case of [an] emergency situation, and you buy this from a private company. This time it was an outcry in many countries, but we do stockpiling all the time for other things. We have emergency supplies for natural disasters. . . . [During] the Cold War we used to have all this stockpiling of everything—clothes, food, oil, everything—and of course this is something that came from the private sector. So there is something wrong here in our explanation about the role of the private sector in developing and providing security. So to me when I look back [on] all of this, it was technically a success story, [but] public-wise it was not. Let's learn from this, we need to ap-

ply this going forward on areas like antibiotics and other viral threats and even threats of bioterrorism. That we need to explain this all in a much better way to the general public. (Bergstrom 2013)

The publics, in other words, are still likely to be quite confused as to whether or not their governments should continue to stockpile the antiviral. With time, government decisions about stockpiling have only become more complicated, not less so.

Roche and the Lessons from Tamiflu

What about Roche? What lessons does the company, in turn, take away from its experiences with Tamiflu? Roche has managed to dramatically reverse the commercial fortunes of Tamiflu on the back of such health security considerations. In fact, the company ended up achieving quite handsome revenues from the antiviral's second life as a highly lucrative medical countermeasure against pandemic flu. Yet—and highly significantly—this does not mean that Roche will also develop other new medical countermeasures in the future. Roche does believe that pharmaceutical companies have an important role to play in this area, but the company also makes it quite clear that it would take on a new medical countermeasure project only if it aligns with Roche's wider business strategy. Generally speaking, two Roche spokespeople point out, the company will prioritize those diseases and conditions where they have a good understanding of the biology, as well as an ability to target some relevant part of it with either a small or large molecule intervention (Rollerhagen and Braxton 2016: 9).

If a new medical countermeasure were to fit with these principles, and with Roche's broader business strategy, the company would likely pursue it. That was certainly true for Tamiflu, where the company was mostly pursuing the lucrative market for seasonal flu. Roche has since had some discussions with BARDA in the United States regarding the potential development of an intravenous formulation of oseltamivir. Yet if those wider conditions are not met, the company is unlikely to prioritize such products, and—rather tellingly—there are no active agreements for medical countermeasures at the time of writing (Rollerhagen and Braxton 2016: 8).

Nor are medical countermeasures likely to be much of a priority for the company in the foreseeable future. The process of developing them remains too risky and too uncertain commercially. As the company further explains,

"The pharma business model already involves a significant level of investment risk. While the risks associated with the development of a medicine to treat a known disease is one thing, developing a medical countermeasure to mitigate a pandemic or attack which may or may not happen increases the investment risk still further. While such developments are crucial, the funding model of the industry makes such research investments very challenging" (Rollerhagen and Braxton 2016: 9). As one looks across the company as a whole, Tamiflu will probably go down very much as a commercial exception for Roche and not at all as the rule. Roche, in short, is still not particularly interested in the whole field of medical countermeasures—even after all of the money it has made from Tamiflu.

More generally Roche's experiences with Tamiflu thus suggest that governments will continue to face an uphill struggle in trying to engage large pharmaceutical companies in the quest to develop new medical countermeasures. That lack of engagement by large pharmaceutical companies continues to be a defining feature, and also major obstacle, to the development of new medical countermeasures moving forward. After all, those large pharmaceutical companies possess immense—even unparalleled—expertise in terms of their technical and production know-how about pharmaceutical products. They also have considerable funding at their disposal as well as many decades of experience designing new medicines. The prospects for developing new medical countermeasures could thus be greatly improved in the future by the closer involvement of large pharmaceutical companies in those efforts.

With only a few notable exceptions, however, "Big Pharma" continues to eschew the area of medical countermeasures. Not much has changed in that regard, even after the lucrative Tamiflu experience, exposing real limits to the power of governments to shape the priorities of large commercial pharmaceutical companies. Indeed, it remains uncertain whether any government today even has the power to persuade a large pharmaceutical company like Roche to develop a medical countermeasure that the company would not already want to develop for other reasons.

Nor is there really any easy way for governments to get around this challenge—especially without generating new tensions in so doing. One option, of course, would be for governments to simply constitute such a medical countermeasure market artificially. They could conceivably use significant public funds in order to make advance commitments that they will purchase a set number of medical countermeasures at a predetermined price. Doing so would certainly help reduce uncertainty and increase commercial rewards for a company developing a new medical countermeasure. This was broadly the approach taken by the George W. Bush administration through its BioShield program. Much ink has already been spilled over the billions of dollars pledged for new medical countermeasure development under Project BioShield in the United States. Yet in a commercial context where it can, according to some industry estimates, cost on average in the range of $800 million to $ 1.5 billion to develop a new drug or vaccine (Cole 2013: 24), Project BioShield's funding of a $5.6 billion dollar special reserve fund over 10 years of procurement seems fairly modest—given the broad range of potential health security threats that have to be considered.

What is more, even this level of funding has already attracted significant political controversy—indicating that there are economic and political limits to pursuing such a strategy. The financial sums that would be required to constitute such markets artificially across a whole range of biological threats would rapidly attain dimensions likely to exceed what citizens would tolerate in terms of "shifting" public funds to pharmaceutical companies. Politically, it could start to look as though pharmaceutical companies were trying to enrich themselves from the security concerns of the taxpayer. The attempt of many governments to control public expenditure after a financial crisis also makes such an approach increasingly unrealistic. So there are very real political, and increasingly also financial, limits to pursing such a strategy of trying to artificially constitute a medical countermeasure market through the use of public funds.

Short of utilizing the public purse to artificially create such a market, governments wishing to encourage the development of new medical countermeasures are essentially left with two other options. First, they could try to prioritize the development of medical countermeasures for those threats where such parallel commercial markets do exist—much as they do in the case of flu. For diseases where such a dual commercial and medical countermeasure market exists, a new drug could have both "normal" and health security applications. The experience with neuraminidase inhibitors suggests that for diseases with such a dual market, it is possible for governments to acquire new medical countermeasures even without having to actively incentivize companies to do so—because the commercial market will do so on its own. The one rather obvious drawback with this strategy, however, is that there are only a very limited number of health security threats that possess such a parallel commercial market—and most do not. It would simply leave many other health security threats unaddressed.

A second option would be for governments to encourage pharmaceutical companies to develop more broad-spectrum medical countermeasures. These would consist of new drugs that may simultaneously work across a range of different diseases, conditions, and threats. We have already seen how one of the key attractions of neuraminidase inhibitors is that they showed activity across a range of different influenza viruses, thus increasing the potential size of the market. Stretching that principal further, if new medical countermeasures could be developed that work against a number of different diseases, this could again be a commercially much more attractive proposition and would make the market both more predictable and more sizable. It would effectively represent a different way of doubling up and building a bigger market. Such a strategy might work, for example, in cases where a potential biothreat generates symptoms or biological reactions similar to those for which commercial drugs are already available (Wizemann et al. 2010: 133–134).

Again, however, there are obvious issues with such an approach—not least whether it is actually scientifically possible to develop such treatments. Even where such a strategy could work scientifically, there would still be a need for a supplementary strategy to deal with the large number of threats where this is not the case. There are just no easy options for governments wishing to procure new pharmaceutical defenses for their populations. Even after all the formative experiences with Tamiflu, developing new medical countermeasures will likely remain an uphill struggle for governments moving forward.

Yet new international outbreaks alerts have continued to come in fast and thick since the H1N1 pandemic. The year 2012 witnessed the emergence of human fatalities caused by a new coronavirus leading to MERS. The disease was first reported in Saudi Arabia and kills around 3 to 4 out of every 10 people who are reported to be infected. Since then cases have also been reported in Europe, the Middle East, and Asia. In 2013 instances of lethal human infections with a new avian H7N9 influenza virus arose in China, again generating considerable international alarm and causing more than 200 deaths in China already. The world then also experienced its largest outbreak of Ebola to date, causing high-level international concern and prompting another meeting of the United Nations Security Council. In 2015, the world was caught off guard once more—this time by the unexpected spread of Zika virus in South America and beyond. Protective medical countermeasures were not available at the height of any of those outbreaks because many of the underlying problems associated with their development and use remain unresolved. Even as they close the books on Tamiflu, therefore, governments need to think hard about how they could do better for their populations against an array of biological dangers in future.

Looking Ahead to the Next One: Building a Medical Countermeasures Enterprise

Will governments ever get to a point where they could rapidly make lifesaving new medical countermeasures available to populations in response to such deadly outbreaks? One key benefit of revisiting the whole Tamiflu story is that it reveals what major challenges would first need to be overcome. Ten such challenges have been identified in total—spread across three different groups: development challenges, acquisition challenges, and deployment challenges. If governments want to rapidly make new medical countermeasures available to their populations during future outbreaks, they need to be able to address *all* of these challenges first. The ten key challenges can be succinctly recounted now.

First, there are the initial development challenges associated with designing a new medical countermeasure. Those early challenges are *scientific*, as we have seen just how demanding the scientific development of new medical countermeasures can be. Going through this process takes a considerable amount of time, and success often involves a mixture of rational drug design and serendipity. These early challenges are also *economic* because developing new medical countermeasures is very risky and expensive, and yet there is no commercial market for most of these products. Unless a way of sharing the commercial risks can be found, financing their development will remain difficult for commercially operating companies. Finally, these early challenges also include navigating the *late-stage development* processes for pharmaceutical products, such as clinical trials, manufacturing, and so forth. With large pharmaceutical companies unlikely to prioritize medical countermeasures, many promising drug candidates will be overlooked and never be properly developed into full-fledged medical countermeasures.

If all those initial hurdles can be overcome and a new medical countermeasure is successfully developed, a second set of challenges comes into play about how governments would then transform such products into a functioning medical countermeasure capability. Here there are additional *regulatory* challenges that arise in actually getting the new product officially approved, so that governments can then proceed to acquire them for their stockpiles. Governments also face further challenges here in properly gauging their levels of *demand* for such products, given that it can oscillate wildly with fluctuating events on the ground, and it may simply be too late to leave their procurement until an emergency occurs. Even when governments manage this problem through advance stockpiling of medical countermeasures, they still have to consider the complex *logistical* challenges around how they would rapidly get the right number of medical countermeasures to the right people at the right time—and when normal distribution channels may well have become severely disrupted.

Should an emergency then occur, and a new medical countermeasure actually has to be deployed to the population at large, there is yet a third set of challenges that quickly comes into play. Depending on the scale of the outbreak, there will likely be a *scaling up* challenge in terms of manufacturing and production. Global demand for any medical countermeasures can increase dramatically during an outbreak or crisis, introducing new challenges around how to rapidly scale up production capacity to meet such a surge in international demand. If it is not possible to meet that demand, the resulting inequality in terms of international access can quickly generate new international diplomatic tensions and lead to calls for allowing generic production—also raising tensions around *intellectual property* and the protection of *patents*. During such a crisis, there is also a further challenge in terms of dealing with the *liabilities* for possible injuries that might arise, because rapidly rolling out a new medical countermeasure to a large number of people during a health emergency could lead to the emergence of harmful side effects. Especially for products destined for use in such health emergencies, there will likely also be strong calls for *all* the clinical trial data to be made publicly accessible so as to enable independent scrutiny about their effectiveness and safety, making *data access* a final challenge that can emerge at that point. Any government wishing to secure their populations pharmaceutically in the future will thus need to successfully manage a large number of different challenges simultaneously. That is one key lesson to emerge from the whole Tamiflu story.

Just as important, however, is that many of these challenges also differ in crucial respects from those usually associated with more routine pharmaceutical development. At almost every stage in the life course of a new medical countermeasure, the introduction of security logics into commercial processes of pharmaceutical development generates new issues and problems. Economically, the unpredictability of health-based security threats makes it much more difficult for companies to build viable business models around the costly development of new medical countermeasures. From the regulatory perspective, the comparative rarity or dangerousness of the pathogens involved also makes it much more difficult to conduct the clinical trials that would normally be required for gaining regulatory approval. On the production and manufacturing side, governments trying to manage a crisis may urgently require access to a volume of medical countermeasures far exceeding what routine production systems can supply in a short period of time. Logistically, governments may also be unable to rely on existing pharmaceutical distribution systems to get medical countermeasures to their citizens during an emergency. The legal picture similarly becomes more complicated in a security context because governments may have to act in extraordinary ways during an emergency (e.g., using drugs that are not yet approved) and because the large volume of people suddenly taking a medical countermeasure could provoke overwhelming lawsuits if harmful side effects subsequently surface. From virtually every angle, then, the complex entanglement of pharmaceutical and security logics generates new tensions that differ in key respects from those associated with more routine pharmaceuticals. Existing systems for developing and handling pharmaceutical products may therefore not work very well for medical countermeasures. That too is an important lesson to emerge from the whole Tamiflu story.

All of these challenges coalesce to form a vexing Gordian knot of policy issues around medical countermeasures in the twenty-first century. There is not just the large number of different challenges that have to be considered. There are also all the intricate interconnections between various stages in the life course of a medical countermeasure that have to be factored in. On top of that, there is the sheer breadth of different issues, actors, and professional fields involved in the effort. Medical countermeasures evidently live very complex social lives and any government wishing to protect its populations pharmaceutically will therefore need to do so much more than just ensure pharmaceutical companies develop a few new products; they will also have to put into place effective governance mechanisms across *all* of the many policy challenges we have encountered along the way.

How could all of this ever be done in practice? A final lesson to emerge here from the Tamiflu story is that there can be no quick fix or "magic bullet" policy solution that will suddenly spur pharmaceutical companies into developing more medical countermeasures in the future. As should be evident by now, there are simply too many competing challenges, actors, interests, and tensions involved. Governments wishing to encourage the commercial development of new medical countermeasures will instead have to design a much broader and more comprehensive policy framework that simultaneously deploys a multiplicity of measures. Governments will effectively have to mobilize, adapt, and redistribute the various levers of the state in such a way that it has the overall effect of more strongly incentivizing pharmaceutical companies to develop such new medical countermeasures in the future. That would require nothing short of a bold, new, and wide-ranging political initiative that is willing to do many things differently in relation to pharmaceuticals, that can galvanize the many different stakeholders involved in such an effort, and that can also continuously orchestrate all of these many moving parts toward the common purpose.

Can any government feasibly introduce such a bold initiative capable of untying the Gordian knot around medical countermeasures? So far the US government has tried harder than most by launching what it calls the medical countermeasures enterprise—precisely in order to reflect the fundamentally risky but also bold and wide-ranging nature of the political undertaking required to realize the medical countermeasure vision. The stakeholders involved in that enterprise today include a diverse range of federal government departments (Health and Human Services, Defense, Homeland Security, Agriculture, Veterans Affairs, etc.), state and local governments, industry, academia, professional societies, regulators (e.g., the FDA), public health institutions (e.g., the CDC) and so forth.

The design of that US medical countermeasures enterprise consists of at least five interrelated elements. First, it entails the new pharmaceutical *stockpiles* created by the US government—like the National Pharmaceutical Stockpile, which subsequently evolved into the Strategic National Stockpile. Second, it consists of new *funds* that the government has made available to purchase new medical countermeasures for the stockpile through the BioShield program and subsequent federal appropriations—thereby adding a financial incentive for their development. Third, it includes new *regulatory mechanisms* introduced by the government for granting approval for new medical countermeasures like the "animal rule," which allows their effectiveness to be demonstrated in animal models. Fourth, it encompasses new *legal protections* for medical countermeasures developers (and others) against lawsuits for injuries that might be sustained through the widespread use of such medical countermeasures. Finally, it also includes a whole new *institution*—the Biomedical Advanced Research and Development Authority—tasked by the government (and funded with around $500 million per year) to work more closely with companies and help them overcome the "valley of death" associated with late-stage development (Baker-Hostetler 2016). Largely via a piecemeal and protracted process of trial and error, the US government has ended up spawning a bold new—and in many ways quite exceptional—medical countermeasure regime operating outside of the more conventional boundaries of pharmaceutical development and regulation (Elbe et al. 2014).

That medical countermeasure enterprise is certainly not perfect and continues to evolve. Yet mostly by working with small and medium-sized pharmaceutical companies, that enterprise has already helped to produce a number of new medical countermeasures, including 24 products cleared, approved, or licensed since 2007, as well as 14 products already procured for the Strategic National Stockpile (Hatchett 2016b: 5). It remains difficult, of course, to know exactly how successful these new products would be in practice, because many of them have never had to be used so far. Yet there can be no doubt that progress has been made in broadening the array of medical countermeasures now available to the US population.

Overall, then, the US experience with building this new medical countermeasures enterprise clearly confirms that there are no quick fixes or policy interventions to encourage the commercial development of new medical countermeasures. There are just too many steps, costs, risks, and uncertainties involved in the process and too many complex interdependencies that also exist between those various life-cycle stages. Securing populations pharmaceutically would no doubt be a tall order for any government—and even the US governments has experienced a number of significant setbacks along the way. At the same time, the US experience does also show that it can be done. Progress can be made when governments design wider pharmaceutical regimes that remain sensitive to the many different challenges involved. In many ways, the key lesson thus to emerge from the US experience is that the Gordian knot around medical countermeasures can only be untied through the creation of a bold new pharmaceutical regime designed specifically for that purpose.

Governing Global Health Security: Preparing for the Next Pandemic

Could a similar pharmaceutical enterprise also be built at the international level so as to strengthen global health security more broadly in the twenty-first century? From a more global perspective, it is important to bear in mind that the US medical countermeasures enterprise is geared mostly toward the needs of the United States. While the US government has certainly been at the international forefront of medical countermeasure efforts over the past decade, its principal mission has always been to protect the domestic US population (although it does also participate in some international partnerships).

With significant financial pressures bearing down on its own government budgets, the US medical countermeasures enterprise can at most begin to address some of the threats facing the American population. Its financial and production scale is not nearly large enough to meet the immense international demand that can quickly arise when a new outbreak occurs. During future international health emergencies, it is therefore unlikely that the US system can produce enough quantities of medical countermeasures to help *all* of the people in need around the world. For that same reason, it is also not sustainable for the rest of the world to simply rely upon the pioneering efforts of one country like the United States to do most of this work on medical countermeasures. From the perspective of global health security, one of the bigger political questions for the future is therefore whether the kind of pharmaceutical enterprise spearheaded in the United States could also be internationalized in an effort to share the development costs more equitably and to increase the number of such medical countermeasures that would be available to other populations around the world in the future.

Such a greater degree of internationalization could conceivably help with addressing some of the underlying market challenges that are involved. It is evidently very difficult to create new medical countermeasures through underlying market mechanisms alone. Yet the experience with Tamiflu suggests that a financially more viable business case for medical countermeasures could be constructed when multiple governments are willing to simultaneously commit to stockpiling them in significant numbers. In Europe, for example, there could be scope to build upon the EU decision on cross-border health threats to think about EU-wide systems to address the need for medical countermeasures (European Court of Auditors 2016: 6). Recent experiences with the international Ebola response have also shown that greater levels of international cooperation can be achieved on an ad hoc basis (Roemer-Mahler and Elbe 2016) and that further opportunities also exist to extend some of these lessons from the US medical countermeasures enterprises to other pressing global health challenges such as neglected tropical diseases and antimicrobial resistance (Long et al. 2017; Roemer-Mahler et al. 2017). Realizing all these opportunities in the future, however, would first require achieving a far greater degree of international political cooperation between governments in the area of health security, especially in relation to three pivotal areas.

First, there would need to be a reasonable degree of international consensus on what the major health-security threats facing the world are. The World Health Organization's recent "R&D Blueprint" is a significant step in that direction, and its list of priority diseases is something that could be built upon in that respect. Second, there would also have to be mechanisms for like-minded governments to pool their resources to create a bigger financial incentive for the pharmaceutical industry to engage with medical countermeasures. Finally, it would also require a significant reduction in the legal and regulatory obstacles to the international sharing of pharmaceutical products (and data). Many of these legal and regulatory aspects pivotal to the functioning of the new medical countermeasure enterprise too remain calibrated to the legal jurisdiction of the United States. Significant barriers thus have to be overcome before such medical countermeasures could be shared with other countries, including low-income countries where medical need might be greatest (Marinissen et al. 2014). Across all three areas, a geographically broader system for strengthening global health security in the twenty-first century would first require a greater degree of international cooperation.

Those increased levels of international cooperation around medical countermeasures, in turn, could only be achieved by garnering greater political leadership in this area. In the domestic political context of the United States, the experiences of the Anthrax letters in 2001 and subsequently with highly pathogenic avian flu (H5N1) proved transformative in terms of generating political attention and funding for these issues. More than a decade later, however, there are greater difficulties with sustaining the political momentum behind such efforts at the scale required, even in the United States. Generating equivalent collective action at the international level would be even more challenging still. Governance arrangements for emergencies at the international level still appear very much trapped in such a "boom and bust" cycle, as the international community rapidly moves from grappling with one new outbreak to the next. Comparatively, the international system is also politically much more decentralized and fragmented, consisting of many different countries simultaneously pursuing their competing national interests. Generating international leadership and collective action on medical countermeasures in that context is a qualitatively different—and also much bigger—challenge.

Yet *not* providing such leadership—and simply maintaining the status quo—would also entail considerable costs. Those costs again fall broadly into three areas. First, there have already been a large number of unexpected lethal outbreaks in the twenty-first century, and the expectation is that there will be more in the future. Not having an equivalent medical countermeasures regime at the international level will likely mean that many countries around the world will not have such pharmaceutical defenses at their disposal during later emergencies and that lives could be lost as a result. This is something that may well come to be looked back upon in the future as a valuable—but also missed—opportunity to become better prepared. During any such future outbreak there will likely be immense political interest in scrutinizing what advance measures were taken by governments to develop such medical countermeasures.

A second cost that needs to be considered here is that the current international inequality around access to such new medical countermeasures between high- and low-income countries is already provoking—at times even quite bitter—international political tensions threatening to undermine existing forms of international health cooperation. Amid the height of fears of an imminent H5N1 pandemic in 2006, for example, the Indonesian government ceased sharing its lethal H5N1 virus samples with the rest of the international community over concerns that the government would not have affordable access to new medical countermeasures developed with the help of such biological samples (Elbe and Buckland-Merrett 2017). It marked a particularly stark and intense international political confrontation sparked by unequal access to medical countermeasures. Yet it also showed how the inability to provide other countries with such medical countermeasures can undermine existing forms of international cooperation that high-income countries too depend upon for their health security. In the case of H5N1, it meant that Indonesia started withholding crucial virus samples from the rest of international community, jeopardizing the pandemic preparations of many high-income countries as well. This too represents a significant cost associated with simply maintaining the status quo.

Finally, such international discrepancies in access to medical countermeasures can also create subtler kinds of diplomatic difficulties for countries like the United States. That is because the US government now also has to deal with an increasing number of international requests for access to its medical countermeasures from other countries—requests that need to be handled sensitively and that have the potential to generate new diplomatic tensions if they are turned down. Added together, there is thus quite a considerable cost involved in simply relying on one country to do most of the heavy lifting in developing new medical countermeasures—both for other countries around the world and for the United States. Although generating leadership and political will for internationalizing the medical countermeasure enterprise is a substantial international political challenge, *not* doing so will also incur considerable costs over time. Here the Coalition for Epidemic Preparedness Innovations has recently emerged as an ambitious new attempt to build greater political momentum around such a wider international capability in the area of vaccines.

All of that said, even if such a medical countermeasure enterprise could be built at international level there is also one final—and seemingly more intractable—dilemma residing at the heart of the entire quest to secure populations pharmaceutically: the issue of trust. The desire to protect their populations against health-based security threats is ultimately compelling governments to work much more closely with the pharmaceutical industry and even to accommodate some of the industry concerns about medical countermeasures so as to encourage their greater involvement. Given the central role that industry plays in developing new pharmaceutical products, it is actually very difficult for governments to ignore those industry concerns altogether—especially if they wish to strengthen the pharmaceutical protection of their populations.

Yet the more closely and intensively governments try to partner with pharmaceutical companies to develop new medical countermeasures, the more difficult it becomes for governments to persuade their publics that their independence remains intact. Governments, after all, also need to keep a critical distance from the pharmaceutical industry, to avoid the perception of conflicts of interest, to objectively discharge their regulatory functions, and to ensure that taxpayers receive good value for the money. This problem is only exacerbated by the low reputation that the pharmaceutical industry has in many countries around the world.

In the case of Tamiflu, governments and pharmaceutical companies are still having to contend with the political fallout from the 2009–2010 H1N1 pandemic flu. Especially in Europe, widespread public distrust about pharmaceutical stockpiling has emerged in the aftermath of the Tamiflu "fiasco." More generally, there also remains strong political concern about maintaining scientific independence, and some government institutions even have rules prohibiting them from forming partnerships with industry. Governments thus have to tread a fine political line between cooperating with pharmaceutical companies to ensure that their populations can be protected with appropriate medical countermeasures and not appearing wasteful with public resources to the direct benefit of an industry with a highly uneven political reputation.

The pharmaceutical industry is certainly aware of this problem. Reflecting on the successes and failures of the Tamiflu experience, one prominent industry representative observes: "What of course did not work was the whole public perception around this. And of course in hindsight now that the [H1N1] pandemic was weak we have of course all of us been accused of crying wolf and even some critics of the industry say that we invented this we engineered this, which to me is ridiculous" (Bergstrom 2013). Publics do rely on their governments to make sure that medicines are safe and effective. However, once governments begin to partner more closely with pharmaceutical companies to develop new medical countermeasures and are seen to be politically invested in those products, it becomes much more difficult to convince publics that the requisite independence is preserved. Even when successful, the conflation of public and private interests in the name of strengthening health security generates new issues around public trust.

Yet that same public trust will be absolutely crucial for governments in responding to any future outbreaks, especially when asking citizens to use medical countermeasures. The whole question of how to build and maintain public trust in any international medical countermeasure enterprise is thus a final area that would need to receive greater attention when trying to strengthen global health security more broadly in the twenty-first century. It marks the one key area where resistance to such medical countermeasure efforts tends to crystallize most clearly. In fact, the ultimate viability of any such international medical countermeasure enterprise may well end up standing, or indeed falling, with this whole issue of trust.

Despite some of the successes of the US medical countermeasures enterprise, then, several key obstacles also remain to using its experiences as the basis for a geographically broader strategy to govern global health security in the twenty-first century—especially in terms of greater internationalization, generating political leadership, and the issue of trust. On a deeper level, moreover, all of these obstacles in moving forward again also seem linked to the closer play of security logics in the area of medical countermeasures. For is it not precisely because the provision of security is widely seen to be the preserve of national governments and states that the security framing has ended up encouraging a medical countermeasure response shaped very much along the lines of individual countries—rather than mirroring the more global aspirations of the lethal pathogens themselves? Is it not also the security framing—with its oscillating cycle of threat and apathy—that makes it so much more challenging politically to forge a sustainable and longer-term approach in this area? Is it, finally, not the imperatives of security that are compelling governments to work more closely with the pharmaceutical industry—albeit in ways that then also make it much more difficult for governments to maintain public trust in terms of properly carrying out its regulatory functions of the industry and its products? In either case, there is certainly much unfinished business in the quest to secure populations pharmaceutically, and the whole effort also faces a number of countervailing pressures in moving forward in the twenty-first century. Much work therefore still remains to be done before governments can arrive at a point where they could rapidly make lifesaving new medicines available to their populations in response to future outbreaks.

Epilogue

Pharmaceuticals, Security, and Molecular Life

How is it, in the end, that the ability to develop, stockpile, and distribute new medical countermeasures has become so much more central to security policy in the twenty-first century? What is the deeper significance of this whole "pharmaceuticalization" of security that is unfolding before our eyes? On the surface of things, the pharmaceutical turn in security is simply made possible by virtue of our growing medical ability to interfere with biological threats at a tiny, even molecular scale. A closer look at Tamiflu has thus revealed how the antiviral essentially consists of an artificial new molecule that was deliberately designed to interrupt the process of viral replication unfolding inside the human body. Many other medical countermeasures have similarly been designed since to interfere at the molecular scale with the biological processes surrounding lethal pathogens. First and foremost, it is therefore also this technical ability to rationally design and mobilize new molecules in the form of pharmaceutical interventions that helps to explain the pharmaceutical turn in security policy. It would just not be possible without those new pharmaceutical technologies.

Yet that technical capability in turn presupposes a deeper scientific understanding of those many minute biological processes involved in the production and spread of infectious disease. Again, the case of Tamiflu has been highly instructive. It showed that this new pharmaceutical intervention could only be designed *after* scientists had first gained a much better understanding of the precise molecular processes involved in viral replication unfolding inside the human body—especially the role played by the influenza virus's surface proteins such as neuraminidase. Once scientists had understood the vital role played by the neuraminidase and decoded its precise molecular structure, they discovered a "static" site that could form the basis for a new drug target. Scientists could then set about the task of deliberately designing an "artificial" molecule that would bind to that critical site in the neuraminidase and that could inhibit its key role in the process of viral replication. In that sense, our technical ability to develop new pharmaceutical defenses is itself dependent upon a prior—and deeper— scientific understanding of the life processes unfolding at the scale of the molecular. The technical capability is first made possible by the rise of a molecular biology elucidating the molecular dynamics that are pivotal to the stability, survival, and reproduction of lethal pathogens (Morange 1998: 1). Digging a little deeper thus reveals the pivotal role that molecular knowledge also plays in enabling our growing ability to develop new medical countermeasures.

This underlying molecular knowledge also does much more than that, however. It even plays a constitutive role in producing many of the same biological dangers in the first place. Without that same molecular knowledge, after all, we would not even know about the smoldering cocktail of biological danger that lurks just beyond the limits of what we can perceive with the naked eye. Only by first decoding the molecular composition of many viruses and bacteria did it become clear that the molecular profiles of microbes could change over time. Pathogens not only exist, but they can also evolve and even recombine in unexpected ways at the molecular scale— thereby generating new threats to human life in the future. In the case of flu, molecular biology thus revealed that the surface proteins of the influenza viruses are continuously changing in ways that the human immune system will struggle with over time. This knowledge led many experts to conclude that the outbreak of a new flu pandemic is only a matter of time and that it would be prudent to prepare for that eventuality in advance. Thanks to our deeper understanding of the precise molecular processes surrounding influenza viruses, the prospect of another flu pandemic effectively became a question of *when*, not *if*. Here, then, molecular biology also does much more than just help us to develop new pharmaceutical interventions; it also plays a vital role in generating such health security threats in the first place—by initially alerting us to the fact that such biological dangers even exist (even if we cannot see them with our own eyes). The recent expansion of security agendas to explicitly warn of an array of such biological dangers is one expression of the resulting intensification of our profound sense of microbial unease provoked by these new molecular knowledges.

All of this, however, suggests that the pharmaceutical turn in security policy is ultimately bound up with a much more fundamental epistemic shift in our understanding of life. At the heart of this "pharmaceuticalization" of security lies more than just a newfound technical capability or indeed the growing influence of the molecular sciences—but nothing less than the emergence of a whole new *molecular* vision of life that is today reshaping the world we live in. This new "molecular" vision of existence, the sociologist Nikolas Rose argues, can be usefully contrasted with the older, or "molar," model of life (and medicine). The latter tended to revolve mainly around the visible human body—with its limbs, organs, tissues, blood, and so forth. In that context, the human body (enclosed by the natural skin) was conceived as a kind of anatomical unit with "functionally interconnected organs, tissues, functions, controls, feedbacks, reflexes, rhythms, circulations and so forth" (Rose 2001: 13). This "natural" body also formed a clear limit against which our understanding of life and medicine could unfold. With the rise of molecular biology, however, the scale at which we can understand and imagine life has become progressively smaller in the course of the twentieth century—first moving to the level of the cell and its inner workings and then eventually arriving at the domain of atoms and their molecular groupings.

Over time, this pivotal transition has also begun to shape and change our understanding of life, or biological existence, in profound ways. "Life" now comes to be seen more and more as something that is fundamentally governed by the complex interplay of such elaborate (but also minute) molecular processes. Indeed, life is reconceptualized as a "set of intelligible vital mechanisms among molecular entities that can be identified, isolated, manipulated, mobilized, recombined, in new practices of intervention, which are no longer constrained by the apparent normativity of a natural vital order" (Rose 2007: 5–6; see also Dillon and Reid 2001; Kay 1993, 2000). Increasingly, the life sciences are capable of studying those processes, identifying the molecular dynamics critical to health and disease and even developing new ways of intervening upon those molecular processes. The politics of life today, Rose argues in this vein, "addresses human existence at the molecular level: it is waged about molecules, amongst molecules, and where the molecules are themselves at stake" (Rose 2001: 17).

Yet whereas Rose and others see the societal implication of this development mainly in terms of a pivotal shift from population health to the individual management of a "somatic" self (Rose 2001: 17), the story of Tamiflu reveals that these molecular knowledges are also transforming much broader and population-based rationalities of security that governments are deploying at the outset of the twenty-first century (Braun 2007; Hester 2016). Those same knowledges are today also fanning new concerns about biological threats to national security and are even enabling the concomitant construction of a whole new medical countermeasures enterprise in the United States. Much as the security rationalities of the twentieth century eventually became profoundly colored by physics with the advent of nuclear weapons, so too molecular biology is beginning to shape the security strategies of the twenty-first century. As one influential historian of molecular biology puts it, "Hardly a common term in the 1950s, molecular biology is now expected to take the dominant role in the twenty-first century that physics played in the twentieth. Our understanding of life, health and disease is as much dependent on knowledge produced by molecular biologists as the fabrication of food and drugs, trials in court, and new ways of waging war" (de Chadarevian 2002: 1).

Precisely herein, then, also lies the deeper significance of the whole Tamiflu story in the end. It reveals that even the ways in which we imagine and practice security are now becoming shaped by this molecular vision of life. Security too is beginning to acquire a molecular form. Or, to put it slightly differently, security policy is changing because our underlying conception of life is also changing.

References

Abbasi, Kamran. (2014). The Missing Data That Cost $20bn. *BMJ* 348. https://doi.org/10.1136/bmj.g2695.

Abbott, Tony. (2005). Bracing for the Worst. Country Report for Pandemic Flu Conference in Ottawa. 25 October.

Abraham, John. (2010). Pharmaceuticalization of Society in Context: Theoretical, Empirical and Health Dimensions. *Sociology* 44(4): 603–622.

Aebersold, Paul. (2012). FDA Experience with Medical Countermeasures under the Animal Rule. *Advances in Preventive Medicine*, vol. 2012, article ID 507571. doi:10.1155/2012/507571.

AFP. (2005). Rumsfeld Recuses Himself from Avian Flu Decisions. 2 November.

Aldis, William. (2008). Health Security as a Public Health Concept: A Critical Analysis. *Health Policy and Planning* 23: 369–375.

AP. (2002). Rumsfeld Reveals Assets, but Balks at Paperwork. 19 June.

Australia DOH. (2014). National Medical Stockpile. Australian Government Department of Health. Available at http://www.health.gov.au/internet/main/publishing.nsf/Content/health-pubhlth-strateg-bio-factsht_stckpile.htm. [Accessed 5 March 2014.]

Avorn, Jerry. (2005). *Powerful Medicines: The Benefits, Risks, and Costs of Prescription Drugs*. New York: Vintage Books.

BakerHostetler. (2016). Government Contracts Quarterly Update—February 2016. 29 February. Available at https://www.bakerlaw.com/alerts/government-contracts-quarterly-update-february-2016.

BARDA. (2011). BARDA Strategic Plan: 2011–2016. Washington, DC: Biomedical Advanced Research and Development Authority. Available at http://www.phe.gov/about/barda/Pages/2011barda-stratplan.aspx. [Accessed 8 April 2014.]

Barry, Andrew. (2005). Pharmaceutical Matters: The Invention of Informed Materials. *Theory, Culture & Society* 22(1): 51–69.

Bartfai, Tamas, and Graham Lees (2006). *Drug Discovery: From Bedside to Wall Street*. London: Elsevier.

———. (2013). *The Future of Drug Discovery: Who Decides Which Diseases to Treat*. London: Elsevier.

Baumgartner, Anita. (2000). Link in weichere Werbewelten. Available at http://www.ktipp.ch/themen/beitrag/1015668/Link_in_weichere_Werbewelten. [Accessed 30 August 2012.]

Bergstrom, Richard. (2013). Presentation at Workshop on Pandemic Flu Controversies. Brighton: University of Sussex. 11 January.

BIJ. (2010a). Press Coverage of WHO Investigation. Bureau of Investigative Journalism, 11 June. Available at https://www.thebureauinvestigates.com/2010/06/11/press-coverage-of-who-investigation/.

———. (2010b). WHO Swine Flu Advisors Had Links to Drug Companies. Bureau of Investigative Journalism, 7 June. Available at https://www.thebureauinvestigates.com/2010/06/07/who-swine-flu-advisors-had-links-to-drug-companies/.

Binzer, P. (2008). The PREP Act: Liability Protection for Medical Countermeasure Development, Distribution, and Administration. *Biosecurity and Bioterrorism* 6(4): 293–298.

Bittar, Christine. (2001). Tamiflu's Roadshow. Brandweek, 12 March. Available at http://66.197.58.78/Tamiflu_article_3.htm.

Boseley, Sarah. (2015). Second Study Raises Questions over the Benefits of Tamiflu. *Guardian*, 30 January. Available at https://www.theguardian.com/society/2015/jan/30/tamiflu-study-questions-drugs-usefulness-roche-lancet.

Bradsher, Keith. (2005). Pressure Rises on Producer of a Flu Drug. *New York Times*, 11 October. Available at http://www.nytimes.com/2005/10/11/business/11drug.html?pagewanted=print&_r=0.

Braun, Bruce. (2007). Biopolitics and the Molecularization of Life. *Cultural Geographies* 14(1): 6–28.

Buse, Kent, and Gill Walt. (2000). Global Public-Private Partnerships: Part I—A New Development in Health? *Bulletin of the World Health Organization* 78(4): 549–561.

Business Wire. (2001). Gilead Board of Directors Appoints James M. Denny as Chairman. 22 January.

———. (2008). Roche Introduces Program to Facilitate Corporate Pandemic Stockpiling of Tamiflu. Available at http://www.businesswire.com/news/home/20080626005707/en/Roche-Introduces-Program-Facilitate-Corporate-Pandemic-Stockpiling#.VcEcAnh91UE. [Accessed 4 August 2015.]

Butler, Declan. (2014). Tamiflu Report Comes under Fire. *Nature* 508: 439–440.

Cabinet Office. (2008). *The National Security Strategy of the United Kingdom: Security in an Interdependent World.* London: Cabinet Office.

———.(2010). *A Strong Britain in an Age of Uncertainty: The National Security Strategy.* London: Cabinet Office.

Caduff, Carlo. (2015). *The Pandemic Perhaps: Dramatic Events in a Public Culture of Danger.* Oakland: U of California P.

Carpenter, Daniel. (2010). *Reputation and Power: Organizational Image and Pharmaceutical Regulation at the FDA.* Princeton, NJ: Princeton UP.

Cavaleri, Marco. (2016). The Regulatory Framework for Licensure of Medical Countermeasures during Public Health Emergencies. Presentation at IMI Stakeholder Forum, Brussels, 28 and 29 September 2016. Available at http://www.imi.europa.eu/sites/default/files/uploads/documents/Events/SF2016/biopreparedness_cavaleri_regulatory_framework_licensure_emergencies.pdf.

CDC. (2005). Pandemic Flu: Key Facts. Centers for Disease Control and Prevention, 17 October. Available at ftp://ftp.cdc.gov/pub/avian_influenza1/Appendix%20section%20of%20notebook/CDC%20Pandemic%20Influenza%20Fact%20Sheet.pdf.

————. (2012). Seasonal Influenza. Centers for Disease Control and Prevention. Available at http://www.cdc.gov/flu/about/qa/disease.htm. [Accessed 9 November 2012.]

Clarke, Adele, Laura Mamo, Jennifer Fosket, Jennifer Fishman, Janet Shim (Eds). (2010). *Biomedicalization: Technoscience, Health and Illness in the U.S.* Durham, NC: Duke UP.

Clinch, B., J. Smith, A. Kenwright, B. Surujbally, and J. Harding. (2014). Roche Feedback on "Neuraminidase Inhibitors for Preventing and Treating Influenza in Healthy Adults and Children." 26 October. Available at https://editorial-unit.cochrane.org/cochrane-review-neuraminidase-inhibitors-influenza.

Clinical Development Scientist. (2015). Interview by author. 29 June.

Cochrane Neuraminidase Inhibitors Review Team. (2011). Does Oseltamivir Really Reduce Complications of Influenza? *Clinical Infectious Diseases* 53(12): 1302–1303.

Cohen, Deborah. (2009). Complications: Tracking Down the Data on Oseltamivir. *BMJ* 339: b5387.

————. (2013). Roche Offers Researchers Access to All Tamiflu Trials. *BMJ* 346: f2157.

————. (2014). Oseltamivir: Another Case of Regulatory Failure? *BMJ* 348: g2591.

Cohen, Deborah, and Philip Carter. (2010). Conflicts of Interest: WHO and the Pandemic Flu "Conspiracies." *BMJ* 340: 1274–1279.

Cole, Jennifer (Ed). (2013). *Pharmaceutical Resilience: Proceedings of the Workshop on Pharmaceutical Resilience for Serious Infectious Disease.* 5 February. London: Royal United Services Institute. Available at https://rusi.org/sites/default/files/201305_cr_pharmaceutical_resilience.pdf.

Couzin-Frankel, Jennifer. (2015). Tamiflu Helps, Newest Study in Long-Running Debate Says. *Science*, 29 January. Available at http://news.sciencemag.org/biology/2015/01/Tamiflu-helps-newest-study-long-running-debate-says.

Davies, Sara E. (2008). Securitizing Infectious Disease. *International Affairs* 84(2): 295–313.

Davies, Sara, Adam Kamradt-Scott, and Simon Rushton. (2015). *Disease Diplomacy: International Norms and Global Health Security.* Baltimore: Johns Hopkins UP.

De Chadarevian, Soraya. (2002). *Designs for Life: Molecular Biology after World War II.* Cambridge: Cambridge UP.

Dillon, Michael, and Julian Reid. (2001). Global Liberal Governance: Biopolitics, Security and War. *Millennium* 30(1): 41–66.

Dobson, Joanna, Richard Whitley, Stuart Pocock, and Arnold Monto. (2015). Oseltamivir Treatment for Influenza in Adults: A Meta-Analysis of Randomised Controlled Trials. *Lancet* 385(9979): 1729–1737.

DOH. (2009). Use of Antivirals in an Influenza Pandemic: Scientific Evidence Base Review. Available at http://www.dh.gov.uk/en/Publicationsandstatistics/Publications/PublicationsPolicyAndGuidance/DH_125318. [Accessed 19 November 2012.]

Dolan, Kerry A., and Zina Moukheibe. (2003). The Golden Age of Antiviral Drugs. *Forbes*, 27 October. Available at http://www.forbes.com/forbes/2003/1027/098.html.

Doshi, Peter. (2009). Neuraminidase Inhibitors: The Story behind the Cochrane Review. *BMJ* 339: b5164.

Doshi, Peter, Tom Jefferson, and Chris Del Mar. (2012). The Imperative to Share Clinical Study Reports: Recommendations from the Tamiflu Experience. *PLoS Med* 9(4) (10 April): e1001201. Available at https://doi.org/10.1371/journal.pmed.1001201.

Doshi, Peter, Mark Jones, and Tom Jefferson. (2012). Rethinking Credible Evidence Synthesis. *BMJ* 344: d7898.

Drugdevelopment-technology.com. (2012). Small Players, Big Drugs—Pharmaceutical SMEs Take the Innovative Edge. Drugdevelopment-technology.com, 12 April. Available at http://www.drugdevelopment-technology.com/features/featuredrug -pharmaceutical-sme-big-pharma-innovation/.

Dumit, Joseph. (2012). *Drugs for Life: How Pharmaceutical Companies Define Our Health.* Durham, NC: Duke UP.

ECDC. (2016). *ECDC Preliminary Scientific Advice: Expert Opinion on Neuraminidase Inhibitors for Prevention and Treatment of Influenza: Review of Recent Systematic Reviews and Meta-Analyses.* Stockholm: European Centre for Disease Prevention and Control.

Elashoff, Michael. (2012). Interview by author. 31 March.

Elbe, Stefan. (2009). *Virus Alert: Security, Governmentality and the AIDS Pandemic.* New York: Columbia UP.

———. (2010). *Security and Global Health: Towards the Medicalization of Insecurity.* Cambridge: Polity.

Elbe, Stefan, and Gemma Buckland-Merrett. (2017). Data, Disease and Diplomacy: GISAID's innovative contribution to global health. *Global Challenges* 1: 33–46. doi:10.1002/gch2.1018.

Elbe, Stefan, Anne Roemer-Mahler, and Christopher Long. (2014a). Medical Countermeasures for National Security: A New Government Role in the Pharmaceuticalization of Society. *Social Science and Medicine* 131: 263–271.

———. (2014b). Securing Circulation Pharmaceutically: Antiviral Stockpiling and Pandemic Preparedness in the European Union. *Security Dialogue* 45(5): 440–457.

EMA. (2016). Opening Up Clinical Data on New Medicines. European Medicines Agency, 20 October. Available at http://www.ema.europa.eu/docs/en_GB/document_library /Press_release/2016/10/WC500214989.pdf.

EMA Officer. (2013). Interview by author. 16 October.

EMEA. (2005a). Background Information on the Procedure. Available at http://www .ema.europa.eu/docs/en_GB/document_library/EPAR_-_Procedural_steps_taken _before_authorisation/human/000402/WC500033104.pdf. [Accessed 23 August 2012.]

———. (2005b). Scientific Discussion. Available at http://www.ema.europa.eu/docs /en_GB/document_library/EPAR_-_Scientific_Discussion/human/000402 /WC500033103.pdf. [Accessed 19 November 2012.]

Enemark, Christian. (2017). *Biosecurity Dilemmas: Dreaded Diseases, Ethical Responses, and the Health of Nations.* Washington, DC: Georgetown UP.

Epstein, Helen. (2011). Flu Warning: Beware the Drug Companies! *New York Review of Books,* 12 May. Available at http://www.nybooks.com/articles/archives/2011/may /12/flu-warning-beware-drug-companies/.

EU. (2013). Presidency Confirms Agreement on Strengthening Responses to Serious Cross-Border Health Threats. 15 May. Available at http://www.eu2013.ie/news /news-items/20130516crossborderhealthupdateengonly/.

European Commission. (2011). *Stakeholder Consultation on Health Security in the European Union.* 9 September.

European Court of Auditors. (2016). *Dealing with Serious Cross-Border Threats to Health in the EU: Important Steps Taken but More Needs to Be Done.* Luxembourg: European Court of Auditors.

European Influenza Expert. (2012). Interview by author. 29 November.

European Ombudsman. (2010). Summary of Decision on Complaint 2560/2007/ BEH against the European Medicines Agency (EMA). Available at https://www .ombudsman.europa.eu/en/cases/summary.faces/en/5646/html.bookmark. [Accessed 6 July 2017.]

———. (2011). *The European Ombudsman: Guide to Complaints.* Available at http:// www.ombudsman.europa.eu/en/resources/staffguide.faces#/page/1. [Accessed 26 January 2015.]

Fassbender, Melissa. (2016). BARDA Talks Medical Countermeasure Manufacturing. Outsourcing-Pharma.com, 25 April. Available at http://www.outsourcing -pharma.com/Contract-Manufacturing/BARDA-talks-medical-countermeasure -manufacturing.

FDA. (1999a). Food and Drug Administration Center for Drug Evaluation and Research: Antiviral Drugs Advisory Committee. 24 February.

———. (1999b). Letter to Hoffmann-La Roche, Inc. NDA21-087. 27 October.

———. (1999c). Medical Review for Zanamivir. Available at http://www.accessdata.fda.gov /drugsatfda_docs/nda/99/021036-medreview8.pdf. [Accessed 30 September 2013.]

———. (2000). Letter to Joanna McNamara. 14 April. Available at http://www .fda.gov/downloads/Drugs/GuidanceComplianceRegulatoryInformation /EnforcementActivitiesbyFDA/WarningLettersandNoticeofViolationLetterstoPha rmaceuticalCompanies/UCM166329.pdf.

———. (2002). New Drug and Biological Drug Products; Evidence Needed to Demonstrate Effectiveness of New Drugs When Human Efficacy Studies Are Not Ethical or Feasible. *Federal Register* 67(105) (31 May).

———. (2005). Tamiflu Pediatric Adverse Events: Questions and Answers. Available at http://www.fda.gov/drugs/drugsafety/postmarketdrugsafetyinformationforpatien tsandproviders/ucm107840.htm. [Accessed 26 January 2015.]

———. (2006). Meeting of the FDA Advisory Pediatric Advisory Committee. 16 November.

———. (2010a). FDA Warns about Fraudulent Tamiflu. FDA News Release, 17 June. Available at http://www.fda.gov/NewsEvents/Newsroom/PressAnnouncements /ucm216148.htm.

———. (2010b). Tamiflu and Relenza Emergency Use Authorization Disposition Letters and Question and Answer Attachments. 22 June. Available at http://www.fda.gov /Drugs/DrugSafety/PostmarketDrugSafetyInformationforPatientsandProviders /ucm216249.htm.

———. (2014). FDA Medical Countermeasure Initiative. Program Update Fiscal Year 2014. Available at http://www.fda.gov/downloads/EmergencyPreparedness/Counter terrorism/MedicalCountermeasures/AboutMCMi/UCM453168.pdf. [Accessed 23 February 2016.]

———. (2015). FDA Approves Vaccine for Use after Known or Suspected Anthrax Expo- sure. Available at http://www.fda.gov/NewsEvents/Newsroom/PressAnnouncements /ucm474027.htm?source=govdelivery&utm_medium=email&utm_source =govdelivery. [Accessed 23 February 2016.]

FDA Reviewer. (2015). Email Correspondence. 18 June.

Feddersen, Timothy. (2007). Roche and Tamiflu: Doing Business in the Shadow of a Pandemic. Kellog School of Management. Available at http://graduateinstitute .ch/webdav/site/mia/shared/mia/cours/IA005/Roche%20and%20Tamiflu.PDF. [Accessed 24 August 2012.]

Ferguson, N. M., D. A. Cummings, S. Cauchemez, C. Fraser, S. Riley, A. Meeyai, S. Iamsirithaworn, and D. S. Burke. (2005). Strategies for Containing an Emerging Influenza Pandemic in Southeast Asia. *Nature* 437: 209–214.

Finnemore, Martha, and K. Sikkink. (1998). International Norm Dynamics and Politi- cal Change. *International Organization* 52 (Autumn): 887–917.

Flyer, Paul. (2013). Interview by author. 27 September.

Forbes. (2014). Donald Rumsfeld Goes Tax Protester on IRS, but Should Aim at Congress. 17 April. Available at http://www.forbes.com/sites/robertwood/2014/04/17/donald -rumsfeld-goes-tax-protester-on-irs-but-should-aim-at-congress/#1cb16b823640.

Fox, Maggie. (2007). Interview—Flu Threat Offers New Business for Tamiflu Maker. Reuters, 23 July. Available at http://in.reuters.com/article/2007/07/24/idINIndia -28622120070724.

Franz, D. R., and R. Zajtchuk. (2002). Biological Terrorism: Understanding the Threat, Preparation, and Medical Response. *Disease a Month* 48(8): 493–564.

Fuyono, Ichiko. (2007). Tamiflu Side Effects Come under Scrutiny. *Nature* 446: 358–359.

Gaffney, Alexander. (2012). In First for Animal Rule Pathway, FDA Approves GSK's Rax- ibacumab. *Regulatory Focus*, 17 December. Available at http://www.raps.org/focus -online/news/news-article-view/article/2649/in-first-for-animal-rule-pathway-fda -approves-gsks-raxibacumab.aspx.

Gallagher, James. (2014). Tamiflu: Millions Wasted on Flu Drug, Claims Major Report. *BBC News*, 10 April. Available at http://www.bbc.co.uk/news/health-26954482.

GAO. (2016). *High-Containment Laboratories: Improved Oversight of Dangerous Pathogens Needed to Mitigate Risk*. Report by the US Government Accountability Office, 30 August. Available at http://www.gao.gov/products/GAO-16-642.

Garfield, Simon. (2009). Catch It! Bin It! Profit from It! *Observer*, 25 October. Avail- able at http://www.guardian.co.uk/world/2009/oct/25/swine-flu-vaccines-profit /print.

Ghosh, Arijit, and Wahyudi Soeriaatmadja. (2006). Japan to Spend $30 Mln to Stock- pile Tamiflu for Asian Nations. *Bloomberg News*, 2 May.

Gilead Sciences. (2010). George P. Schultz. Available at http://www.gilead.com/bod _shultz. [Accessed 2 July 2010.]

———. (2016). Personal Correspondence with Andrew Whitaker, senior director, Alli- ance Management, Gilead Sciences. 1 June.

Goldacre, Ben. (2012). *Bad Pharma: How Drug Companies Mislead Doctors and Harm Patients*. London: Fourth Estate.

————. (2014). What the Tamiflu Saga Tells Us about Drug Trials and Big Pharma. *Guardian*, 10 April. Available at http://www.theguardian.com/business/2014/apr /10/Tamiflu-saga-drug-trials-big-pharma/print.

————. (2015). Interview by author. 29 July.

Goodman, Jordan, and Vivien Walsh. (2001). *The Story of Taxol: Nature and Politics in the Pursuit of an Anti-Cancer Drug*. Cambridge: Cambridge UP.

Google Trends. (2013). Google Trends search performed on "Tamiflu." Available at http://www.google.co.uk/trends/explore?q=Tamiflu#q=Tamiflu&cmpt=q. [Accessed 2 September 2013.]

Gottron, Frank. (2014). The Project BioShield Act: Issues for the 113th Congress. CRS Report R43607. Available at http://fas.org/sgp/crs/terror/R43607.pdf. [Accessed 26 March 2015.]

Gøtzsche, Peter C., and Anders W. Jørgensen. (2011). Opening Up Data at the European Medicines Agency. *BMJ* 342: d2686.

Hama, Rokuro. (2005). 3 Boys Died from Adverse Reactions Probably Related to Tamiflu. 25 November 2005. Available at http://www.npojip.org/english/no59.html.

————. (2008). Fatal Neuropsychiatric Adverse Reactions to Oseltamivir: Case Series and Overview of Causal Relationships. *International Journal of Risk & Safety in Medicine* 20: 5–36.

————. (2014). Interview by author. 23 May.

Hama, Rokuro, and C. L. Bennett. (2017). The Mechanisms of Sudden-Onset Type Adverse Reactions to Oseltamivir. *Acta Neurologica Scandinavica* 135: 148–160. doi:10.1111/ane.12629.

Hamied, Yusuf. (2003). Access to Medicines at Affordable Prices. First Margi Memorial Lecture. 9 November.

————. (2014). Interview by author. 25 February.

Harrington, Joseph E., Jr., and Edbert B. Hsu. (2010). Stockpiling Anti-Viral Drugs for a Pandemic: The Role of Manufacturer Reserve Programs. *Journal of Health Economics* 29: 438–444.

Hatchett, Richard. (2016a). PHEMCE-Supported Drug Achieves FDA Approval. ASPR Blog. 21 March. Available at http://www.phe.gov/ASPRBlog/pages /BlogArticlePage.aspx?PostID=180.

————. (2016b). State of BARDA. Presentation at the BARDA 2016 Industry Day, Washington, DC, 18 October. Available at https://www.medicalcountermeasures.gov /media/36904/01_hachett_state-of-barda-address.pdf.

Hayashi, Keiji. (2009). Hayashi's Criticism on Previous Cochrane Review. Available at http://www.bmj.com/content/suppl/2009/12/07/bmj.b5106.DC1/jeft726562.ww1 _default.pdf. [Accessed 2 July 2017.]

————. (2014). Interview by author. 23 May.

Healy, David. (1997). *The Antidepressant Era*. Cambridge, MA: Harvard UP.

————. (2004). *Let Them Eat Prozac: The Unhealthy Relationship between the Pharmaceutical Industry and Depression*. New York: New York UP.

Heneghan, C. J., I. Onakpoya, M. A. Jones, P. Doshi, C. B. Del Mar, and R. Hama et al. (2016). Neuraminidase Inhibitors for Influenza: A Systematic Review and Meta-Analysis of Regulatory and Mortality Data. *Health Technology Assessments* 20(42).

Hernán, Miguel, and Marc Lipsitch. (2011). Oseltamivir and Risk of Lower Respiratory Tract Complications in Patients with Flu Symptoms: A Meta-Analysis of Eleven Randomized Clinical Trials. *Clinical Infectious Diseases* 55(3): 277–279.

Hester, R. J. (2016). Biology as Opportunity: Hybrid Rule from a Molecular Point of View. In Shelley Hurt and Ronnie Lipschutz (eds.), *Hybrid Rule and State Formation: Public-Private Power in the 21st Century* (pp. 175–202). New York: Routledge.

———. (forthcoming). Pre-empting Biological Danger: How Security Policies Get under Our Skin. Unpublished manuscript.

HHS. (2011). Strategic National Stockpile (SNS). Available at http://chemm.nlm.nih.gov/sns.htm. [Accessed 4 August 2015.]

———. (2012). 2012 HHS PHEMCE Strategy and Implementation Plan. Washington, DC: US Department of Health and Human Services. Available at http://www.phe.gov/Preparedness/mcm/phemce/Pages/strategy.aspx. [Accessed 13 March 2013.]

———. (2014). Project BioShield Annual Report to Congress January 2014–December 2014. Washington, DC: US Department of Health and Human Services, Office of the Assistant Secretary for Preparedness and Response.

Hirota, Y. (2008). [Interim Report of Investigations about the Frequency of Associated Symptoms with Influenza] (in Japanese). In *Report of Research on Health Science*. Tokyo: Ministry of Health, Labour, and Welfare of Japan, 2008.

Houseago, Harry. (2009). Ode to Tamiflu. Available at http://www.telegraph.co.uk/news/health/swine-flu/5296590/Swine-flu-Ode-to-Tamiflu-by-Hugo-Houseago.html. [Accessed 19 April 2016.]

Hoyt, Kendall. (2012). *Long Shot: Vaccines for National Defense*. Cambridge, MA: Harvard UP.

Hurt, A. C., and H. Kelly. (2016). Debate Regarding Oseltamivir Use for Seasonal and Pandemic Influenza. *Emerging Infectious Diseases* 22(6): 949–955.

Influenza Scientist. (2014). Interview by author. 15 September.

IOM. (2010). *Medical Countermeasure Dispensing: Emergency Use Authorization and the Postal Model*. Workshop Summary. Washington, DC: Institute of Medicine.

Jack, Andrew. (2006). Feeling the Strain. *Financial Times*, 2 September.

———. (2009). Flu's Unexpected Bonus. *BMJ* 339: 720–721.

———. (2010). Roche Accused over Illegal Tamiflu Deals. *Financial Times*, 21 May.

———. (2014). Tamiflu: "A Nice Little Earner." *BMJ* 348: g2524.

Jefferson, C., F. Lentzos, and C. Marris. (2014). Synthetic Biology and Biosecurity: Challenging the "Myths." *Frontiers in Public Health* 2: 115. doi:10.3389/fpubh.2014.00115.

Jefferson, Thomas. (2012). Complaint to European Ombudsman. 15 October. Available at http://www.bmj.com/Tamiflu/ombudsman.

Jefferson, Thomas, Peter Doshi, Matthew Thompson, and Carl Heneghan. (2011). Ensuring Safe and Effective Drugs: Who Can Do What It Takes? *BMJ* 342: c7258.

Jefferson, Thomas, M. Jones, P. Doshi, C. Del Mar, L. Dooley, and R. Foxlee. (2010). Neuraminidase Inhibitors for Preventing and Treating Influenza in Healthy Adults (Review). Cochrane Library, issue 2.

Jefferson, Thomas, M. A. Jones, P. Doshi, C. B. Del Mar, R. Hama, M. J. Thompson, E. A. Spencer, I. J. Onakpoya, K. R. Mahtani, D. Nunan, J. Howick, and C. J. Heneghan. (2014). Neuraminidase Inhibitors for Preventing and Treating Influenza in Adults and Children. Cochrane Database of Systematic Reviews, issue 4, art. no. CD008965.

Jefferson, Thomas, Mark Jones, Peter Doshi, Elizabeth Spencer, Igho Onakpoya, and Carl Heneghan. (2014). Oseltamivir for Influenza in Adults and Children: Systematic Review of Clinical Study Reports and Summary of Regulatory Comments. *BMJ* 348: g2545.

Jones, Mark. (2011). Does Oseltamivir Really Reduce Complications of Influenza? *Clinical Infectious Diseases* 53(12): 1302–1303.

Kaiser, L., C. Wat, T. Mills, P. Mahoney, P. Ward, and F. Hayden. (2003). Impact of Oseltamivir Treatment on Influenza-Related Lower Respiratory Tract Complications and Hospitalizations. *Arch. Intern. Med.* 163(14) (28 July): 1667–1672.

Kamradt-Scott, Adam. (2015). *Managing Global Health Security: The World Health Organization and Disease Outbreak Control.* Basingstoke: Palgrave.

Kaplinsky, R. (2000). Spreading the Gains from Globalisation: What Can Be Learned from Value Chain Analysis. IDS Working Paper 110. Available at http://www.ids.ac .uk/files/Wp110.pdf. [Accessed 25 July 2015.]

Kay, Lily E. (1993). *The Molecular Vision of Life: Caltech, the Rockefeller Foundation, and the Rise of the New Biology.* New York: Oxford UP.

———. (2000). *Who Wrote the Book of Life? A History of the Genetic Code.* Stanford, CA: Stanford UP.

Kelly, Heath, and Benjamin Cowling. (2015). Influenza: the Rational Use of Oseltamivir. *Lancet* 385: 1700–1703.

Kendrick, Malcolm. (2007). *The Great Cholesterol Con: The Truth about What Really Causes Heart Disease and How to Avoid It.* London: John Blake.

Kittelsen, Sonja. (2013). *The EU and the Securitization of Pandemic Influenza* (Doctoral dissertation). Aberystwyth University, Aberystwyth.

Klenk, Hans Dieter. (2012). Influenza Virology. In M. von Itzstein (Ed.), *Influenza Virus Sialidase—A Drug Discovery Target* (pp. 1–29). Milestones in Drug Therapy. Basel: Birkhäuser Verlag GmbH.

Kurki, Pekka. (2015). Interview by author. 9 July.

Lakoff, Andrew. (2005). *Pharmaceutical Reason: Knowledge and Value in Global Psychiatry.* Cambridge: Cambridge UP.

Laurance, Jeremy. (2005). Suicides Linked to Tamiflu—So Is Only Weapon against Bird Flu Safe? *Independent*, 15 November. Available at http://www.independent.co.uk /news/world/asia/suicides-linked-to-Tamiflu--so-is-only-weapon-against-bird-flu -safe-515406.html.

Laver, Graeme. (1999). Interview by Mark Willacy. Australian Broadcasting Corporation, 28 July. Available at http://www.abc.net.au/pm/stories/s39728.htm.

———. (n.d.). Email Correspondence. Available at http://virologyhistory.wustl.edu/laver .htm. [Accessed 12 February 2015.]

Laver, Graeme, and Elspeth Garman. (2002). Pandemic Influenza: Its Origin and Control. *Microbes and Infection* 4: 1309–1316.

Laver, William Graeme, Norbert Bischofberger, and Robert Webster. (2000). The Origin and Control of Pandemic Influenza. *Perspectives in Biology and Medicine* 43(2): 173–192.

Lean, Geoffrey, and Jonathan Owen. (2006). Donald Rumsfeld Makes $5 Million Killing on Bird Flu Drug. *Independent on Sunday*, 12 March. Available at http://www

.independent.co.uk/news/world/americas/donald-rumsfeld-makes-5m-killing-on
-bird-flu-drug-469599.html.

Li, Jie Jack. (2009). *Triumph of the Heart: The Story of Statins*. Oxford: Oxford UP.

Light, Donald. (2010). Bearing the Risks of Prescription Drugs. In Donald W. Light
(Ed.), *The Risks of Prescription Drugs* (pp. 1–39). New York: Columbia UP.

Lightfoot, Nigel. (2009). UK Biodefence Medical Countermeasures Portfo-
lio. Presentation at GHSI Public Health Emergency Medical Countermeasures Workshop, Washington, DC, 4–5 November. Available at https://www
.blsmeetings.net/2009GHSImeetingsMCM/presentations/Bio/Lightfoot
-UKMCMPortfolio.pdf.

Livre Blanc. (2013). *Le livre blanc sur la défense et la sécurité nationale*. Paris: Direction de
l'information légale et administrative.

Löfgren, Hans, and Owain Williams (Eds.). (2013). *The New Political Economy of Pharmaceuticals: Production, Innovation and TRIPS in the Global South*. Basingstoke:
Palgrave.

Long, Christopher, Anne Roemer-Mahler, and Stefan Elbe. (2017). *Towards New Antibiotics: Key Insights from BARDA in the United States*. Policy Brief. Centre for Global
Health Policy, University of Sussex. Available at https://www.sussex.ac.uk/webteam
/gateway/file.php?name=long-roemer-mahler-elbe-2017-towards-new-antibiotics
-key-insights-for-barda-in-the-united-states.pdf&site=346. [Accessed 11
May 2017.]

Longini, Ira, Jr., M. Elizabeth Halloran, Azhar Nizam, and Yang Yang. (2004). Containing Pandemic Influenza with Antiviral Agents. *American Journal of Epidemiology*
159(7): 623–633.

Love, James. (2005). CPTech Statement on Roche/Gilead Licensing of Tamiflu Patents. 5 November. Available at http://www.cptech.org/ip/health/tamiflu
/cptech11052005.html.

Lu, Z. K., J. Samuel, B. A. Kessler, R. Schulz, J. Bian, and J. D. Brian Chen et al. (2014).
Systematic Approach to Pharmacovigilance beyond the Limits: The Southern Network on Adverse Reactions (SONAR) Projects. *Adv. Pharmacoepidemiol Drug Saf.*
3(149). doi:10.4172/2167-1052.1000149.

MacKellar, Landis. (2007). Pandemic Influenza: A Review. *Population and Development
Review* 33(3): 429–451.

MacKenzie, Debora. (2007). Japan Bans Tamiflu for Teenagers. *New Scientist*, 23 March.
Available at http://www.newscientist.com/article/dn11451-japan-bans-Tamiflu
-for-teenagers.html#.VK-neYeQ6Ag.

———. (2009). *BMJ* Criticisms of Tamiflu Questioned. *New Scientist*, 11 December.
Available at https://www.newscientist.com/article/dn18271-bmj-criticisms-of
-tamiflu-questioned/.

Magrini, Nicola, and Maria Font. (2007). Direct to Consumer Advertising of Drugs in
Europe. *BMJ* 335: 526.

Marinissen, Maria Julia, Lauren Barna, Margaret Meyers, and Susan E. Sherman.
(2014). Strengthening Global Health Security by Developing Capacities to Deploy
Medical Countermeasures Internationally. *Biosecurity and Bioterrorism* 12(5):
284–291.

Matheny, Jason, Michael Mair, Andrew Mulcahy, and Bradley T. Smith. (2007). Incentives for Biodefense Countermeasure Development. *Biosecurity and Bioterrorism* 5(3): 228–238.

McCarthy, Michael. (2014). 26 Nations Join US Global Health Security Agenda. *BMJ* 348: g1589. Available at http://www.bmj.com/content/348/bmj.g1589. [Accessed 16 January 2015.]

McInnes, Colin, and Simon Rushton. (2013). HIV/AIDS and Securitization Theory. *European Journal of International Relations* 19(1): 115–138.

McKillop, Tom. (1999). Our Worst Fears Were Fully Justified. *Financial Times*, 6 October.

McNeill, Donald, Jr. (2005). Indian Company to Make Generic Version of Flu Drug Tamiflu. *New York Times*, 14 October. Available at http://www.nytimes.com/2005/10/14/health/14virus.html.

Mielczarek, Agnieszka. (2015). Potential Use of the Joint Procurement Mechanism. Presentation to workshop on the Joint Procurement of Medical Countermeasures / High-Level Hearing on the Implementation of the Council Recommendation on Seasonal Influenza Vaccination. 29 April. Luxemburg: European Commission Directorate-General Health & Food Safety. Available at http://ec.europa.eu/health/preparedness_response/docs/ev_20150429_co03_en.pdf.

MMWR Weekly. (1997). Isolation of Avian Influenza A (H5N1) Viruses from Humans—Hong Kong, May–December 1997. *MMWR Weekly* 46(50) (19 December): 1204–1207.

Morange, Michael. (1998). *A History of Molecular Biology*. Translated by Matthew Cobb. Cambridge, MA: Harvard UP.

Mounier-Jack, Sandra, and Richard Coker. (2006). How Prepared Is Europe for Pandemic Influenza? Analysis of National Plans. *Lancet* 367: 1405–1411.

Mounier-Jack, Sandra, Ria Jas, and Richard Coker. (2007). Progress and Shortcomings in European National Strategic Plans for Pandemic Influenza. *Bulletin of the World Health Organization* 85(12).

Moynihan, Ray, and Alan Cassels. (2005). *Selling Sickness: How the World's Biggest Pharmaceutical Companies Are Turning Us All into Patients*. New York: Nation Books.

MUGAS. (2014a). MUGAS (Multiparty Group for Advice on Science) Vision. Available at http://mugasfoundation.net/mugas-vision/. [Accessed 10 August 2015.]

———. (2014b). MUGAS website. Available at http://mugas.net. [Accessed 10 August 2015.]

Muthuri, Stella G., et al. (2014). Effectiveness of Neuraminidase Inhibitors in Reducing Mortality in Patients Admitted to Hospital with Influenza A H1N1pdm09 Virus Infection: A Meta-Analysis of Individual Participant Data. *Lancet Respiratory Medicine* 2(5): 395–404.

NAO. (2013). *Access to Clinical Trial Information and the Stockpiling of Tamiflu*. National Audit Office. 21 May. London: Stationary Office.

National Academies of Sciences, Engineering, and Medicine. (2017). *Global Health and the Future Role of the United States*. Washington, DC: National Academies Press.

Nguyen-Van-Tam, Jonathan. (2010). Foreword: Oseltamivir for Seasonal, Avian and Pandemic Influenza: 10 Years of Clinical Experience. *Journal of Antimicrobial Chemotherapy* 65 (Suppl. 2): ii.3–4.

———. (2014). Principal Author of PRIDE Study Responds to News Story in the *BMJ* Claiming That the Study Was Based on "Flawed" Analysis. *BMJ* 348: g2935.

————. (2015). Practical Issues Related to Pandemic Deployment of Antivirals. Presentation. Available at http://www.flucentre.net/core/?p=425. [Accessed 25 January 2015.]

Nguyen-Van-Tam, Jonathan, Peter J. M. Openshaw, and Karl G. Nicholson. (2014). Antivirals for Influenza: Where Now for Clinical Practice and Pandemic Preparedness? *Lancet* 384(9941): 386–387.

NICE. (1999). *Zanamivir (Relenza) in the Management and Treatment of Influenza.* London: National Institute for Clinical Excellence. Available at http://www.nice.org.uk/proxy/?sourceUrl=http%3A%2F%2Fwww.nice.org.uk%2FniceMedia%2Fpdf%2FZanamivir+(Relenza).pdf. [Accessed 4 August 2015.]

————. (2000). *Guidance on the Use of Zanamivir (Relenza) in the Treatment of Influenza.* National Institute for Clinical Excellence. November.

————. (2003a). *Guidance on the Use of Oseltamivir and Amantadine for the Prophylaxis of Influenza.* National Institute for Clinical Excellence. September.

————.(2003b). *Guidance on the Use of Zanamivir, Oseltamivir and Amantadine for the Treatment of Influenza.* National Institute for Clinical Excellence. February.

————. (2009). *Amantadine, Oseltamivir and Zanamivir for the Treatment of Influenza.* National Institute for Health and Clinical Excellence.

Nicholson, Anna, Scott Wollek, Benjamin Kahn, and Jack Hermann. (2016). *The Nation's Medical Countermeasure Stockpile: Opportunities to Improve the Efficiency, Effectiveness, and Sustainability of the CDC Strategic National Stockpile: Workshop Summary.* Washington, DC: National Academies Press.

Nicoll, Angus, and Marc Sprenger. (2011). Learning Lessons from the 2009 Pandemic: Putting Infections in Their Proper Place. *European Journal of Epidemiology* 26(3): 191–194.

Nunes, João. (2014). *Security, Emancipation and the Politics of Health: A New Theoretical Perspective.* Abingdon: Routledge.

Okamoto, Etsuji. (2010). Is Oseltamivir (Tamiflu) Safe? Re-examining the Tamiflu "Ado" from Japan. *Pharmacoeconomics & Outcomes Research* 10(1): 17–24.

O'Neill, Graeme. (1989). Synthetic Molecule Disables the Flu Virus. *New Scientist*, 24 June, 42.

Ortiz, Justin, Laurie Kamimoto, Ronald E. Aubert, Jianying Yao, David K. Shay, Joseph S. Bresee, and Robert S. Epstein. (2008). Oseltamivir Prescribing in Pharmacy-Benefits Database, United States, 2004–2005. *Emerging Infectious Diseases* 14(8): 1280–1283.

PAC. (2013). Public Accounts Committee—Minutes of Evidence HC 295. Available at http://www.publications.parliament.uk/pa/cm201314/cmselect/cmpubacc/295/130617.htm. [Accessed 10 August 2015.]

Palmer, James. (1999). Letter to Heidi Jolson. 2 March.

Parker Waichman LLP. (2015). Tamiflu® (Oseltamivir Phosphate) Class Action Lawsuit. Available at http://www.yourlawyer.com/topics/overview/Tamiflu. [Accessed 27 March 2015.]

Petryna, Adriana, Andrew Lakoff, and Arthur Kleinman. (2007). *Global Pharmaceuticals: Ethics, Markets, Practices.* Durham, NC: Duke UP.

PHAC. (2012). National Emergency Stockpile System. Public Health Agency of Canada. Available at http://www.phac-aspc.gc.ca/ep-mu/ness-eng.php. [Accessed 5 March 2014.]

PharmaTimes. (2003). UK Launch for Roche's Tamiflu. *PharmaTimes*, 24 January.

PHEMCE. (2013). The Public Health Emergency Medical Countermeasures Enterprise Review. US Department of Health and Human Services. Available at http://www .phe.gov/Preparedness/mcm/enterprisereview/Pages/default.aspx. [Accessed 27 July 2015.]

Piester, Todd. (2008). Strategic National Stockpile: Pandemic Influenza Countermeasures. Presentation. Centers for Disease Control and Prevention. 21 August. Available at http://www.google.co.uk/url?sa=t&rct=j&q=&esrc=s&source =web&cd=1&cad=rja&uact=8&ved=0CCEQFjAA&url=http%3A%2F%2Fwww .cdc.gov%2Fphin%2Flibrary%2Fresources%2Ftools%2Fcra%2F9.19 .08%2520SNS%2520Countermeasures.pps&ei=Mvu4VIvYIcOu7AaitoDADQ&usg =AFQjCNEib_U0_opy7qKBbhK_6sQ4EPacJQ&sig2=ou0XTCxW9f4WLbPZ _LX97Q&bvm=bv.83829542,d.ZGU.

Pilling, David. (1999). Glaxo Ponders Effects of Relenza Refusal. *Financial Times*, 2 October, 15.

PMLive. (2013). Roche Releases All Tamiflu Trial Data to Cochrane. 5 April. Available at http://www.pmlive.com/pharma_news/roche_releases_all_tamiflu_trial_data _to_cochrane_470108.

Pollack, Andrew, and Tom Wright. (2005). Accord on Sharing Flu Vaccine Production. *New York Times*, 17 November.

Prior, Stephen. (2004). Who You Gonna Call? Responding to a Medical Emergency with the Strategic National Stockpile. Report Commissioned by the National Defense University, Center for Technology and National Security Policy. June. Available at http:// www.dtic.mil/cgi-bin/GetTRDoc?AD=ADA476356. [Accessed 16 January 2015.]

Reddy, David. (2010). Responding to Pandemic (H1N1) 2009 Influenza: The Role of Oseltamivir. *Journal of Antimicrobial Chemotherapy* 65(Suppl 2): ii35–40.

Reuters. (2005). EBay Stops Tamiflu Sale on Web as Drug Price Soars. 18 October. Available at http://www.redorbit.com/news/health/275417/ebay_stops_Tamiflu_sale _on_web_as_drug_price_soars/index.html.

Riordan, Michael. (2013a). Email Correspondence. 15 October.

———. (2013b). Interview by author. 17 October.

Roberts, Stephen, and Stefan Elbe. (2017). Catching the Flu: Syndromic Surveillance, Algorithmic Governmentality and Global Health Security. *Security Dialogue* 48(1): 46–62.

Roche. (2005). Factsheet Tamiflu. 15 December.

———. (2007). Media Release. 26 April. Available at http://www.roche.com/media /media_releases/med-cor-2007-04-26.htm.

———. (2012). Preparing for and Responding to Influenza Pandemics: Roles and Responsibilities of Roche. Available at http://www.roche.com/roles _responsibilities_influenza.pdf. [Accessed 25 February 2013.]

Roemer-Mahler, Anne, and Stefan Elbe. (2016). The Race for Ebola Drugs: Pharmaceuticals, Security and Global Health Governance. *Third World Quarterly* 37(3): 487–506.

Roemer-Mahler, Anne, Stefan Elbe, and Christopher Long. (2017). *New Medicines for Neglected Tropical Diseases: The Lessons from Biodefence*. Policy Brief. Centre for

Global Health Policy, University of Sussex. Available at https://www.sussex.ac.uk /webteam/gateway/file.php?name=roemer-mahler-elbe-long-2017-new-medicines -for-neglected-tropical-disease-the-lessons-from-biodefense.pdf&site=346. [Accessed 11 May 2017.]

Rollerhagen, Sonja, and Daniel Braxton. (2016). Letter from Roche Responding to Questions. 4 January.

Rose, Nikolas. (2001). The Politics of Life Itself. *Theory, Culture & Society* 18(6): 1–30.

———. (2007). *The Politics of Life Itself: Biomedicine, Power, and Subjectivity in the Twenty-First Century.* Princeton, NJ: Princeton UP.

Rumsfeld, Donald. (1998). Fax to George Schulz. 9 November. Available at http://library .rumsfeld.com/doclib/sp/216/To%20George%20Shultz%20re%20Gilead%20 Board%2011-09-1998%20(II-141-1).pdf#search="Gilead".

———. (1999). Fax to Condoleezza Rice. 29 March. Available at http://library .rumsfeld.com/doclib/sp/217/1999-03-29%20to%20Condi%20Rice%20re%20 Gilead%20Board.pdf#search="Gilead".

Rushton, Simon, and Jeremy Youde. (2015). *Routledge Handbook of Global Health Security.* London: Routledge.

Russell, Sabin. (2005). Flu Vaccine Maker Won't Share Patent; Roche Rejects Calls to Allow Production of Generic Versions. *San Francisco Chronicle*, 13 October. Available at http://www.sfgate.com/health/article/Flu-drug-maker-won-t-share-patent -Roche-rejects-2576163.php.

Samii, Ramina, and Luk Van Wassenhove. (2008). *Fighting the Flu: Tamiflu Stockpiling: A Pandemic Preparedness Policy.* INSEAD.

Sampaio, Cristina. (2015). Interview by author. 21 July.

Schlatter, Reto. (1999). Bei Roche und Glaxo steigt das Fieber. *PME* 40/99. Available at http://www.pme.ch/de/artikelanzeige/artikelanzeige.asp?pkBerichtNr=33232. [Accessed 23 January 2015.]

Schmit, Julie. (2005). Avian Flu Scare Has Tamiflu Maker Navigating Minefield. *USA Today*, 7 December.

Schneider, Reto. (2001). Das Rennen um GS4104: Wie ein Medikament entwickelt, getestet und vermarktet wird. *NZZ Folio: Die Zeitschrift der Neuen Zuercher Zeitung.* 1 April. Available at http://www.nzzfolio.ch/www/d80bd71b-b264-4db4 -afd0-277884b93470/showarticle/81bb3c96-9216-4eb5-b602-7e0937369c79 .aspx.

Schulz, Nick. (2005). Bird Flu in Hand for Bush? *Washington Times*, 12 October.

Schwartz, Nelson. (2005a). Rumsfeld's Growing Stake in Tamiflu. *CNN Money*, 31 October.

———. (2005b).The Tamiflu Tug of War. *Fortune*, 14 November. Available at http:// archive.fortune.com/magazines/fortune/fortune_archive/2005/11/14/8360685 /index.htm.

SEARO. (2006). Regional Production of Oseltamivir: Reviews of the Current Situation. Report of an Informal Meeting, New Delhi, India, 30–31 March. Available at http://apps.searo.who.int/PDS_DOCS/B0287.pdf.

SEC. (2005). Annual Report Pursuant to Section 13 or 15(D) of the Securities Exchange Act of 1934 for the Fiscal Year ended December 31, 2005. Gilead Sciences. Available at http://www.sec.gov/Archives/edgar/data/882095/000119312506045128/d10k .htm. [Accessed 3 March 2015.]

Sheridan, Desmond. (2016). *Evidence-Based Medicine: Best Practice or Restrictive Dogma*. London: Imperial College Press.

Shimazawa, Rumiko, and Masayuki Ikeda. (2015). Development of Drug-Approval Regulations for Medical Countermeasures against CBRN Agents in Japan. *Health Security* 13(2): 130–138.

Silverman, Ed. (2015). The Dispute over Tamiflu Is Revived by Yet Another Analysis. *Wall Street Journal*, 2 February. Available at http://blogs.wsj.com/pharmalot/2015 /02/02/the-dispute-over-Tamiflu-is-revived-by-yet-another-analysis/tab/print/.

Smith, Frank. (2014). *American Biodefense: How Dangerous Ideas about Biological Weapons Shape National Security*. Ithaca, NY: Cornell UP.

Smith, James. (2009). Point-by-Point Response from Roche to *BMJ* Questions. *BMJ* 339: b5374.

Smith, James, and S. Sacks. (2009). Incidence of Neuropsychiatric Adverse Events in Influenza Patients Treated with Oseltamivir or No Antiviral Treatment. *International Journal of Clinical Practice* 63(4): 596–605.

Spurgeon, David. (2005). Roche Canada Stops Distributing Oseltamivir. *BMJ* 331: 1041.

Stanton, John. (2005). Big Stakes in Tamiflu Debate. *RollCall*, 15 December. Available at http://www.rollcall.com/issues/51_64/news/11597-1.html.

Strong, P. M. (1990). Epidemic Psychology: A Model. *Sociology of Health and Illness* 12(3): 249–259.

Swaine, Jon, and Rebecca Smith. (2009). Swine Flu: Online Pharmacies Report Huge Surge in Demand for Tamiflu. *Telegraph*, 27 April. Available at http://www.telegraph .co.uk/health/swine-flu/5231337/Swine-flu-Online-pharmacies-report-huge-surge -in-demand-for-Tamiflu.html.

Takenaka, T. (2001). Classical vs. Reverse Pharmacology in Drug Discovery. *BJU International* 88(Suppl. 2): 7–10.

Tegnell, Anders. (2012). Interview by author. 29 November.

Tierney, Eugene, and David Reddy. (2005). Tamiflu—Seasonal and Pandemic Use 2005. Presentation. Available at http://www.roche.com/med_mb091105etdr.pdf. [Accessed 10 August 2015.]

Tinari, Serena, Harry Haner, and Reto Padrutt. (2011). The Tamiflu Saga—A Pandemic Business. Script. Available at http://attentiallebufale.it/wp-content/uploads /2011/01/RSI-Script-Tamiflu-English1.doc. [Accessed 19 January 2015.]

Toovey, Steven, et al. (2008). Assessment of Neuropsychiatric Adverse Events in Influenza Patients Treated with Oseltamivir: A Comprehensive Review. *Drug Safety* 31(12): 1097–1114.

———. (2012). Post-Marketing Assessment of Neuropsychiatric Adverse Events in Influenza Patients Treated with Oseltamivir: An Updated Review. *Advances in Therapy* 29(10): 826–848.

Trakatellis, Antonio. (2007). *Pandemic Influenza in the EU: Are We Sufficiently Prepared?* Brussels: European Parliament.

Turner, Robin. (2006). Preparing for the Next Influenza Pandemic. Presentation at the Copenhagen Business School. 4 December.

Turner, Sarah. (2005). Roche Sales Up 20% as Tamiflu Sought. *Wall Street Journal*, 19 October.

US Congress. (2005). Hearing before the Subcommittee on Health of the Committee on Energy and Commerce, House Of Representatives, 109th Congress. First Session. 26 May. Available at http://www.gpo.gov/fdsys/pkg/CHRG-109hhrg21642/html/CHRG-109hhrg21642.htm.

US Senate. (2005). Funding Needs for Pandemic Influenza Preparedness. Hearing before a Subcommittee of the Committee on Appropriations, US Senate, 109th Congress, 2 November.

———. (2006). Pandemic Influenza Preparedness. Hearing before a Subcommittee of the Committee on Appropriations, US Senate, 109th Congress, 31 January.

Van Gelder, Alex. (2005). Patent Nonsense on Avian Flu. *Boston Globe*, 31 October. Available at http://www.boston.com/news/globe/editorial_opinion/oped/articles/2005/10/31/patent_nonsense_on_avian_flu/.

Van Koeveringe, Jan. (2006). Address to the Annual General Meeting of Shareholders of Roche Holding Ltd. 27 February.

Varghese, J., W. Laver, and P. Colman. (1983). Structure of the Influenza Virus Glycoprotein Antigen Neuraminidase at 2.9 Å Resolution. *Nature* 303: 35–40.

Vetterli, Martin. (2009). Die Glaubenspille Tamiflu. *Beobachter*, issue 19. Available at http://www.beobachter.ch/justiz-behoerde/buerger-verwaltung/artikel/grippe_die-glaubenspille-Tamiflu/. [Accessed 4 August 2015.]

Von Itzstein, Mark. (2007). The War against Influenza: Discovery and Development of Sialidase Inhibitors. *Nature* 6: 967–974.

Wall Street Journal. (2005). Schumer's Statement on Roche. 18 October. Available at http://www.wsj.com/articles/SB112965799254572133.

Walsh, Diana. (2005). Customs Seizes Fake Tamiflu / Nation's First Haul of Bogus Bird Flu Pills Traced to China. *San Francisco Chronicle*, 19 December. Available at http://www.sfgate.com/health/article/SOUTH-SAN-FRANCISCO-Customs-seizes-fake-Tamiflu-2556274.php.

Ward, Penelope. (2015). Interview by author. 14 July.

Ward, Penelope, Ian Small, James Smith, Pia Suter, and Regina Dutkowski. (2005). Oseltamivir (Tamiflu) and Its Potential for Use in the Event of an Influenza Pandemic. *Journal of Antimicrobial Chemotherapy* 55(Suppl. S1): i5–i21.

Washington Post. (2002). Rumsfeld: Over $20 Million in Stock Sold to Avoid Conflicts. 19 June.

Webster, Robert G. (2010). William Graeme Laver. 3 June 1929–26 September 2008. *Biographical Memoirs of Fellows of the Royal Society* 56: 215–236.

WEF. (2006). Global Risks 2006. Davos: World Economic Forum. Available at http://www.weforum.org/pdf/CSI/Global_Risk_Report.pdf. [Accessed 4 August 2015.]

West, Diane. (2000). Chasing the Flu(s) Away: A Tamiflu Case Study. *Pharmaceutical Executive*, March, 120–124.

White House. (2002). The National Security Strategy of the United States of America. Available at http://www.state.gov/documents/organization/63562.pdf. [Accessed 16 January 2015.]

————. (2006). The National Security Strategy of the United States. Available at http://georgewbush-whitehouse.archives.gov/nsc/nss/2006/. [Accessed 16 January 2015.]

————. (2016). Fact Sheet: United States Leadership to Advance the Global Health Security Agenda. Available at https://www.whitehouse.gov/the-press-office/2016/10/12/fact-sheet-united-states-leadership-advance-global-health-security. [Accessed 17 October 2016.]

WHO. (2005). Avian Influenza: Assessing the Pandemic Threat.

————. (2007). A Safer Future: Global Public Health Security in the 21st Century. The World Health Report 2007. Geneva: World Health Organization.

————. (2011a). H5N1 Avian Influenza: Timeline of Major Events. Geneva: World Health Organization. Available at http://www.who.int/influenza/human_animal_interface/avian_influenza/H5N1_avian_influenza_update.pdf. [Accessed 4 August 2015.]

————. (2011b). Pandemic Influenza A (H1N1): Donor Report. 1 March.

Whyte, Susan Reynolds, Sjaak van der Geest, and Anita Hardon. (2002). Social Lives of Medicines. Cambridge: Cambridge UP.

Williams, Simon, Jonathan Gabe, and Peter Davis (Eds). (2009). Pharmaceuticals and Society: Critical Discourses and Debates. Oxford: Wiley-Blackwell.

Williams, Simon J., Paul Martin, and Jonathan Gabe. (2011). The Pharmaceuticalisation of Society? A Framework for Analysis. Sociology of Health and Illness 33(5): 710–725.

Wizemann, Theresa, Megan Reeve Snair, and Jack Herrmann. (2016). Rapid Medical Countermeasure Response to Infectious Diseases: Enabling Sustainable Capabilities through Ongoing Public- and Private-Sector Partnerships: Workshop Summary. Washington, DC: National Academies Press.

Wizemann, Theresa, Clare Stround, and Brouce Altevogt. (2010). The Public Health Emergency Medical Countermeasures Enterprise: Innovative Strategies to Enhance Products from Discovery through Approval. Workshop Summary. Washington, DC: Institute of Medicine.

WTO. (2003). World Trade Organization, Implementation of Paragraph 6 of the Doha Declaration on the TRIPS Agreement and Public Health, WT/L/540. 30 August. Available at http://www.wto.org/english/tratop_e/trips_e/implem_para6_e.htm.

Yeh, Brian. (2007). Influenza Antiviral Drugs and Patent Law Issues. CRS Report for Congress. 18 November. Available at http://www.ipmall.info/hosted_resources/crs/RL33159_070816.pdf.

Yokota, S., T. Fujita, M. Mori, A. Nezu, A. Okumura, and M. Hosoya et al. (2007). Epidemiologic Survey of Influenza-Associated Complications (I): Clinical Assessment of Symptoms and Signs, and Medication. Nihon Syounikagakkaizatsushi 111: 1545–1558.

Zamiska, Nicholas, and Jason Dean. (2005). Generics Challenge Roche's Tamiflu Claims. Wall Street Journal, 3 November. Available at http://www.wsj.com/news/articles/SB113098216326386983?mod=_newsreel_3.

Index